D0174458

RESPONSES
TO
ELIE WIESEL

RESPONSES
TO
ELIE WIESEL

Edited by Harry James Cargas

PERSEA BOOKS
NEW YORK

Published in cooperation with the Anti-Defamation League of B'nai B'rith

Also, for Judy and Adam Aronson, friends

For information, address the publisher:
Persea Books
225 Lafayette St., New York, N.Y. 10012

Cloth, ISBN: 0-89255-031-7
Paper, ISBN: 0-89255-032-5
Library of Congress Catalog Card Number: 77-94055
Printed in the United States of America

ACKNOWLEDGMENTS

CONTENTS

A CONVERSATION WITH ELIE WIESEL

by Lily Edelman

We begin our conversation while Israel and the Jewish people are fighting once again for survival, for life itself. How do you feel about this?

No matter what happens in our generation, all events seem more acute because of our immediate past. We always return to that nocturnal event for we see in it a measurement, a yardstick. Because of this historic perspective, we view things differently. All events are inter-related, all Jews are inter-dependent. What takes place in Jerusalem affects us here. What we do here affects Jerusalem. When Jews speak of Jews they say: we. Not you—and surely not: they. We fight, we appeal, we help. We rebel against the cruel oppressor in Russia. We pray for redemption. We face Egyptian tanks in the Sinai, Russian missiles in the Golan. No act is isolated. All that is being done is somehow inscribed in a general pattern—in a common design.

Take an example: Why have the Russians extended so much military assistance to Egypt—from where they had been expelled? I think I know why: They meant to punish Israel for the embarrassment we caused them with Russian Jewry.

To the enemy we are one people. Pharaoh and Haman, Hitler and Stalin—all have used the same language, involving the same arguments, insisting on the oneness of our people: And the irony is that they are right, they have to be right—for our sake. When we are united, we receive the Law. When we are not, we are attacked by Amalek.

In other words: When the enemy attacked on Yom Kippur, their target was not only Israel but all Jews.

What were your first reactions?

Sadness, immense sadness. Four wars in twenty-five years is an abomination. I was overcome by strange feelings of uselessness, helplessness. People were fighting, people were dying, and here I sit trying to create words.

But then the Jew in me took over, and I found my bearings. As a Jew I know I must never say "I" but "we." I participate in the struggle of all Jews everywhere as they participate in my tales. And that for me is the essence of being Jewish. We live more than one life, on more than one plane. We are wherever hope is being invoked and formulated. We have to continue.

What then is the specific function of a writer in the Jewish struggle, in the human struggle?

Everyone writes for different reasons and with different aims. Mine is not to create but to re-create. I believe the purpose of literature is to correct injustice. People were killed ... I try in my books to bring them back to life or at least to bring their death back to life. People suffered ... I try to give meaning to their suffering. I write to surprise, not to inform. If I open a book and am not overcome by its mystical quest, by a question put directly to me, then that book is not for me. In my own work I try to put in as much interrogation as possible, as much thirst, as much search for life and justice, for truth and beauty, for the past that becomes future.

In your foreward to an important new anthology, The Literature of American Jews, *edited by Theodore Gross, you talk about these writers, as trying to change the world and acting as a humanizing element in the course of history. Why is this a specifically Jewish function?*

For almost three thousand years, the Jewish people had no army, no political leverage, nothing. The only power we have had is the word, and with it we managed not only to influence history but to stay alive. No other people has had such an impact on events. Therefore the writer has a frightening, a gratifying but awesome task: words and their use. Because God created the world with the word, Jews view that word as holy. We are the only people that picks up a sacred book and kisses it; we believe our tradition to be the only revealed tradition, handed down by God, not by man.

What if anything have American Jewish writers contributed thus far toward maintaining the sacredness of the word?

These are contemporaries, and I do not like to be critical. But unfortunately American Jewish literature is sometimes lacking in this element of sacredness. Some of the writers distort what is Jewish, with too much vilification, too little understanding. Once upon a time a Jew had to know something in order to write. Now, people write who don't know anything about the Jews. It is so easy to write. But that's more than a Jewish problem: In America, too many people "write." More books are printed and published than are "written."

What about the moral message of writers? A recent editorial, based on Jeb Magruder's calling his Watergate deeds "a question of slippage," makes the point that the whole country if not the whole world seems to have slipped into the same kind of morass. Does a writer have any responsibility in this area?

Ideally he should assume such responsibility. But, on the contrary, he often becomes a victim of that slippage, a part of it. He uses the same words. But that's not new. One of the crimes committed a generation ago was the crime against language, the corruption of language: The Germans used the most beautiful words to cover the blackest crimes. Even that wasn't new. After all, for hundreds of years the Catholic Church tortured and burned people to save their souls. That's the legacy. Auschwitz didn't come in a void, but as a chain of events. If one can accept a saint in the church like Saint Louis, who was a murderer—he burned the Talmud, what didn't he do when he went to Jerusalem with the Crusades! Can one imagine today Pope Pius XII's being considered for sainthood? And, unfortunately, writers are affected by the pollution around them.

What then is the problem? Why do we produce so few writers who can lift the heart?

We have no moral authority of leadership, and this affects all of us, especially our young people. Whom should we look up to? I think it will take generations and generations to realize what we lost. Much of our moral and spiritual leadership in America still derives from Eastern Europe and those few survivors who came over before or after World War II. In another generation we won't even have them, and then our Judaism will be even emptier than now. I foresee a serious spiritual crisis in this country. The American Jewish community is going to go down because the moral reserve and the spiritual and intellectual baggage that are required simply won't be there.

How do you feel, by the way, about being included in an anthology of American Jewish literature? Do you think of yourself as an American Jewish writer?

If I have to define myself, I think of myself first as a Jew and second as a writer: and as a writer I belong everywhere. Nothing that is Jewish could be alien to my concern. I wish I could write about the fate of the Arab Jews, which is forgotten, and I may yet do so. When I wrote *The Jews of Silence,* I did not see myself as a Russian Jew but I could and did identify with the Jews of Russia. Whenever Jews are experiencing Jewish history, whenever Jewish history goes through them, then I try to identify with them. The issue for me is to be an antenna to capture Jewish history. A generation ago, no doubt, Jewish history centered in Eastern Europe. In 1948 it was in Israel. In the early '60s it was in Russia. Now, it's in Israel again.

Will you one day devote a major work to the American scene?

Of course. After all, I have lived here now since 1956 and am part of the American Jewish community. My closest friends live in America. But for the moment, I have not yet solved my problems with myself; the true self that I am belongs neither to France, to America, nor to any other place, but to a world that is not here. I believe one cannot speak of one's past, and yet I have spoken about it; and then I decided once again to remain silent. My dilemma revolves around the question of how to transform that past into something which has nothing to do with it. And this is in a sense what I have tried to do in my new book, *The Oath.* That's what literature is, an eternal metamorphosis.

Actually, we say "God created the world" with one word, a word that includes all the others. The composition is different, the structure and inner tension are different. We cannot fool ourselves or other people. I can use exactly the same words, but if the context that surrounds these words is different, then it becomes a different book. And yet, I have used exactly the same words and am actually always speaking about the same events. But if we know how to go about it, if the grace and spirit are on us, then we can turn out something that seems new.

The Oath, *of course, is new and yet in a way it is a continuation of all of your preceding work. What does seem different is a coming to grips with the central problem of transmission of the Jewish tale.*

Yes, that is my main obsession—how to transmit. If we cannot transmit, we are dead. The difference between death and life is that life transmits, death stops. I have dealt with this obsession in my other books too, but in *The Oath* I try to open a way. There is so much despair in my other books, so much darkness, that many young people often question me: Why shouldn't we commit suicide? That is their legacy. Just today in my seminar at City College, some of my students asked: Is this what being Jewish means—to be surrounded all the time by danger? And of course the questions are even more acute today in the new war. If to be Jewish means to be surrounded all the time by enemies—who are as eternal as we are—then why go on? Why not stop right away? And so I feel it my responsibility not only to give them a tale but to try to create an opening and to turn being Jewish into an instrument of life. So I am groping, I am searching, and my idea now, which may be a solution for the moment, is simply to redeem death, to redeem evil. In other words, what I try to say is this: Fate is cruel; what we can and must do is impose a human meaning on that fate. The moment I give my despair to someone that gift may become to him a reason for hope. This theme of transmission is explored more fully in this new work than in all my other books.

The other attempt I have made here is to link universal history to Jewish history. I have said here more directly than before that whatever happens to the Jews happens to all mankind. People thought they could kill Jews and remain alive, and they were wrong. When they kill Jews, they kill themselves. And that is what they have done: They have killed themselves.

Does that explain your choice of the Talmudic quote at the front of The Oath: *"Had the peoples and the nations known how much harm they brought upon themselves by destroying the Temple of Jerusalem, they would have wept more than the children of Israel"?*

Correct. So many people died, so many will die.

While all your major characters are concerned with some aspect of transmission, they seem to have different roles. The father, who is the scribe of Kolvillag, says over and over again that his task is not to interpret or comment but merely to chronicle. In one of your essays in One Generation After, *you spoke about the Jewish passion to record everything on paper. Why is this so important?*

In Hebrew the word *sofer* means both scribe and writer. In other words, a writer is a scribe. In Jewish tradition the task was to transcribe only what was heard and seen—a difficult task because it allowed for no mistakes. The Talmud tells how the brilliant scribe Rabbi Meir was told by his master Rabbi Ishmael: "Be careful. Should you omit or add one single word you may destroy the world." This was an exaggeration, of course, but it proves the point about the scribe's being the instrument of the events he recorded.

Is that regarded as a lower echelon of transmission?

No, everything that has to do with writing is sacred. Since the event itself is already a witness, a testimony, it must be communicated in its purest form. Later on come the commentaries on commentaries, the interpretations. But first is that first word, which must be basic and austere. That's why I try to capture in my writing what we call the *tzimtzum* or condensation—one word instead of hundreds.

What is the origin of pinkas, *the name given the book the chronicler keeps?*

Pinkas is a Hebrew word meaning "book." In Eastern Europe each community kept its own *pinkas.* The one in *The Oath* is of course invented. I have tried in all my work to be that kind of chronicler, to provide the basis for interpretation.

What role does Moshe the Madman, one of your favorite friends, play in this work?

Moshe makes the event happen. The father is the chronicler, Moshe is the event, and Azriel the son inherits the chronicle. And, of course, one generation later, the young narrator receives their common testimony.

Do you see Moshe as a prophet?

Moshe is eternal, he is immortal because he appears in every book. And now he has to bring the Messiah but did not do so. He doesn't bring the Messiah, not yet. So he becomes mad—as does anyone who tries to bring the Messiah before his time. But because of his humanity, Moshe lives on. He knows what no one else knows, he sees what no one else can see. He is the mystery of the tale, the mystic, the poet.

Why is madness such an important presence in your work?

For many reasons, but mainly because rationalism is a failure and betrayal. When we study what happened a generation ago, we cannot but think that it was prepared by the rationalists. If Darwin, the scientist, for example, had not reduced man to the state of an animal, maybe people would have thought twice before killing human beings. Even Darwin wasn't the first. If the Church hadn't seen the Jew as subhuman, maybe the Germans would have thought twice too. The Holocaust could not have happened had there not been this combination of factors. Once you can rationalize everything you can also rationalize murder. Rationalism failed philosophically because we still don't understand what happened. It also failed theologically, and it failed humanly. So what else remains? Madness. If there is one word that can include all the other words about the Holocaust that word is madness—madness from the victim's point of view, madness from the executioner's point of view, madness from God's point of view, from man's point of view. The winds of madness were blowing. Creation itself was contaminated. But then, I like to think that my madmen are pure and beautiful, madmen who try to save the world and not to destroy it, to help, not to hurt. And because they were captured by the evil forces I try to give them back to the pure forces. All the messengers are mad, all the saints are mad. When too much harm is done to them, I give them back their role.

In other words, madness can be a force for evil or a force for good?

Absolutely. Hitler, *lehavdil,* was mad and so were his troopers. But there were good madmen too. The Jews were mad: To want to survive in such an evil world is madness.

Do you see madness as a sort of transcendence of all the boundaries that usually inhibit people?

Yes, madness is a liberation of the self. What is my madman? He is not clinical but a mystical madman, attaching his self to that of the universe, of mankind. This is his madness: He becomes one with the world, one with man, one with God.

You said earlier that you like to surprise, and Moshe's marriage, after his long period of solitary isolation, is an episode that certainly takes one by surprise. Does his ability to give himself so completely to one person foreshadow the later gift of his life to save the community?

Certainly. What does the tale of Moshe really mean? Simply that man cannot redeem the world, that he must try. If I save one person, I have saved the world. That's a basic Jewish teaching.

In *The Town Beyong the Wall*—and *The Oath* is more a continuation of that book than any of the others—all the tensions, all the relationships, are always "I and thou," the dialogue of two persons who are one. In the end of *The Town*, the narrator, Michael, decides that the only way for him to be saved is to save another madman, the deaf mute in the prison cell, and to bring him back to sanity. If I have any moral message, this is it: Try to save one person. In *The Oath* it is one person—Moshe the Madman—who wants to save the whole world. And when he realizes that he cannot save the world, he wants at least to save his wife.

What about the old man, Azriel? What is his role?

Azriel incarnates all the others. He receives all their testimonies and becomes all the others. As a child he was taught by both his father the scribe and by Moshe the Madman. This really means that with each generation we grow richer and our task greater. Example: It was easy for Abraham, who became the rebel. It was more difficult for Isaac because he had to spread his own words plus those of Abraham. Jacob had to be not only Abraham and Isaac but also Jacob. Our task is the most difficult—we have to be all our forebears and more.

The difficulty for me in the beginning was to dream about Jerusalem and to fear a Holocaust. My generation then lived through both the Holocaust and the resurrection of Israel. But my students, for example, most of whom are the children of survivors, have the greatest challenge of all: These young people have to combine all that went before, just as Azriel has to be himself as well as Moshe as well as his father and the entire community. Of course, it is paralyzing. But what a mission!

Would it be correct to call Azriel a Wandering Jew?

No, the Wandering Jew is not a Jewish but a Christian concept, growing out of a medieval legend about a Jewish cobbler who taunted Jesus on the way to the crucifixion and was cursed to wander thereafter until Jesus' return. In our own tradition, the Jew as a wanderer is usually symbolized by the *Lamed Vavnik,* the Just Man. But I adopt another term for Azriel—*Navenadnik*—which in Hebrew means beggar or wanderer. In the Hasidic tradition, before the Just Man could be revealed he had to become a *Navenadnik,* wandering about and hiding his own identity so as to attract and help others anonymously. Since the *Shekhinah,* the divine presence, is everywhere, the wanderer travelled around gathering all the sparks and repairing things everywhere. In Azriel's encounter with Abrasha, both wanderers are trying to correct injustice but by vastly different methods.

You certainly allow for human differences. "All men are messengers," you say, even Yancsi, the Christian boy whose disappearance triggers the pogrom against the Jews in Kolvillag.

Yancsi is also an event. This is the human tragedy: Both good and evil testify to God's existence.

What about the young man who asks questions, the narrator, who wants to commit suicide? What does he add to the task of transmission?

That young man is everyone. In 1945, 1946, 1947 I went through the same kind of depression, asking: What for? What's the use? And today the situation is more discouraging. My young man is a special person—he is the son of a survivor, a tragic figure who feels left out, useless. I made him unclear intentionally. From time to time when he comes on stage, he is strong, especially when he describes his mother, who is obsessed with the son who died and feels guilty because she didn't go after that other child and save him. And my young man has a single question: Where do *I* fit in? He arouses our pity because he doesn't even have the consolation of being a witness. He represents all my students and all the young people who are so perplexed today.

Why does Azriel eventually break his oath of silence?

He becomes interested in this young man, and that's what saves him. This is to me a beautiful truth: One thinks one gives, and one really receives. To give is to receive, Rebbe Nachman of Bratzlav once said. This old man who thinks he is saving the young man suddenly realizes at the end that it is he himself who is really being saved. You see, a pure gesture—no matter what or where—remains pure because it contains beauty and truth and justice.

Why did Moshe exact the oath of silence in the first place?

As you remember, the book begins with Azriel's saying "No, I will not speak, I will not speak, I will not speak." And it ends by his giving the tale of Kolvillag to the young man. Why the oath of silence in between? He explains to Azriel's father, the scribe, that he does not believe in the written word because it is too easily distorted. He believes only in silence. Here he reflects my own ambivalence about having written about the Holocaust. Many of us go around with guilt feelings: Maybe we shouldn't have written a word. For years and years I spoke about the need for silence. Only one of my books, *Night,* deals directly with the Holocaust; all the others reveal why one cannot speak about it. The Holocaust is a sacred subject. One should take off one's shoes when entering its domain, one should tremble each time one pronounces the word.

After the war, most of the survivors did in fact refuse to speak. Some of us wrote, but with a certain severity of style—brief sentences and understatements. Our guilt derives now from the feeling that perhaps we should not have spoken at all, especially in the light of some of the vulgarity that surrounds this theme today. The Holocaust has suddenly become a fashionable subject, a household word. Theologians make theology out of it, philosophers make philosophy out of it, politicians make politics out of it, JDL warns "Never again." The subject has become an instrument to be used. And this I deeply resent.

And at the same time some of us think that perhaps we were wrong. Perhaps we should not have written about it because no one could or would understand anyway. Because we did succeed, at least in part, to create a certain awareness of the Holocaust, others began to misuse the subject, misunderstand, misinterpret, and distort. it. As a result, I often tell myself that in 1945 all of us, all the survivors, should perhaps have gathered in a conclave in a forest somewhere and decide that whoever survived should not speak. Maybe we would have achieved much more that way. That's why I put so much stress in this book on the oath of silence.

How can one distinguish between silence and indifference? How can silence become a weapon against indifference and evil? Doesn't silence make "business as usual" easier?

It depends. Of course, my silence is meant to be a very eloquent silence, a screaming silence, a shouting silence. When a man says he has much to say but doesn't care and turns away, that is indifference. But when a man says, "I have much to say but I am not going to say a word," that suggests the power of silence. I remember a true story: Before going to his post, Israel's first ambassador to Russia was told by President Weizmann; "You will not be able to speak to the Jews in Russia. But there is one thing you can do, and that is to remain silent. Let your silence be heard from one corner of the world to the other." Silence of this kind can become a gesture, an act, a deed, a testimony against indifference, silence with a capital "S." In *The Jews of Silence*, silence becomes a character in the tale, a presence.

There are many different shades of silence: the silence of the fool and that of the wise man. What is the difference between the two? The fool is silent because he has nothing to say. But the wise man is silent because he has too much to say. Two different silences.

How can the listener differentiate between them?

One must attain a certain awareness and realize that what counts is what one does around the silence. A mediocre man may surround silence with empty words, but a poet surrounds his silence with words containing layers of silence, dramatic tension, visions of horror, acts of gratitude. Though I speak of silence in all my other books, I develop the theme to the fullest in *The Oath*.

Does this resemble in any way the use of blank space in Oriental painting, which becomes a presence only when perimetered by something that makes one see that space?

The Berditchever once said that when God gave the Torah He gave not only the words but also the blanks between the words. The task of man is to be a blank between the words, a messenger, a link between God and man, between man and man, between present and past.

In One Generation After, *you closed with the following passage: "And now, teller of tales, turn the page. Speak to us of other things. Your mad prophets, your old men drunk with nostalgic waiting, your possessed—let them return to their nocturnal enclaves. They have survived their deaths for more than a quarter of a century; that should suffice. If they refuse to go away, at least make them keep quiet. At all costs. By every means. Tell them that silence, more than language, remains the substance and the seal of what was once their universe, and that, like language, it demands to be recognized and transmitted."*

With those words I did say farewell to the theme of the Holocaust—as such. I have not returned to it—as such. Why did I or others write about the Holocaust in the first place? Out of a certain sense of mission. Certainly not for other reward. The truth is that all Holocaust writers know in a way that they are doing the "wrong" thing.

In addition, people say, well, they write too much about the Holocaust. This is one of the most vulgar and obscene remarks we can hear these days, and it has had its effect on certain writers—especially in Europe. I must confess that I find it maddening that Jewish writers today have to justify themselves for writing about Jews and Jewish themes. No one dares to ask why Faulkner writes about the South, why Hemingway wrote about the civil war in Spain, why Goethe wrote about Germans, or Musset about the French. Ten books can be written about a single murder, and no one resents that. But writers who have survived the Holocaust are asked to justify themselves for taking on that lonely obligation.

Of course, one doesn't have to listen to all the voices. One listens to one's own voice, and what counts in my work are the voices I hear. And those voices do not come from this world or from this time. I justify myself to myself alone. Yet, I did change because I simply felt that ten books around and on the subject were enough for me. But, of course, I would lie if I were to say the I do not write in the shadow of that event. On the contrary. It is still there and there I hope it will remain forever. No theme is more important or more overpowering. The fate of one person who died during that period would be enough for ten Prousts and ten novels. So just imagine ...

Man can understand only through words. Jews have never believed in statues, we have never believed in buildings. Judaism is words. We come back to the beginning. If the American Jewish community is experiencing so many difficulties and so many defeats, especially with our young, it is perhaps because there are too many buildings. Judaism is not buildings, Jewish building is in words, we build words. The only way for us to communicate what happened in the past is through words, whether of past glory or of past disaster. Only words.

Do you sense any new awareness today of the need to return to the words?

I receive hundreds of letters from young people (the average age of my readers is 16 or 17, which gives me a sense of reward), who want to know. They represent in their questions a tremendous return to the word. What is art, after all? Art is tension, ambiguity, telling and not telling. When a thousand words are pressed into a single line, a poem is born. In literature the weight of silence determines the weight of art.

This talk about how much to tell and not to tell leads me to a personal question: What of the Holocaust experience are you going to teach your little Elisha? What are you going to teach this very important survivor's son about his Jewish past?

Everything. The first thing I did after his birth was to write him a letter. And I have written him many letters since. He must go through what I went through. I want him to have the same childhood I had.

How is that possible? You're not in Sighet.

Through the words, through the words. They are more than geography. I want him to learn what I learned: *ahavat Yisrael*, love of the Jews, which is the principal commandment in Judaism. That I want him to receive—from the very beginning. That's what I received—from the very beginning.

because we are commanded to love Jews, we must love all Jews—those who died as well as those who are alive. I will begin teaching him at the age of three what I learned at that age.

Where will you start?

The moment he is at an age to understand I will tell him the significances of names in Judaism—and what his names Shlomo Elisha represent. That means I will be telling him of people he can no longer know but whom he incarnates. And through these names I shall tell him about his grandfather and what happened over there. And I don't think I'll spare him anything, except that I'll try to do it in a subtle, understated, condensed and austere way—as in my writing. And he will come to know that it is not a curse but a privilege to bear such names to be the continuator of such a tradition. The rest is up to him. He will give the commentary.

ELIE WIESEL'S ANTI-EXODUS

by Lawrence S. Cunningham

In a course entitled "Religion and the Novel," I assigned, as preliminary reading, Elie Wiesel's *Night*. The reaction of the students was almost unanimous: Why this book? It is not a novel; it tells the truth; why should an autobiography be read in a course that deals with fiction? My immediate response was to paraphrase an answer that Wiesel himself once gave to a question put to him by a Hasidic rebbe in Tel Aviv: Some true stories are false and some false stories are true. But there is a further point. Is it so clear that Wiesel's book is biography after all? It does tell his story and the story of his father and the story of his youth in Sighet and the story of the end of his childhood in the camps of Nazi Germany. In that sense it does tell the truth about him. What *Night* does not do is to follow the accepted canons of autobiography as that term is understood in the broadest sense of that term. *Night* does not tell of the growth of a person even in the sense that Joyce does in *A Portrait of the Artist as a Young Man*. Whatever else *Night* might be, it is not a *Bildungsroman*. In fact, what one comes to see is that *Night* is not a story of someone's life (i.e., *bios graphe*), nor of the unfolding of the consciousness of life and growth, but rather of someone's death: the death of God, of history, of one's father and of meaning. Wiesel has written, not a biography, but a thanatography.

Writing about death presents an almost insurmountable problem: How evoke death on the page when death is, par excellence, the most ineffable and imcommunicable human experience? Man may be drawn to death; he may philosophize about it; he may, as Freud so cogently argues, struggle against it; he may even have felt its wing touch him, as did Wiesel and others. But to describe the very act of dying is impossible. The best that one can do, through an apophatic exercise, is deny and distort everything that supports the whole structure of the experience of living. In that way man gets some sense of death. Robert Jay Lifton has written most wisely on this point. He has described the near transcendental experience of those who have lived in the order of death as "the replacement of the natural order of living and dying with the unnatural order of death-dominated life" (*Death in Life* [Vintage], p. 30).

The natural order of Wiesel's life was the God-intoxicated milieu of the Hungarian town of Sighet. This particular town was, like his own early life, insulated, timeless, unchanging. The events that began to unfold in 1943-44 provided the immediate context out of which the natural order of Hungarian Judaism was changed and inverted into the death-dominated life of the camps. What has been largely overlooked is that Wiesel, writing some years after these events, frames the story of that inversion in terms of the oldest "biography" of his own people: the story of the Exodus. The life-giving biblical myth of election, liberation, convenant, and promise becomes the vehicle for telling the story of the unnatural order of death-domination. It is as if Wiesel, either consciously or unconsciously, felt constrained to write a near parody of the Exodus story in order to give reality and urgency to the story that he feels is his vocation to tell and tell again.

The village of Sighet was a settled one. There was a rural rhythm, a sense of God's worship being done; a feeling of fraternity; and a longing for the Messiah. This village, as Wiesel remembers it and describes it, was a happy and secure place. An angel came to that village and told the people to pack up and flee, for death would come to them. The angel was Moche the beadle, a simple man who sought God in the mysteries of the cabala and who had seen, further to the west, the face of evil in the form of execution squads who shot Jews before open ditches. Unlike the angel of Passover, this messenger was thought to be crazy; nobody listened.

But Moche had, in fact, been right. The orders came for the Jews to pack their possessions in haste and get ready to leave. There was a rumor among some that they would be sent to work in brick factories to the west. In this particular form of the Exodus, a people were to go out to make bricks as slaves, not to leave behind such an enforced work. But even that was to prove an optimistic rumor. The people left in haste, but they left in cattle cars for the west. During the train journey there was to be another mad visionary, Madame Schacter, who cried out to her fear-crazed companions: "Jews, listen to me! I can see a fire! There are huge flames! It is a furnace!" But she was insane, and her insanity was exacerbated by hunger, thirst, crowding and the stench of many humans in a small railroad car. Only when the train stopped at Birkenau, the reception depot for Auschwitz, did people look into the sky and see the guides that Madame Schacter had seen in her lunatic visions: a tall chimney that belched forth both smoke and flame. These flames did not, however, guide the chosen people. These flames signified something obscenely different: "Never shall I forget that smoke. Never shall I forget the little faces of the children whose bodies I saw turned into wreaths of smoke beneath a silent blue sky. Never shall I forget those flames which consumed my faith forever."

When this new "going out" of the Jews was completed, the final destination was the desert. But it was not the biblical desert, where people wandered with a purpose. Here there was no manna sent from heaven to be found as the dew on plants in the morning. Nor was there to be a rain of quail to eat. In this desert the food that was sent "tasted of corpses." Nor was a brazen serpent fashioned and raised up in order for men to look on it and feel the venom of serpents disappear from their veins. In this desert there were other instruments erected and men were told to bare their heads and look on these new instruments: gallows in the courtyards where men were ordered to look up at children hung for camp infractions. And venom coursed through the hearts of the spectators to spew out in their thoughts: Where is God? Where is He? Where is God now?

That question becomes the central one for the inhabitants of the camps, and it is the central question of *Night*. The Jews of old were told to flee the fleshpots of Egypt in order to find God in the desert. They were His people just as He was their God. But in the new convenant of the Anti-Exodus, people came into the desert not to be forged into a people, but to have their peoplehood exterminated. To be chosen in the camp meant to be chosen for the ovens. In an obscene use of the biblical vocabulary, election and "being chosen" meant to be marked for death.

Thus, the ancient dialogue between God and men now turned into a long and progressive silence in which the desert experience of Auschwitz and Buchenwald obscured and muted the presence of God. God became for the people of the desert someone to be accused and screamed at, not Someone who guided them into the wilderness in order to receive their prayer and their worship. The unfolding of this death becomes clearer in the novel if careful attention is paid to the parallel that Wiesel sets up between the death of his father and the death of his God.

The main hope that motivated Wiesel in the first days that he spent in the camp was his desire to remain close to his father, since his father was the last intimate link with the secure life that he had known in Sighet. Being near his father was a sign of the reality of his former life. Only when the rhythm of the life in the camp became clearer to him did he realize what a terrible choice he had made in assuming his filial responsibilities. The prisoner had one goal in mind: to keep strong enough to avoid selection by the camp physicians; all else was of secondary importance to that main purpose. As his father slowly succumbed to the harsh treatment of the camp, Wiesel was forced into a near schizophrenic state of making a choice that involved his own sense of filial piety and his own desire to survive. Every morsel he tendered to his father, every exertion he made to spare him an extra effort, every word of defense that he made before the kapos — every gesture, in short, that he made in behalf of his father—was a gesture that brought himself closer to death. He was torn between the sense of love for his father (and, by analogy, a sense of who he was and what he was, since his father was the link to his earlier life) and his own need to exist. When his father's death actually occurred he himself unflinchingly acknowledged the hitherto latent ambivalences that tore at him then and tore at him 13 years later when he wrote *Night*. It was a complex admission of shame, bitterness, and relief: "I did not weep, and it pained me that I could not weep. But I had now no more tears. And, in the depth of my being, in the recesses of my weakened conscience, could I have searched it, I might perhaps have found something like—free at last!"

When one studies the trajectory of Wiesel's relationship to his father in Auschwitz and Buchenwald, one is struck with the parallel trajectory of his fundamentally ambivalent relationship with the God of the Covenant, the God of Abraham, Isaac, and Jacob. It is as though his own father was the icon of God. At the beginning of the experience in the camp, there was an unquestioned and unambivalent sense of the worship of God (Why do I pray? Why do I breathe!). The question of survival, an increasingly important question even to the point where it became *the* question, puts a strain on this intimate sense of obligation to God: to fast on Yom Kippur was to take a step closer to death since in the camp every day was a fast; to accuse oneself of fault on the Day of Atonement seemed to reverse the natural order of existence since it was the inmate who was grievoulsy and unjustly offended. Slowly but inexorably there is a psychic transformation. One does not call for repentance or forgiveness, not even on Yom Kippur; especially not on that day. By some mad reversal that day becomes a special time to hurl a *j'accuse*. In short, to affirm the ancient covenant and its attendant responsibility is to hasten one's physical and psychical death. It is to hasten the day of "chosenness"—the day when Doctor Mengeles will point his finger of election.

It is at this level that the whole drama of the Exodus becomes totally and completely reversed. The whole dynamic of the Exodus story is based on the idea of a people who must go out in order to worship their God in freedom and security. But the new Exodus ends in what Wiesel calls "the Kingdom of the Night." In the Bible God has found his people before they go to find Him. In the New Exodus, the people not only had found God but served him; they went out only to lose Him. In the biblical experience the people are constituted and elected as a people by their fidelity to God. In this Exodus they are to find that their future means peoplelessness (forgive the neologism but how else can it be said?), framed in terms of a final solution.

In his recent work, *The Seduction of the Spirit,* Harvey Cox has emphasized the crucial importance of telling stories as a fundamental part of "being religious." Elie Wiesel has told his story within the subtle framework of an earlier story so that from this powerful mix of thanatography and liberation myth people may be forced to see the grim visage of postmodern man: the possible death of history; the dying of persons, peoples, and comfortable divinities. God may not be dead for Elie Wiesel; there may be even a possibility of a new Exodus. Be that as it may, *Night* insists that the old order has been overturned and the form of the question has been radically changed. God may still live, but if He does, He has much to answer for.

THE DOMINION
of DEATH

by Lawrence L. Langer

> *The most frightening aspect of our present world is
> not the horrors in themselves, the atrocities, the
> technological exterminations, but the one fact at the very root
> of it all: the fading away of any human criterion....*
> Erich Kahler

> *... a man can cross the threshold of death before
> his body is lifeless.*
> Alexander Solzhenitsyn

> *Death too can be a way of life.*
> Jakov Lind

True art, says Erich Kahler, expanding Erich Auerbach's idea
of "mimesis" or imitation, is and has to be

> an act of conquest, the discovery of a new sphere of
> human consciousness, and thereby of new reality. It lifts
> into the light of our consciousness a state of affairs, a layer
> of existence, that was dormant in the depth of our
> unconscious, that was buried under obsolete forms,
> conventions, habits of thought and experience. And by
> showing this latent reality, by making it visible to us,
> open to our grasp, the work of art actually *creates* this
> new reality as a new sphere of our conscious life. There is
> no true art without this exploratory quality, without this
> frontier venture to make conscious the preconscious, to
> express what has never been expressed before and what
> heretofore had seemed inexpressible.[1]

Once we recognize that critical dogmas of this sort are not to
be measured for their "truth"—if this were the case, most

critical principles would cancel each other out—but for their
relevance, their appropriateness, their consistency with a
given body of material—once we recognize this, then Kahler's
definition of art proves singularly applicable to the literature of
atrocity. All serious art undoubtedly aspires toward the
revelation of a new sense of reality, but the literature we are
concerned with possessed the curious advantage of having
such a "new" reality already available, pressing with equal
force on the conscious and (as we have just seen) the
preconscious life of the artist, and seeking only a way of being
convincingly presented to an audience of contemporary
readers. Normally, nonfiction is excluded from such defini-
tions of art, since by its very nature it seeks to reflect a
historical reality without manipulating or distorting details,
drawing on the very conventions and habits of thought and
experience that Kahler excludes. Most autobiographies, for
example, orient us toward the past rather than shaping fresh
visions of the future. Yet Kahler's terms are broad enough, and
the nature of the Holocaust experience sufficiently unique, to
permit autobiography to be included in his definition of art—
if one could be found.

Most of the autobiographies concerned with *l'univers
concentrationnaire* numb the consciousness without enlarging it
and providing it with a fresh or unique perception of the nature
of reality, chiefly because the enormity of the atrocities they
recount finally forces the reader to lose his orientation altogether and to feel as though he were wandering in a
wilderness of evil totally divorced from any time and place he
has ever known—a reality not latent in, but external to, his
own experience. The most impressive exception to this
general rule is a work that has already become a classic in our
time, an autobiography which, in its compressed imaginative
power and artful presentation of the circumstances of the
author's internment in Auschwitz, yields the effect of an
authentic *Bildungsroman*—except that the youthful protagonist becomes an initiate into death rather than life—Elie
Wiesel's *Night*.

A reader confronted with this slim volume himself
becomes an initiate into death, into the dark world of human
suffering and moral chaos we call the Holocaust; and by the
end he is persuaded that he inhabits the kind of negative

universe which Lear invokes when he enters with Cordelia dead in his arms: "Thou'lt come no more;/Never, never, never, never, never," and is prompted to intone together with Lear: "No, no, no life"—a final rejection of love, of family, of the past, of order, of "normality"—that lies dead on the stage at his feet. Wiesel's *Night* is the terminus a quo for any investigation of the implications of the Holocaust, no matter what the terminus ad quem; on its final page a world lies dead at our feet, a world we have come to know as our own as well as Wiesel's, and whatever civilization may be rebuilt from its ruins, the silhouette of its visage will never look the same.

Night conveys in gradual detail the principle that Hermann Kasack had evoked in his dream: death has replaced life as the measure of our existence, and the vision of human potentiality nurtured by centuries of Christian and humanistic optimism has been so completely effaced by the events of the Holocaust that the future stretches gloomily down an endless vista into futility. The bleakness of the prospect sounds melodramatic but actually testifies to the reluctance of the human spirit to release the moorings that have lashed it to hope and to accept the consequences of total abandonment. Disappointed in a second coming, man has suffered a second going, a second fall and expulsion, not from grace this time but from humanity itself; and indeed, as we shall see in one of the most moving episodes in his harrowing book, Wiesel introduces a kind of second crucifixon, consecrating man not to immortality but to fruitless torture and ignominious death. Yet one is never permitted to forget what is being sacrificed, what price, unwillingly, the human creature has had to pay for *l'univers concentrationnaire,* what heritage it has bequeathed to a humanity not yet fully aware of the terms of the will.

Works like *Night* furnish illumination for this inheritance, an illumination all the more necessary (especially if one is to go on to explore the literature succeeding it) when we consider how unprepared the human mind is to confront the visions it reveals. A book like *Anne Frank: The Diary of a Young Girl,* incontestably more popular and influential than Wiesel's *Night,* by its very widespread acceptance confirms our unpreparedness to respond to the grimmer realities and the imaginative re-creations of the literature of atrocity. In many respects *Anne Frank* is the reverse of *Night*—in its premises, in the nature of the experiences it narrates, and in its conclusions; in fact, it draws on the very "obsolete forms, conventions, habits of thought and experience" which, in Erich Kahler's formulation, the writer must burrow through if he is to create for his reader the new reality we dignify by the name of art.

Of course, the comparison is meant to be objective rather than invidious; Anne Frank was indeed a young girl, and her eventual fate was more terrifyingly final, if no more fearful, than Wiesel's. But her *Diary*, cherished since its appearance as a celebration of human courage in the face of impending disaster, is in actuality a conservative and even old-fashioned book which appeals to nostalgia and does not pretend to concern itself with the uniqueness of the reality transforming life outside the attic walls that insulated her vision. Bruno Bettelheim long ago provoked angry criticusm for suggesting the limitations in the tactics of the Frank family; whether or not it was justified is irrelevant here, but it further confirms the sentimentality of an audience that pursues Anne's reality— like Anne herself—only to the arrival of the "green police," that is unable or unwilling to peer beyond the end of her tale to the "new" reality symbolized by her wretched death in the barracks of Bergen-Belsen.

Anne Frank's *Diary* was written in the innocence (and the "ignorance") of youth, but its conclusions form the point of departure for Wiesel's *Night* and most authors in the tradition of atrocity; indeed, their work constitutes a sequel to hers and ultimately challenges the principle that for her was both premise and epitaph—"In spite of everything, I still think people are good at heart"—a conception of character which dies hard, but dies pitilessly, in *Night* and in literature of atrocity in general. The optimism which nurtured her faith in humanity is symbolized by her family's quarantine from reality during their years of hiding; their real story, and the story of the transformed world that determined their destiny, began after Anne's diary ended. The values it preserves— love, devotion, courage, family unity, charity—are mocked by the fate she suffered (mocked too, one is inclined to add, by the fate of Lear and Cordelia), and to the informed reader only dramatize the inadequacy of heart-warming terms to describe the soul-chilling universe that destroyed her.

Yet Elie Wiesel recognized, as Anne Frank could not, that

the values she celebrated might form an indispensable core for creating a magnetic field to attract fragments of atrocity, so that a permanent tension could be established between the two "forces"—a similar tension exists in some of the dreams we examined—a kind of polarity between memory and truth, nostalgia and a landscape of horror eerily highlighted by the pale reflection from vacant moral spaces. The literary effect is that memory ceases to offer consolation but itself becomes an affliction, intensifying the torment of the sufferer. Or rather, the usual content of memory is replaced by the harsh events of life in the concentration camp, until the past loses the hard edge of reality and the victim finds that both past and future, memory and hope—the "luxuries" of normal existence—are abruptly absorbed by an eternal and terrifying present, a present whose abnormality suddenly becomes routine. At this moment, life becomes too much for man and death assumes the throne in the human imagination.

A prospect like this must have led Camus to begin *The Myth of Sisyphus* with the statement that the only truly serious philosophical problem is suicide. In fact, Camus offers a lucid description of the consequences for man of his familiar world disappearing (consequences which Elie Wiesel presents in greater detail in *Night*):

> in a universe suddenly divested of illusions and lights, man feels an alien, a stranger. His exile is without remedy since he is deprived of the memory of a lost home or the hope of a promised land. This divorce between man had his life, the actor and his setting, is properly the feeling of absurdity.[2]

Too lucid, perhaps: Camus built intellectual defenses against a universe ruled by atrocity and the irrational in an attempt to prevent man's total defeat at its hands; Wiesel's relationship to *l'univers concentrationnaire* was far more tentative, and he was concerned no less with its effect than with its essence. The unreal reality of *Night* and most literature of atrocity exists in a world halfway between Camus's alternatives of suicide or recovery.

Perhaps even *essence* is an inexact word for Wiesel's appeal to the imagination as well as to the intelligence of the reader: asked some years after the liberation if he himself believed what had happened in Auschwitz, he replied, "I do not believe it. The event seems unreal, as if it occurred on a different planet." Even more paradoxically, he commented on the difficulty of coming to terms, not with the Holocaust—"one never comes to terms with it"—but with its tale:

> The full story of the Holocaust has not yet been told [1967!] All that we know is fragmentary, perhaps even untrue. Perhaps what we tell about what happened and what really happened has nothing to do one with the other. We want to remember. But remember what? And what for? Does anyone know the answer to this?[3]

What this ambiguity conceals we may never know, but it emphasizes the difficult struggle between language and truth that every author must engage in when he turns to this theme; and the important distinctions it draws between the Holocaust itself and its tale, "what really happened" and "what we tell about what happened," explains why Wiesel's autobiographical narrative reads more like fiction than "truth," since the power of the imagination to evoke an atmosphere does far more than the historian's fidelity to fact to involve the uninitiated reader in the atmosphere of the Holocaust.

Night is an account of a young boy's divorce from life, a drama of recognition whose scenes record the impotence of the familiar in the face of modern atrocity; at its heart lies the profoundest symbolic confrontation of our century, the meeting of man and Auschwitz (a meeting reenacted by Rolf Hochhuth in the culminating episode of *The Deputy*)—and this confrontation in turn confirms (as in Anthony Hecht's "More Light! More Light!") the defeat of man's tragic potentiality in our time, and the triumph of death in its most nihilistic guise. The book begins with the familiar, a devout Jewish family whose faith supports their human aspirations and who find their greatest solace—and assurance—in the opportunity of approaching, through diligent study, the divine intentions implicit in reality. The premises behind these aspirations are clarified for the boy narrator by Moché the Beadle, a humble, sagelike man-of-all-work in the Hasidic synagogue in the Transylvanian town where the boy grows up:

"Man raises himself toward God by the questions he asks

Him.... That is the true dialogue. Man questions God and God answers. But we don't understand his answers. We can't understand them. Because they come from the depths of the soul, and they stay there until death. You will find the true answers ... only within yourself."[4]

With this counsel, says the narrator, "my initiation began"; but the kind of questions one asks in his dialogue with God are determined by tradition and education and assumptions that have withstood the assault of adversity. Moche's wisdom is tested when he is deported, together with other foreign Jews from the small Hungarian town. One day (having escaped, miraculously, from his captors), he reappears with tales of Jews digging their own graves and being slaughtered, "without passion, without haste," and of babies who were thrown into the air while "the machine gunners used them as targets" (p. 18). The joy was extinguished from his eyes as he told these tales, but on one believed him—including the young narrator.

The inability of humanity to accept the version of reality proclaimed by Moche the Beadle brings us once again to the world of despair transcending tragedy inhabited by King Lear. For just as Lear attributes to the symbols of royalty more power than they possess, and stubbornly refuses to believe that his daughters are capable of the monstrous behavior and attitudes which his situation confirms, so the citizens of Sighet, the narrator's town, depend on the material "items" of their civilization, almost as if they were sacred talismans, for security. Their abandoned possessions, after their deportation, become symbols of a vanished people, a forgotten and now useless culture.

Throughout *Night*, Wiesel displays a remarkable talent for investing the "items" of reality, and of the fantastic "irreality" that replaces it, with an animistic quality, and then setting both on a pathway leading to an identical destination: death. For example, in this description of a landscape without figured, crowded with things but devoid of life—less macabre than Borchert's bomb-ruined Hamburg but equally devastating to the imagination—in this passage, presided over by an indifferent nature, symbols of an exhausted past turn into harbingers of a ghastly future:

> The street was like a market place that had suddenly been abandoned. Everything could be found there: suitcases, portfolios, briefcases, knives, plates, banknotes, papers, faded portraits. All those things that people had thought of taking with them, and which in the end they had left behind. They had lost all value.
>
> Everywhere rooms lay open. Doors and windows gaped onto the emptiness. Everything was free for anyone, belonging to nobody. It was simply a matter of helping oneself. An open tomb.
>
> A hot summer sun. [p. 28]

Just as Lear undergoes a physical disrobing and a spiritual denudation before he gains a measure of self-knowledge and a more valid conception of reality, so the fifteen-year-old narrator of *Night* is gradually deprived of the props which have sustained him in his youth; but his experience is such that self-knowledge (as ultimately for Lear) becomes more of a burden than a consolation, and "a more valid conception of reality" sounds like a piece of impious rhetoric.

The displacement of life by death as a measure of existence is metaphorically reinforced in *Night*—as it is in some of Nelly Sachs's poems—by imagery that has become standard fare for much literature of atrocity, imagery facilitating the transition from one world to the other—the boxcars, for example, in which victims were transported:

> The doors were closed. We were caught in a trap, right up to our necks. The doors were nailed up; the way back was finally cut off. The world was a cattle wagon hermetically sealed. [p.35]

"Liberation" from this hermetic world upon arrival in the camp, however, changes nothing; the "way back" ceases to have meaning, and man must turn his attention to absorbing the nature of the fearful "way ahead," and of finding methods to survive in spite of it, though the price he must pay for his survival is not calculable in figures inherited from the familiar past. He must somehow accommodate himself to an environment dominated by the macabre images of furnace and chimney, of flames in the night and smoke and reeking human flesh; and he must further acknowledge, against all his human impulses and religious training, the authenticity of this harsh, incredible fate:

"Do you see that chimney over there? See it? Do you see those flames? (Yes, we did see the flames.) Over there—that's where you're going to be taken. That's your grave, over there. Haven't you realized it yet? You dumb bastards, don't you understand anything? You're going to be burned. Frizzled away. Turned into ashes." [p. 40]

Those absent no longer touched even the surface of our memories. We still spoke of them—"Who knows what may have become of them?"—but we had little concern for their fate. We were incapable of thinking of anything at all. Our senses were blunted; everything was blurred as in a fog. It was no longer possible to grasp anything. The instincts of self-preservation, of self-defense, of pride, had all deserted us. In one ultimate moment of lucidity it seemed to me that we were damned souls wandering in the half-world, souls condemned to wander through space till the generations of man came to an end, seeking their redemption, seeking oblivion—without hope of finding it. [pp. 45-46]

The narrator's response introduces a tension that permeates the literature of atrocity: "Surely it was all a nightmare? An unimaginable nightmare?" With a desperate insistence he clings to a kind of emotional nostalgia, as if the stability of his being depends on an affirmative answer; but a subsequent experience shatters that stability permanently, and his efforts henceforth are devoted to making the reader relive the nightmare that continues to haunt him.

His world crumbles—as did Ivan Karamazov's—over the suffering of little children: his first night in the camp he sees babies hurled into a huge ditch from which gigantic flames are leaping:

I pinched my face. Was I still alive? Was I awake? I could not believe it. How could it be possible for them to burn people, children, and for the world to keep silent? No, none of this could be true. It was a nightmare.... Soon I should wake with a start, my heart pounding, and find myself back in the bedroom of my childhood, among my books.... [p. 42]

The waking dream, haunted by the omnipresence of death, filled with "truths" unacceptable to reason but vivid, nevertheless, in their unquestionable actuality, leads first to a disorientation—the new inmates of the camp begin reciting the Jewish prayer for the dead *for themselves*—then to an attempt, at least by the young narrator, to discover mental attitudes commensurate with what the mind initially finds incomprehensible. The ritual incantation which marks his inauguration into *l'univers concentrationnaire* inverts the traditional pattern of autobiography and *Bildungsroman* by beginning with a repudiation that depletes the possibilities of life scarcely after it has begun; it signifies not only a boy's despair, but the exhaustion of meaning in a world henceforth unlike anything men have ever encountered:

> Never shall I forget that night, the first night in camp, which has turned by life into one long night, seven times cursed and seven times sealed. Never shall I forget that smoke. Never shall I forget the little faces of the children, whose bodies I saw turned into wreaths of smoke beneath a silent blue sky.
>
> Never shall I forget those flames which consumed my faith forever.
>
> Never shall I forget that nocturnal silence which deprived me, for all eternity, of the desire to live. Never shall I forget those moments which murdered my God and my soul and turned my dreams to dust. Never shall I forget these things, even if I am condemned to live as long as God Himself. Never. [pp. 43-44]

When the author of these words said a decade later that the events seemed unreal, that he did not believe they had happened to him, he emphasized not only their uniqueness, but also the paradoxical situation that life goes on even after it has "stopped," that Wiesel the man survives and talks about what happened—or remains silent—while Wiesel the writer, certainly in *Night,* has transcended history and autobiography and used the imagery of atrocity and his own experience to involve the nonparticipant in the essence of its world. With due respect to the suffering of the victims, one may repeat what has often been reported by students of the Holocaust—after a particular point, catalogues of brutalities and lists of statistics cease to affect the mind or the imagination, *not* because what they seek to convey lacks significance, but because the mind and imagination lack a suitable context for the information. Hence Wiesel's gradual shift in focus to the *implications* of the events, and his dramatic juxtaposition of carefully selected—though always genuine—scenes and feelings, create an indispensable vestibule for anyone wishing to venture farther into the mansion of Holocaust fiction.

When the first night ends, the narrator presumably has left normality behind, and death has infected his future: "The student of the Talmud, the child that I was, had been consumed in the flames. There remained only a shape that looked like me. A dark flame had entered into my soul and devoured it." The flame illuminates a vision of the self which under ordinary circumstances might be called self-knowledge, but here leads to a futility that negates tragedy and prefigures an exile more complete than anything Camus ever conjured up, a human condition that will have to create new terms for its existence, since Auschwitz has irrevocably breached any meaningful alliance between it and the past:

Even *oblivion* and *redemption,* once the sacred and universally recognizable alternatives in Dante's *Inferno* and *Paradiso,* are goals consigned to the limbo of language, words drawn from memory because reality affords no exact vocabulary for what Wiesel wishes to describe; Wiesel's "half-world," in many of its features remarkably like Hermann Kasack's purely imaginary *Totentraum* or Dream of Death, responds to evocation through vague images rather than specific ideas. Language is not reduced to silence, but it must be used more sparingly, and its range of allusion is governed by concrete experiences rather than by abstract conceptions: for example, the word *furnace,* which was not, says Wiesel, "a word empty of meaning: it floated on the air, mingling with the smoke. It was perhaps the only word which did have any real meaning here" (p. 48).

For Stephen Dedalus, words—"A day of dappled seaborne clouds," for instance—unlocked the mysteries of reality and disclosed vistas of beauty that inspired him to affirm his spirit before a hostile or indifferent world and trust his powers of creation to shape the future. In *l'univers concentrationnaire* of Wiesel's narrator, a diametrically opposite principle of negation prevails, whereby events silence the creative spirit, destroy the longings of youth, and cast over reality an all-embracing shadow of death.

One of the dramatic pinnacles of *Night* illustrates with unmitigated horror this reversal of the *Bildungsroman* formula: three prisoners, two men and a young boy, have been "convicted" of sabotage within the camp and are sentenced to be hanged before thousands of inmates. One imagines the boy, a "sad-eyed angel" on the gallows in the middle, the older victims on either side of him, a grotesque and painful parody— though literally true—of the original redemptive sufferer; the sentence is executed, and the prisoners are forced to march by the dangling bodies, face to face with their own potential fate;

> The two adults were no longer alive. Their tongues hung swollen, blue-tinged. But the third rope was still moving; being so light, the child was still alive....
>
> For more than half an hour he stayed there, struggling between life and death, dying in slow agony under our eyes. And we had to look him full in the face. He was still alive when I passed in front of him. His tongue was still red, his eyes were not yet glazed.
>
> Behind me, I heard [a] man asking:
>
> "Where is God now?"
>
> And I heard a voice within me answer him:
>
> "Where is He? Here He is—He is hanging here on this gallows...."
>
> That night the soup tasted of corpses. [p. 71]

More than one boy's life and another boy's faith is extinguished here, and more than soup loses its familiar taste— a rationale for being, a sense of identification with the human species (as well as a divine inheritance), all the feelings which somehow define our world as a "civilized" place of habitation, are sacrificed on this gallows crucifix, until it is no longer possible to establish a connection between one's intelligence and its apprehension of surrounding reality. The ritual of death, the agonizing struggle between living and dying which always has one inevitable outcome, even if some fortunate few should literally survive—for a time—the ritual of death ungraced by the possibility of resurrection, becomes the focus of existence and shrouds reality in an atmosphere of irrational, impenetrable gloom—"Our senses were blunted," as Wiesel wrote earlier; "everything was blurred as in a fog."

Under such circumstances men learn to adopt toward totally irrational events attitudes that one would expect only from insane or otherwise bewildered human beings: the result is that the incredible assumes some of the vestments of ordinary reality, while normality appears slightly off-center, recognizable, one might say, "north-north-west." Neither total confusion nor absolute comprehension, neither a mad world in which men behave sanely, nor a reasonable one in which human conduct seems deranged—this is the schizo-phrenic effect Wiesel achieves in his autobiographical nar-rative. It is scarcely necessary to arrange literal episodes or invent new ones to create the nightmare atmosphere which imaginative works in the tradition will strive for—such is the unique nature of reality in *l'univers concentrationnaire*. For example, shortly after the episode of the hanging of the boy, the Jewish New Year arrives, and Wiesel establishes a counterpoint between the traditional celebration of the in-mates, who offer the familiar prayers of praise—"All creation bears witness to the Greatness of God!"—and his own religious disillusionment, which makes him resemble a solitary shrub on a desolate island of faith, which itself appears diminutive and even slightly ludicrous in an endless sea of atrocity:

> My eyes were open and I was alone—terribly alone in a world without God and without man. Without love or mercy. I had ceased to be anything but ashes, yet I felt myself to be stronger than the Almighty, to whom my life had been tied for so long. I stood amid that praying congregation, observing it like a stranger. [pp. 73-74]

Nevertheless, a short time later the apostate narrator seriously debates with fellow inmates living in the shadow of the crematorium whether or not they should fast on Yom Kippur, the Day of Atonement. No participant in this discussion could appreciate more intensively than the innocent, horrified spectator-reader the scathing irony, not to say the insane logic, of this situation: starving men choosing not to eat. The narrator ultimately nibbles his bread and feels a void in his heart, a void intensified by the futility of religious values in a universe that not only refuses to acknowledge them, but is built on premises so cynical that such values mock the men who espouse them.

For the victims who seek sustenance in their faith are reduced·to a more degrading role by the subsequent episode, a "selection"—which in plain language meant that some men, usually those physically weaker, were periodically designated for death in a ritual that resembled the weeding-out of defective parts in a machine-assembly plant. Men who know in advance that their life depends on the opinion of an SS "doctor" run past this official, hoping that their numbers will not be written down; most pass the "test," but a few are aware that they "fail," that in two or three days they will be taken to the "hospital" and never be seen again. After such knowledge, what humanity? What logic or reason or connection between what men do and what they suffer, can prevail in one's conception of the universe? In one's conception of one's self? For the narrator, existence is reduced to an elemental struggle between acquiescence to death—"Death wrapped itself around me till I was stifled. It stuck to me. I felt that I could touch it. The idea of dying, of no longer being, began to fascinate me." (p. 90)—and the need to live, in order to support his weakening father, broken in health and spirit by the rigorous discipline of the camp.

Ultimately, the contest between Death and the Father, the one representing *l'univers concentrationnaire* with its insidious and macabre dissolution of reasonable longings, the other all those familiar inheritances which constitute the basis of civilized existence—ultimately, this contest assumes symbolic dimensions, as if normalcy in its dying gasp makes one final effort to assert its authority over the gruesome power seeking to dispossess it. But when death intrudes on the imagination to the point where memory and hope are excluded—as happens in *Night*—then this rivalry, with the accompanying gesture of resistance, proves futile; a kind of inner momentum has already determined the necessary triumph of death in a world disrupted beyond the capacity of man to alter it. The extent of the disruption, and the transformation in humanity wrought by it, is painfully illustrated by the cry of SS guards to the prisoners being transported westward in open cattle-cars from Auschwitz (because of the approaching Russian troops) to Buchenwald: "Throw out all the dead! All corpses outside!"— and by the response of those still surviving: "The living rejoiced. There would be more room" (p. 100).

Thus disinherited, bereft of any value that might permit him to confront the inevitable death of his father with at least the dignity of an illusion, and compelled in the depths of his heart to accept the desolate rule of *l'univers concentrationnaire*— "Here there are no fathers, no brothers, no friends. Everyone lives and dies for himself alone." (p. 111)—the narrator helplessly watches his last living link with the familiar world of the past expire and learns that grief has expired with him. Not only have normal feelings lapsed—plunging us into a shadowy realm where men cease to respond to reality by following any predictable pattern—but they have been replaced by attitudes which a "normally" disposed reader, still bound by the moral premises of pre-Holocaust experience, would characterize as verging on the inhuman. But to the reader who has himself submitted imaginatively to the hallucination-become-fact of this experience, the narrator's reaction to his father's death can more accurately be described as one illustration of what happens when human character is pressed beyond the limits of the human: "in the recesses of my weakened conscience, could I have searched it, I might perhaps have found something like—free at last!" (p. 113).

At this moment, to follow Camus's language, man is divorced from his life, the actor from his setting, and the son (in a manner quite different from the conventional *Bildungsroman*) severed from his patrimony and thrust forth onto a stage which requires the drama of existence to continue, though without a script, *sans* director, the plot consisting of a single unanswerable question: How shall I enact my survival in a world I know to be darkened by the shadow of irrational death, before an audience anticipating a performance that will be illuminated by the light of reason and the glow of the future? Out of some such query as this, representing a paradox of private existence, is born a principle of schizophrenic art, the art of atrocity.

The final, haunting moment of *Night* occurs when the narrator, Wiesel himself, following his liberation, gazes at his own visage after lingering between life and death (a result of food poisoning):

> One day I was able to get up, after gathering all my strength. I wanted to see myself in the mirror hanging on the opposite wall. I had not seen myself since the ghetto.

> From the depths of the mirror, a corpse gazed back at me.
>
> The look in his eyes, as they stared into mine, has never left me. [p. 116]

An unrecognizable face from the past and a living death-mask—variations on this confrontation, spanning two worlds with a current linking regret to despair, characterizes the literature that grew out of the nightmare of history which transformed a fifteen-year-old boy into a breathing corpse.

Wiesel's account is ballasted with the freight of fiction: scenic organization, characterization through dialogue, periodic climaxes, elimination of superfluous or repetitive episodes, and especially an ability to arouse the empathy of his readers, which is an elusive ideal of the writer bound by fidelity to fact. His narrative approaches fiction in its ability to evoke rather than describe the two worlds that eventually create a Karamazov-like "double" in the narrator on the final page. It demonstrates more clearly than any other literal account of the Holocaust how powerfully the paradoxes of this historical horror will challenge and exasperate the imagination of the artist—the painter as well as the writer, one might add—who tries to create a form appropriate to its jagged revelations. The young boy who stared at the inarticulate knowledge and suffering in the eyes of his reflection at that crucial moment in his life was destined to become a novelist himself, though his fictional concern with the implications of his ordeal—understandably enough, perhaps—would be more philosophical than dramatic; but the *sensibilité concentrationnaire*, roused by similar knowledge, if not always similar suffering, drew this portion of history into the unlimited aspirations of literary art, and gave it a resonance and universality which only imaginative literature could achieve.

1. Erich Kahler, *The Tower and the Abyss* (New York: The Viking Press, 1967), p. 151.
2. Albert Camus, *The Myth of Sisyphus*, trans. Justin O'Brien (New York: Vintage Books, 1959), p. 5.
3. "Jewish Values in the Post-Holocaust Future," *Judaism* 16 (Summer 1967): 283; 285.
4. Elie Wiesel, *Night*, trans. Stella Rodway (New York: Hill and Wang, 1960), p. 16.

FROM *NIGHT* TO *THE GATES OF THE FOREST:*
The Novels of Elie Wiesel
by Irving Halperin

Elie Wiesel is widely acclaimed as one of the most important and influential writers in the literature of the Holocaust. His books *Night, Dawn, The Accident, The Town Beyond the Wall,* and *The Gates of the Forest* have reached an international audience. He has received a number of literary prizes (the Prix Rivarol in Paris in 1963, the National Jewish Book Council Award in 1964, the Remembrance Award of the World Federation of the Bergen-Belsen Association), and he was the first recipient of the B'nai B'rith prize for "excellence in Jewish literature." In June of 1967, an honorary doctorate of letters was conferred on him by the Jewish Theological Seminary of America.

Yet despite such recognition, his work has been criticized on the grounds that it suffers from overstatement, rhetoric, sentimentality, and a lack of literary inventiveness. This criticism has its source in a critical view which asserts that writers on the Holocaust need to keep their "cool." The familiar prescription of those who espouse this position is for the writer to maintain an ice-cold, surgical detachment from his material. Supporters of the "cool" approach to Holocaust literature argue that the suffering and atrocities of World War II cannot be rendered by direct emotional involvement—indeed, to become too emotional is to risk, they warn, losing control over one's material—therefore, let the writer employ obliqueness, irony, wryness, casual wit, lunatic humor, and subterranean fantasy. In sum, their argument is that the horrors of the Holocaust can be made endurable to the reader only through the manipulation of literary artifice.

Hence some reviewers have reacted predictably to a writer like Elie Wiesel. A. Alvarez (*Commentary,* November 1964) judged Wiesel's *Night* a defective book because it fell back on rhetoric and overstatement. How much better, he argued, is Piotr Rawicz's *Blood from the Sky,* because there the writer uses "diversionary tactics to convey intensities which he could not otherwise express." Elsewhere in the article he praised Rawicz for finding "imaginative ways around the atrocities." Herbert Mitgang called *The Accident* "falsely melodramatic." Another reviewer, Theodore Frankel (*Midstream,* December 1964), concluded that Wiesel's novel *The Town Beyond the Wall* is spoiled by "overwriting, sentimentalizing, and a maudlin philosophy whose shallowness too often contrasts oddly with the terrible misery which evoked it." Joseph Friedman (*Saturday Review,* July 25, 1964) found the "parables and moralizing passages" of *The Town Beyond the Wall* "diffuse and lacking in narrative pressure," but he admired the nonrealistic aspects of the work, especially the "impressionistic opening sequence, a fragmented, hallucinatory abstraction." And Emile Capouya (*Saturday Review,* May 28, 1966), in reviewing *The Gates of the Forest,* remarked that Wiesel's "literary talent, in the narrow sense, is quite meager."

Such evaluations prefigure the complications that arise when the reader is called upon to function as a critic of Holocaust literature. For how is he to judge literary works in this area? Is he simply to look at them as products of the literary imagination? But given the extraordinary nature of their content, how is this possible? And even if it were, what criteria would one use in evaluating them as literature? Should a book like, say, *Night* be subjected to the same kinds of critical standards one would employ for a Hemingway or Fitzgerald novel? Is one to insist that precisely because the content of Holocaust fiction is often macabre, the author has a special obligation to eschew overstatement? Is one to argue that because many of these works are boiling, raging with the compulsion to bear witness to a time of chaos and destruction, the author ought to enforce a logical, astringently formal structure upon his works—to make order out of rage? I believe that David Daiches has offered the most satisying and valid response to these questions, especially as they apply to

Wiesel's books. In a review (*Commentary,* December 1965) of
The Gates of the Forest, he writes:

> It is impossible to discuss Wiesel's novels in the terms
> which one would normally employ in reviewing fiction.
> All his works are clearly autobiographical, directly or
> indirectly, and they represent a genuine and sometimes
> painful endeavor to come to terms with post-Auschwitz
> life. The problem they deal with is central in modern
> experience, so that we are continually led as we read to go
> beyond the novels to reflect on how we ourselves should
> think or feel on this issue. They are thus important
> documents of modern consciousness and as such they
> ought to command the widest possible audience. As for
> myself, I would go further and confess that I cannot tell
> and I do not care whether these are great novels. But they
> are certainly important evidence, great documents, deal-
> ing with something which must perpetually haunt
> everyone old enough to have lived through World War
> II.

Not so much as *literary* works but rather as important
documents of modern consciousness—that is how David
Daiches would reply to critics who raise the question of
Wiesel's books, "But are they art?"

To return to the question of artistic distancing, a sufficient
detachment between the writer and his work is necessary to
fiction. But surely it is no disservice to art to approach such
stories on the Holocaust with the kind of passion *directly*
rendered by a writer like Wiesel. For such tales "writ in
blood," can one not respect the writer who risks underdistance
rather than the reverse? In any event, to argue that since the
literal facts of the catastrophe are often unbearable, they must
be altered and made acceptable to the literary imagination is a
curious prescription. Rather why not insist that the services of
art be employed to make the literal facts of the tragedy even
more unendurable? Is, for example, *The Last of the Just* any the
worse a book because the ending, when Ernie Levy and Golda
go to their deaths in a gas chamber, is presented in a detailed,
realistic manner, without recourse to the strategies and
devices of the literary imagination? Instead of being concerned
about whether the author has used "diversionary tactics" and
"imaginative ways around the atrocities," "pro-cool" critics

might be better advised to determine whether the work is, to cite again the words of David Daiches, "an important document of modern consciousness."

Apart from the question of artistic distancing, is it a service to the facts of the Holocaust to keep a spotlight exclusively trained on the grotesque and bestial aspects of human behavior? Whenever men were at their worst, whenever they were without compassion or understanding, this, one adduces from reading the "pro-cool" reviews, is fertile ground for artistic invention. The assumption here seems to be that the literary treatment of the inhuman makes for far more interesting reading than a presentation of admirable human conduct. Indeed, it is as though these reviewers were highly skeptical that exemplary behavior in the camps or ghettos can be rendered without the writer's falling into sentimentality.

Now obviously the realm of the perverse and inhuman is an appropriate theme for Holocaust literature. But it is too bad that these same critics have not pointed out the abundance of impressive human relationships that is recorded in this body of literature: the warm responsiveness registered between Viktor Frankl and his fellow prisoners (*From Death-Camp to Existentilism*); Eugene Heimler and the sixteen children he protected in Buchenwald (*Night of the Mist*); Micklos and Weinstock (*The Seven Years*); Primo Levi and an Italian civilian (*If This Is a Man*); Tania and Eva (*Tell Me Another Morning*); Henriques and Hirsch (*Breaking-Point*); and Daniella and Fella (*House of Dolls*). The abundance of these relationships in the camps and walled ghettos lends support to the belief sounded in the last lines of Camus's *The Plague:* "What we learn in a time of pestilence: that there are more things to admire in man than to despise."

Moreover, those writers whose characters attempt to climb out of the pit of degradation and bestiality often take greater literary risks than those whose characters and situations emphasize the grotesque and bestial in human behavior. It can be easy for the writer to be icily dispassionate in writing on the sadistic, unfeeling temperament of Nazis. Much harder and difficult it can be to delineate the attempts of prisoners to be "worthy" of their suffering. Much harder and difficult and risky it is for the writer to render the loss of faith in a young man (like the protagonist of *Night*) imprisoned within the absolute hell of Auschwitz.

So that if one puts some of the "cool" writers beside Elie Wiesel, they seem rather unsatisfactory. Wiesel's books are powerful, painful documents of moral force. They sear through the defenses of the reader and strike at him like blows. They can leave one hurt, depressed, even suicidal. At the least, they make the reader feel on his pulses the writer's agony and anger in writing on the recent past.

Granted that Wiesel, by explicitly probing into the moral center of Holocaust experiences, is immersed in an undertaking that certainly involves the artistic risk of being sentimental and rhetorical. However, I think it is ill-advised to raise the question of his works posed or implied by some critics: "But are they art?" Surely there must be standards, other than artistic distancing, obliqueness, etc., for judging such powerful documents of moral force. Wiesel is an important writer not by the rules of contemporary fiction but because his books excite us to intense reflection. Clearly, they have suggested some of the most crucial, if unanswerable, questions pertinent to the Holocaust.

From night (an infernolike atmosphere of suffering and despair) to a gate (the possibilities for individual redemption) —that is the route taken by the narrator-survivors of Elie Wiesel's five novels. From the walls of a concentration camp to the openness of a forest, symbol of the marginal and conditional presence of purity in the universe. The gate? It is the door, the way, leading, hopefully, to redemption. But the problem is that there are many gates in the Wieselean world and for each seeker only one way is right. At any rate, Wiesel's protagonists are in search of *the* gate, and the essential movement and direction of the five novels is from the dark night of the soul *toward*—but not *to*—spiritual rebirth.

It is not an easy road; along the way there are many trials. For a time the archetypal protagonist-survivor of the novels considers the "gate" of suicide as a way out of his unhappiness; later he considers going mad to blot out his grief and shame as a survivor. The worst trials of all are those times when he sees himself as a cursed soul condemned to wander in a nether world without respite and without hope of ever finding redemption. Thus, within this perspective, the "right" gate is at the poles from the cycles of hopeless wandering.

While the protagonist-survivor is in search of his own gate, what is it he "does" along the way? Essentially, he

confronts the questions: What is the meaning of the Holocaust? the meaning of the suffering that afflicts Holocaust
survivors? They are questions no longer asked of God by the
Wieselean survivor; not asked of Him because "God may be
dead." Or, if not dead, then indifferent to the tragic fate of
European Jewry. And yet the survivor needs to think that
there is sense in asking the question, What is the meaning of
such individual and collective tragedy? Because he feels if there
is not even the semblance of an answer to this question, then
life itself and the will to live are unworthy.

But over the course of the five novels, the Wieselean
narrator does not come even close to answering such questions, with the possible exception of a brief moment in *The
Gates of the Forest* when a Williamsburg Hasidic rabbi tells him
that human suffering is God's way of testing man, and that
man's responsibility is to withstand such trials, for "at the end
of such suffering, God awaits us."

Prior to that moment, the narrator generally feels alone
and isolated in a world without God. He has escaped being
turned into ashes but looks at himself as a kind of cursed ghost
wandering in a twilight world halfway between the Holocaust
dead and the living of the present who do not want to hear his
message. The living do not want to listen because his presence
disturbs and frightens them. This does not surprise him, for
even in his own eyes he is a "poisoned messenger" from the
realm of the dead; Auschwitz, Buchenwald are still *in* him.
As the price for having survived, he is seared by guilt. Thus in
The Gates of the Forest, Gregor, a survivor, thinks: "He who is
not among the victims is with the executioners."

But if the Wieselean protagonist is haunted by ghosts, he
ultimately resolves to fight them. Without such resolution and
effort his journey in search of redemption would be lacking in
tension. The fact is, however, that he does grapple with the
demons of his past; and the degree to which he ultimately
succeeds in partly exorcising them may be determined by
looking at the endings of the first and fifth novels. In *Night*, on
being liberated at Buchenwald, the narrator looks into a
mirror, observing that "a corpse gazed back at me." Hence the
last image of the first novel underscores a mood of despair and
the book ends on a note of unqualified blackness; *Night* ends in
night.

Now *The Gates of the Forest* hardly ends in light; the narrator is still an unhappy, tortured man. And yet the difference is this: in the final moments of the book, Gregor goes to a synagogue to recite Kaddish for his father who died in Buchenwald; and this act indicates an emergent openness to the possibilities for some future renewal of religious faith.

From Buchenwald to the synagogue, from the image of a corpselike face in a mirror to the grandiloquent and serene words of the Kaddish—these are the key beginning and terminal road markers along the route taken by the five novels. But of course this is to see them from an all-too-wide overview. What is needed—and what now follows—is a detailed examination of each of the five novels.

Night defines the nature and charts the consequences of a loss of faith in the protagonist, Eliezer, as incident by incident, layer by layer, his trust in God and man is peeled away. It is this "peeling down" process which constitutes the essential structure of *Night* and enables us to see it as a whole; the purpose of what follows is to adumbrate this process.

Eliezer as a boy in Sighet, a small town in Transylvania, absorbed the religious beliefs of his teacher, Moché the beadle, at a Hasidic synagogue. Moché prescribed that one should pray to God for "the strength to ask Him the right questions."

> "Man raises himself toward God by the questions he asks Him," he [Moché] was fond of repeating. "That is the true dialogue. Man questions God and God answers. But we don't understand His answers. We can't understand them. Because they come from the depths of the soul, and they stay there until death. You will find the true answers, Eliezer, only within yourself!" (P. 16.)

Later, as a result of his experiences during the Holocaust, Eliezer would cease especting to get answers to his questions; indeed, he would come to say that question and answer are not necessarily interrelated. Then what should men do—stop asking such questions? Not at all. The protagonists in the later novels, in *The Town Beyond the Wall* and *The Gates of the Forest*, contend that men must continue to pose them. But not to God, who, in the eyes of the Wieselean narrator, remained silent during the Holocaust. Rather, these questions must come out of the depths of men and be addressed to other men. For to be human, to exercise one's humanity, is to go on

posing such questions, even in the face of the Absurd, of
Nothingness.

But such recognition for the protagonist was in the distant
future. Meanwhile, in the beginning of *Night*, the boy Eliezer
did not question Moché's teachings. He believed that as long
as Jews studied and were pious no evil could touch them. The
Germans proved he was mistaken when they occupied Sighet
in the spring of 1944. In consequence, the first of Moché's
teachings jettisoned by Eliezer was the notion that a Jew
should live lowly, self-effacing and inconspicuous. Certainly
Moché was an "invisible" man. The narrator says of him;
"Nobody ever felt embarrassed by him. Nobody ever felt
encumbered by his presence. He was a past master in the art of
making himself insignificant, of seeming invisible."

And yet remaining "invisible" did not help Moché; the
Germans systematically disposed of him along with Sighet's
entire Jewish population. In the beginning of the Occupation,
Jews were ordered to wear yellow stars, then they were driven
out of their homes and herded into ghettos. A "Jewish
council" and Jewish police were imposed on them. Some of the
populace desperately attempted to escape annihilation by
stationing themselves in such places and at such tasks that
would keep them out of sight. And they further deluded
themselves by thinking: The Germans—after all, this was the
twentieth century—would oppress them up to a certain point
and no further. So the popular advice was: Just do what they
tell you; they only kill those who put up resistance. But in the
end, packs on their backs, the Jewish community was marched
off to a transport center, jammed into cattle wagons, and sent
off to concentration camps. Meekness, staying "invisible,"
had not worked. And it is as though Wiesel laments that here
was another instance wherein the Jew contributed to his
agelong fate as victim and "specialist" in suffering. Ought
not the time come when the Jew will make history itself
tremble—when, if need be, *he* will be the executioner? In sum,
Eliezer learned from having undergone the Occupation and
deportation, that it is useless to employ the disguises of the
"invisible" Jew. And this recognition constituted the first
major puncture of his heretofore innocent faith in the teachings
of Moché.

Belief in God the fifteen-year-old Eliezer had before he

came to Auschwitz. But there, in *anus mundi*, that faith was consumed in the flames that consumed children. There "God" was the official on the train ramp who separated life from death with a flick of a finger to the right or left. Yet some Jews continued to urge children to pray to God. "You must never lose faith," they said to Elizer, "even when the sword hangs over your head. That's the teaching of our sages."

But could the sages have imagined the limitless depravity of the Nazis? Could they, in all their wisdom, have counseled a boy of fifteen on how to react to the mass burning of children? To see a child's head, arms, and legs go up in flame—that is an indisputable fact, a measurable phenomenon.

Did He care that children were being consumed by fire? This is the question raised by the narrator of *Night*. And if He does nothing to prevent the mass murder of children, Eliezer cries out: "Why should I bless His name?" This outcry is the sign of, as François Mauriac says in his foreword to the book, "the death of God in the soul of a child who suddenly discovers absolute evil." And this breakdown of religious faith calls forth Eliezer's resolve "never to forget."

> Never shall I forget that night, the first night in camp, which has turned my life into one long night, seven times cursed and seven times sealed. Never shall I forget that smoke. Never shall I forget the little faces of the children, whose bodies I saw turned into wreaths of smoke beneath a silent blue sky.
>
> Never shall I forget those flames which consumed my faith forever.
>
> Never shall I forget that nocturnal silence which deprived me, for all eternity, of the desire to live. Never shall I forget those moments which murdered my God and my soul and turned my dreams to dust. Never shall I forget these things, even if I am condemned to live as long as God Himself. Never. (Pp. 43-44.)

So, too, on the eve of Rosh Hashanah, Eliezer, who until then had always been devoted to this holiday, thinks, bitterly:

> Why, but why should I bless him? In every fiber I rebelled. Because He has had thousands of children burned in His pits? Because He kept six crematories working night and day, on Sundays and feast days? Because in His great might He had created Auschwitz,

> Birkenau, Buna, and so many factories of death? How
> could I say to Him: "Blessed art Thou, Eternal, Master of
> the Universe, who chose us from among the races to be
> tortured day and night, to see our fathers, our mothers,
> our brothers, end in the crematory? Praised be Thy Holy
> Name, Thou Who hast chosen us to be butchered on
> Thine Altar?" (P. 73.)

After Auschwitz, Eliezer could no longer speak of God's goodness or His ultimate purposes.

What is the immediate consequence of this loss of faith? Eliezer feels as though he were a lost soul condemned to wander in a haunted realm of darkness. Here the word "darkness" needs to be underscored, for it is a world at the poles from the one of "light" which Eliezer, as a student of the Cabbala and Talmud, inhabited in Sighet. By day the Talmud, and at night, by candlelight, he and his teacher Moché would study together, searching for "the revelation and mysteries of the cabbala." There was not only candlelight when they studied; the Talmud, the Zohar, the cabbalistic books themselves were light; they illuminated the nature of the "question" and suggested the answer; they seemed to draw Moché and Eliezer toward the shining realm of the eternal "where question and answer would become one."

But the light in *Night* is of brief duration; the atmosphere of the book is almost entirely that of blackness. The fires of Auschwitz consume the light, the religious faith, of Eliezer and leave him a "damned soul" wandering through a darkness where question and answer would *never* become one.

What other kinds of disillusionment are experienced by Eliezer? I have already pointed out two—his realization that to be an "invisible" Jew did not protect one from the Nazis and, second, his turning away from God on witnessing the mass burning of children at Auschwitz. There was also his loss of faith in both the myth of twentieth-century civilized man and the tradition of the inviolable bonds between Jewish parents and children. Before coming to Auschwitz, Eliezer had believed that twentieth-century man was civilized. He had supposed that people would try to help one another in difficult times; certainly his father and teachers had taught him that every Jew is responsible for all other Jews. Until the gates of a concentration camp closed upon him he had no reason to doubt that the love between parents and children was characterized by sacrifice, selflessness, and utmost fealty.

But Auschwitz changed all that. There he was forced to look on while a young boy was tortured and then hanged—his death taking more than a half hour of "slow agony." There dozens of men fought and trampled one another for an extra ration of food. In one instance, he saw a son actually killing his elderly father over a portion of bread while other prisoners looked on indifferently. In Auschwitz the conduct of most prisoners was rarely selfless. Almost every man was out to save his own skin; and to do so he would steal, betray, buy life with the lives of others.

Eliezer's progressive disillusionment did not come about simply because of what he witnessed in Auschwitz; he did not only observe the breakdown of faith; he himself in part caused it to happen. Consider Eliezer's thoughts and conduct with respect to his father when both were concentration camp prisoners. Eliezer feels that his father is an encumbrance, an albatross, who jeopardizes his own chances for survival. The son himself is ailing, emaciated, and in attempting to look after the older man strains his own limited physical resources. Moreover, such efforts make him dangerously conspicuous— always a perilous condition for concentration camp prisoners. And yet he despises himself for not having lifted a hand when his elderly father was struck by a Kapo. He had looked on, thinking: "Yesterday I should have sunk my nails into the criminal's flesh. Have I changed so much, then?"

Eliezer's conflict of wanting to protect his father and, conversely, to be separated from him, is so desperate that when the father is on the verge of dying, the son feels ashamed to think: "If only I could get rid of this dead weight, so that I could use all my strength to struggle for my own survival, and only worry about myself." Again, when the dying man is struck with a truncheon by an officer, Eliezer, fearing to be beaten, stands still, like one paralyzed. Finally, when his father is taken off to the crematoria, the son cannot weep. Grief there is in him and yet he feels free of his burden. Thus another illusion is discarded by a boy who had been reared in a tradition that stresses loyalty and devotion to one's parents.

The death of his father leaves Eliezer in a state of numbness; he feels that nothing more can affect him. But there remains still another illusion he is to shed—the belief that on being liberated the prisoners would be capable of avenging themselves on the enemy. They had endured so much in order to live to the day of liberation. How often had the prisoners spoken to one another about what they would do to the Germans. And yet when Buchenwald is liberated, Eliezer observes with anger and disgust that his fellow prisoners are concerned only with bread and not revenge.

He has lost not only his father but also faith in God and humanity. Many of his previously untested beliefs in the staying powers of the "invisible" Jew, the unquestionable justice of God, the built-in restraints of twentieth-century civilization, and the enduring strength of familial bonds between Jewish parents and children have been peeled away. He will have to journey for a long time and through many lands before arriving at that point of retrospective clarity when he can even first frame the "right questions" concerning his season in hell. He will need to stand before some "false" gates before he can turn away from them. And yet, all through this time, he is to hold fast to the belief that his teacher Moché instilled in him: that there *is* an "orchard of truth," and that for entering the gate to this place every human being has his own key. One function of the Wieselean novels that follow *Night* is to trace the protagonist-survivor's journey in search of such a gate.

In *Night*, Eliezer was a boy of fifteen in Auschwitz. Elisha, the protagonist of Wiesel's second novel, *Dawn*, is a young man of eighteen in Palestine. Seeing himself as a messenger from the dead among the living, Elisha attempts to exorcise the past but cannot; neither can he give himself to the living; he continues to wander in an underground world between the living and the dead. Having seen God and civilized man "die" at Auschwitz, he has few illusions left—and yet he still maintains the slim hope that redemption may be ahead.

In the beginning of *Dawn*, Elisha, as a member of the terrorist movement in Palestine, seeks to be persuaded that if he places himself on the other side of the gun, he will be able to exorcise the "night" in his past. Never again does he want to be helpless before an oppressor. He would like to believe that by killing the enemy—in this case the English—he can exoricise memories of having been the victim during the Holocaust.

The man who urges Elisha to become an "executioner" is Gad, a leader in the terrorist movement. Gad considers himself a messenger from the future, and he wants Elish's future; that is, he exhorts Elisha to fight for a Jewish homeland in Palestine. And the most direct way of doing this, Gad urges, is to strike terror into the hearts of the English occupying forces. He urges his fellow terrorists to hate the enemy and to let the latter be fully apprised of the depth and measure of this hate. An elemental hate which would be justified, Gad insists, because through its long history of persecution, the Jewish people have never learned to hate their persecutors, and they were kept in perennial bondage as victims. Until the Jew became the executioner, he would go on being the victim. Hate against the enemy now offered possibilities for a drastic alteration in the future course of Jewish history. Since God is dead, they, the terrorists, would take upon themselves His awesome power of separating life (in this case the lives of the English in Palestine) from death.

> "On the day when the English understand that their occupation will cost them blood they won't want to stay," Gad told us ... "The commandment *Thou shalt not kill* was given from the summit of one of the mountains here in Palestine, and we were the only ones to obey it. But that's all over; we must be like everybody else. Murder will not be our profession but our duty. In the days and weeks and months to come you will have only one purpose: to kill those who have made us killers. We shall kill in order that once more we may be men." (Pp. 29-30.)

The novel turns on Elisha's test of Gad's views. An English officer, a Captain John Dawson, has been captured by the terrorists and condemned to be executed in retaliation for the previous executions of Jewish resistance fighters by the British—specifically for a Jewish fighter whom the British have lately sentenced to death. Elisha has been ordered by the commander of the terrorists to be the executioner; and the execution is to take place at the same time that the Jewish fighter is scheduled to be hanged in the prison at Acre. The

English believe that the Jews are bluffing, that they are not really prepared to go through with the execution, to extract an eye for an eye. After all, the British assume, aren't they long accustomed to turning the other cheek? But this time the British have misjudged the new kind of toughened Jew that had been bred and formed in the Yishuv (community) of Palestine.

Elisha, however, is not one of those who were raised in Palestine. His early years as a European Jew and his experiences in concentration camps have marked him. As a boy he was taught not to hate Amalek but merely to remember him; he was instructed not to fight with Gentiles but rather to keep out of their way. "Man should belong to the persecuted and not the persecutors," he well may have read in the Talmud. And in the camps he found it prudent to remain inconspicuous, "invisible." Yet even as he girds himself for the task of executing Dawson, he hears in the foreground of his consciousness the injunction: "Thou shalt not kill." Not that as a member of the terrorist movement he hadn't killed before; in the past he had ambushed and shot to death English soldiers. However, then the English had been armed, and at least they had been capable of firing back. But John Dawson is helpless and Elisha, acting alone, would have to look him in the eyes and pull the trigger. He fears he might not feel enough hate to do this. And even if he did pull the trigger, would he not then become, in his own eyes, a kind of SS guard shooting down a defenseless prisoner? Moreover, it troubles Elisha that in killing Dawson he may be judged by the spirit of the Holocaust dead and found guilty; that is, found wanting by the moral and religious standards of his parents and former teachers. They would have enjoined him to be kind and merciful to others. They, who had been murdered by the Nazis, would have said that it is never justified for a Jew to become an executioner. And so, as the dawn on which he has been ordered to kill the British officer approaches, Elisha is haunted by the faces of the Holocaust dead.

Why do they judge me of all people? he cries out within himself. Had he not also been a victim, a prisoner in the camps? Had he voluntarily chosen to return from the kingdom of the dead bearing a poisoned message for the living? So why should he be judged? Rather let God be judged, He who had turned his back on the world of men.

But it is not only the dead, he recognizes, who judge him for having survived the camps or for having accepted the order to execute the English soldier; it is also his own silence. That is, his self-imposed alienation from the uncomprehending, "uninitiated" living who were not "there" condemns him.

Finally, when Elisha comes face to face with Dawson a short while before the dawn of the scheduled execution, his exposure to terrorist ideology is put to the supreme test. With this result—he finds himself unable to hate Dawson. Momentarily it appears he will not be able to go through with the execution. And even though he finally does kill Dawson, this act does not bring the young survivor to the promised new "dawn" that Gad had described; Elisha still remains in "night," still views himself as a corpselike messenger from the dead condemned to "wandering in the half world" of the living. Previously, he had hoped that by killing a man who was one of the enemy, he would put an end to his own cursed existence as a "messenger." He had allowed himself this thin hope, and now it too had collapsed. By killing Dawson he had entered a "gate"—only to find himself still lost in an interior wilderness. And just as at the end of *Night* Eliezer beholds a "corpse" on looking at himself in a mirror, Elisha discovers that a frightening "tattered fragment of darkness, hanging in midair, the other side of the window" is actually his own face. Darkness is the note on which the first two novels conclude.

There is still another "false gate" which the protagonist-survivor will enter in the third novel, *The Accident*. Thereupon he will learn that suicide is no solution for his anguish. Now it may be argued that suicide was a justified act for some prisoners of the death camps. Here one thinks of some inmates of Treblinka who took their own lives rather than endure further suffering. They stood up on chairs, attached belts to their necks and the ceilings of their huts and then kicked away the chairs. It was their way of exerting one of the few freedoms the Nazis could not deny them—the freedom of determining the nature and circumstances of their own deaths.

So, too, it is difficult to condemn the suicide attempt of Eliezer, the narrator of *The Accident,* who practically invited a taxi to strike him down while he was crossing a New York street. Why should he, a survivor, be expected to fight for his life, to hold fast to the Talmudic dictum—"therefore choose life"? For the facts are that Eliezer has suffered the loss of his parents, relatives, friends, all victims of the Holocaust. He has been disillusioned by God and man. And he feels guilt and self-incrimination for having survived.

But if Eliezer wants to die, the presence of Wiesel is clearly felt in the story, and he prefers that his protagonist live. To live, to die—it is out of these alternating pressures that the book receives its focal tension. We have already seen that the question "to kill or not to kill" generated tension in *Dawn;* and we will shortly observe that the central tension in the novel directly following *The Accident, The Town Beyond the Wall,* has its source in the protagonist's obsessive question—"to go or not to go mad?" It may be instructive, therefore, to examine the response of Eliezer to the question "to live or not to live?"

At the outset of the story, Eliezer is actually waiting for an accident to happen to him. In a sense he already has been slowly dying ever since his liberation from a Nazi extermination camp. His girl friend, Kathleen, tries, uselessly, to edge him out of his "sickness unto death." She would want him to enjoy the physical pleasures of the everyday world. Eat! she urges him; for it disturbs her that Eliezer has little interest in food. But what she wants for him, he does not want for himself; he is hungry for neither food nor life. Filled with self-disgust for having survived when so many who were close to him did not, he continually thinks of the dead. It is as though he wanted the dead to judge him, to find him guilty. Not the living, because they were not "there" and hence are not worthy to make such judgment. So if he does not owe the living explanations for his agony, neither need he address his "questions" to them, nor seek their counsel; before the living he need maintain only a silence. Or, perhaps better yet, remove his poisonous presence altogether from their sight by committing suicide.

It is at this point, when he is unable to respond to Kathleen's love or to her pleas to *choose* life, that the accident occurs.

After being struck by the taxi and suffering broken bones along the entire left side of his body, internal hemorrhage, and brain concussion, he nevertheless manages, miraculously, to live. A miracle like that other one wherein he survived Buchenwald. In both instances, following the accident and following liberation from the camp, he had been brought back to life from the edge of the grave; and in both instances he half resented having survived.

His will to die stems not only from a sense of guilt at having survived but also from revulsion in seeing himself as a "poisoned" messenger. It is as though Eliezer assumes that by his very presence, he is a mirror to frighten others, to prevent them from forgetting what the Holocaust past was. He who once enjoyed the warm, familial atmosphere of the shtetl, especially as it was embodied in his pious, loving grandmother, now feels empty, cold, emotionally numb; and he believes that his very presence poisons in others the possibilities for joy and hope.

It is not only his "poisoned" presence, Eliezer believes, that frightens others, but also his messages, the stories he tells of the German Occupation, the long night in Buchenwald and Auschwitz, constrain his auditors, those who were spared his suffering, to interrogate their own lives. And indeed, at one point Eliezer says to a resident doctor following the accident:

> My legends can only be told at dark. Whoever listens questions his life.... The heroes of my legends are cruel and without pity. They are capable of strangling you. (P. 73.)

"Whoever listens questions his life"—this might well be an emblematic warning to readers of Wiesel's works. For his stories, probing the darker reaches of human experience, can profoundly disquiet the reader. Whoever turns to this writer can expect to have his most basic assumptions questioned. It is not simply that Wiesel asks such age-old questions as, for example, What is the meaning of suffering? Other writers could ask the same question and not at all affect the reader. Rather it is because of *who* he is, a man who has suffered beyond the scope or endurance of most men, that he poses such questions with searing, authoritative force.

But to return to *The Accident,* while Eliezer feels compelled to be the interrogator, there are those who seek to offer him, if not answers to his questions, friendship and love.

For one, his girl friend Kathleen. She pits, unsuccessfully, the warmth of her affection against his defenses. The struggle between them generates the dialectical tension of this section of the book. Live! she exhorts when she pleads with him to eat. Live! she says with her body when they make love. But why live? he counters. Simply to eat another meal, to lie down for another few hours' sleep, to work yet another day? No, he would not—unless he could, like Tolstoy, following his suicide attempt during his fifties, find a moral sanction for life itself. But where is this sanction to come from? Certainly not from a belief in God, for where was He when twelve-year-old girls were forced to sleep with the SS? Nor from enduring suffering in the belief that it is a trial which strengthens and ennobles us. For on the basis of what he had witnessed in the camps, suffering often brought out the worst in people, made devils of them and not saints. Not for him Dostoevsky's view that one must be "worthy" of one's suffering.

While Eliezer, his broken body encased in plaster, lies in a hospital, Kathleen and the resident doctor persist in urging him to fight for his life. It is as though all three are characters in a medieval morality play where the forces of life are deployed against the forces of death. If Eliezer is not responsive to the efforts of Kathleen and the doctor, it is not because he distrusts or deprecates their motives. He knows them to be generously well intentioned; but, nevertheless, they are powerless to alter his fundamental condition of despair. Clearly, they want him to bury the dead within himself and turn his face toward the possibilities of the present. But Eliezer cannot forget the dead. Even if he could, even if he could settle for a "normal," satisfying life, sooner or later the past would pursue him with double vengeance, with so much force that he would risk going mad.

> "I think if I were able to forget I would hate myself [Eliezer says to Kathleen, speaking about his experiences in the camps]. Our stay there planted time bombs within us. From time to time one of them explodes. And then we are nothing but suffering, shame, and guilt. We feel ashamed and guilty to be alive, to eat as much bread as we want, to wear good, warm socks in the winter. One of these bombs, Kathleen, will undoubtedly bring about madness. It's inevitable. Anyone who has been there has

brought back some of humanity's madness. One day or
another, it will come back to the surface." (P. 105.)

Actually, Eliezer's prognosis of the prospects before him,
if he wills to live, is convincing. A survivor like him might for
a time be able to turn his back on the recent past and to impose
on his daily life a patina of normalcy. To all outward
appearances, such a person might seem to be ably functioning
in his environment. The survivor might have the illusion that
finally he is clear of the past. Then one day, perhaps twenty or
thirty years later, he would be forced to turn and again
confront the horrors of the Holocaust. And such confrontation might well result in madness.

But if Kathleen and the doctor are not successful in their
efforts to convince Eliezer to "choose life," for a time it seems
that his friend, Gyula, might be. The latter, a painter of
Hungarian origin, has a vital, tough-minded temperament,
and for Eliezer he is a "living rock." By contrast with his
friend's sense of futility and resignation, Gyula actively
chooses "to pit himself against fate, to force it to give human
meaning to its cuelty." For Gyula, what a man must do is
clear: God died during the Holocaust but man survived and
lives on; and the best proof of this assertion is the perpetuation
of meaningful human relationships, like his with Eliezer. The
artist tries to convince his friend that men must do whatever
they can to alleviate human suffering; further, as a Jew he is
especially obliged to do so. Such a commitment, Gyula
believes, takes one away from self-involved concerns and
turns him toward others; indeed, to be human is to *respond* to
another human being. In this perspective, Eliezer's will to die
is a negation, a denial, of such response. The would-be suicide
has given up, rejected the possibilities for both individual
growth and human relationship; whereas the man who has
chosen life keeps "moving, searching, weighing, holding out
his hand, offering himself, inventing himself."

To dramatize his point of view, Gyula, in completing a
portrait of his friend, burns it in the hospital room. The gesture
is obviously intended to be symbolic: the face of the man in the
portrait reflects a vast suffering, and the painter wants Eliezer
to exorcise that part of himself which is haunted by by the past.
But though the portrait has been burned, the ashes remain, and
so the third novel ends on the same dark chord as the first

two—the anguish of a survivor who remains a corpselike, poisoned messenger from the dead.

And yet even though Eliezer continues to be imprisoned within the dark night of the soul, as a consequence of the accident and his ten weeks' stay in the hospital, he finally learns that suicide is a "false gate." In rejecting his previous notion that suicide is a courageous and necessary act in a cruelly absurd and meaningless post-Auschwitz world, he has peeled off another illusion. This does not mean, however, that he is ready to approach the right gate, the one which, as cabbalistic legend has it, leads into the orchard of truth. On the contrary, the road directly ahead will lead him to still another false gate—this one marked madness. That cycle is covered by the fourth novel, *The Town Beyond the Wall,* to which we will now turn.

"I HAVE A PLAN—TO GO MAD." Dostoevsky—this is the epigraph of *The Town Beyond the Wall.* And it is the protagonist's attraction to and ultimate rejection of madness as a possible means to the right gate which helps inform the book with an intense dialectical rhythm. At the outset of the story, as though looking to Dostoevsky's highly disturbed characters in *The Possessed,* Michael, the protagonist, wonders whether by abandoning himself to madness he actually would be revolting against his burdensome role as a poisoned messenger. Madness might blot out his need to ask questions of the Holocaust; it might allow him to be numb in heart and mind. In any event, the possibility of madness as a deliverance from shame and guilt attracts Michael, just as Eliezer of *The Accident* was drawn to the possibility of suicide as a way out of his suffering.

But is madness really the way to *the* gate? Michael begins to question as the novel unfolds. Would it really liberate him from his agony? Supposing that it led to even greater torment? Then perhaps to be afflicted by madness would be a more unendurable existence than to continue assuming the burdens of the messenger. True, the latter wanders in a twilight world without much hope of redemption; but the madman experiences the torture of being chained to the wall in an inner chamber of horrors. If such were to be his circumstances, would not suicide be infinitely more desirable than madness?

But if not through madness, by what other means could

one reach and enter *the* gate? This question is precisely what a large part of the book is concerned with—the testing of various alternatives to madness.

The increasing pressure on Michael to go mad comes from the merciless interrogation and torture he is subjected to by police of the postwar Iron Country town of Szersencse-város, the place of his birth and boyhood and where he has been jailed on the suspicion of being a spy. The police officials are determined to learn by what means he entered the country; for such information they promise to go easy on him. But he is no less determined not to break down under their questioning, because the information they seek would endanger the life of Pedro, his Spanish friend and an accomplice in effecting Michael's illegal crossing of the border. Still, the gestapo-type methods of interrogation and torture by these Iron Country officials are so painful that there are moments when he is tempted to let himself fall into the oblivion of madness. He is forced to stand in a cell (ironically called "the temple"), facing a wall. The intent here is to keep him on his feet eight hours at a stretch, day and night, without food or drink, until he is ready to give the police the information they want. He is not permitted to move, to take even a step, to cross his legs or lean against the wall. It is an ordeal calculated to break even the most hardened prisoner within twenty-four hours, but Michael endures the pain, stalling for time so that Pedro can get out of the country safely.

His torture at the wall needs to be seen in other than merely literal terms. The wall is not only a wall in a jail but, symbolically, the dead-end anguish of European Jewry during the Hitler years. It may also represent the sum total of the satanic means—the gas chambers, burning ditches, gas wagons, deadly serums, machine-gun mass executions—used to destroy the bodies of Jews. And Michael's refusal to be broken at the wall is emblematic of those European Jews who, as the narrator remarks, "more than others, possess the secret of survival, the key to the mystery of time, the formula of endurance."

Neither are the attempts of the Iron Country police to make Michael talk meaningful only at the literal level. The interrogation is not simply imposed on him from the outside, it is also self-imposed; that is, the interrogation may be seen as a metaphor for Michael's unrelenting, painful inner probing regarding the Holocaust. He poses unanswerable questions concerning God, man, meaning, evil, suffering, expiation; and the disquieting force of these questions often threatens his tenuous grip on sanity.

In the end, what largely helps Michael to resist the approach of madness is his recollection of Pedro's belief that just as each man has the power to sentence himself to an internal prison of his own making, so, too, he has the capacity and will to free himself from it. Pedro, whose characteristic vibrant *élan* and tenacious will to survive remind the reader of similar qualities in Gyula of *The Accident,* would opt to pit himself against the forces of fate. Free yourself! he would have said to Michael. Yes, but how, by what means? the latter wonders, helplessly, underscoring the question that is the basis for the unifying principle of the book—a testing of various alternatives to suicide.

What alternatives? For one, silence—that is, emotional withdrawal from others. The vast silence of the survivor who does not wish to be judged for having survived by those who were not "there." Who has nothing to "explain" how it was in the camps. Through silence he can best define himself in relation to the past. But the trouble is that the living feel anxious and threatened in the presence of his silence; and they regard it as a form of hostility against them. Then, too, a sensitive man like Michael cannot remain indefinitely silent, emotionally detached from others; he is all too aware of their loneliness and inner needs. And so ultimately it is necessary that he respond in language and gesture and deed to the suffering of men. Silence is sometimes provisonally necessary for the Wieselean protagonists if they are to hear within themselves the "right" questions concerning the Holocaust past, but in the long run the desideratum for a man is, as Gyula said in *The Accident,* to hold out a hand to others.

Another alternative: Michael attempts to confront those who were indifferent to the fate of the Jewish people during the Nazi occupation of East European countries. Representative of these indifferent ones was the spectator in the window of a house adjoining the old synagogue of Szersencseváros. This spectator, a middle-aged man, sat there with a bland, unperturbed expression day after day as Jews were hunted down in the streets, beaten, and dragged off to the deportation center. Years after the war, Michael remembered—could not forget—that face as it had appeared in looking down at his parents and himself with their packs on their backs.

> A face in the window across the way. The curtains hid the rest of him; only his head was visible. It was like a balloon. Bald, flat nose, wide empty eyes. A bland face, banal, bored: no passion ruffled it. I watched it for a long time. It was gazing out, reflecting no pity, no pleasure, no shock, not even anger or interest. Impassive, cold, impersonal. The face was indifferent to the spectacle. What? Men are going to die? That's not my fault, is it now? I didn't make the decision. The face is neither Jewish nor anti-Jewish; a simple spectator, that's what it is. (P. 150.)

A "simple spectator" in the sense that he is a symbolic embodiment of the "average man" in World War II who, by his passivity and moral indifference to the suffering and murder of the oppressed, was guilty of complicity with the murderers. At the time of the deportation, Michael could not understand how this man could sit at his window looking down at the processions of human agony as though he were merely watching a theatrical performance or a pageant. Did he not *feel* anything? The murderers and the victims Michael could understand; the connections between them had their own kind of logic, twisted though it might be. But the nature of this spectator eluded his comprehension.

To confront the spectator and perhaps take revenge upon him, Michael leaves his residence in Paris and returns to Szersencseváros. Rather than continue feeling guilt and shame for having survived, he would hate and judge the spectator. Which is to say, he wants no longer to countenance himself as victim. But on coming into the presence of the spectator with his bland, bored face, Michael immediately discovers that he is unable to hate him; contempt alone is what he feels for the other. The spectator, then, is unworthy of hatred, which ought to be reserved for sentient human beings and not one who may be likened to "a stone in the street, the cadaver of an animal, a pile of dead wood." Further, Michael's inability to hate the spectator largely stems from his own characteristic aversion to being "judged" by the living for having survived;

and partly from the complicated bonds connecting the executioner, victim, and spectator. True, the executioner is far more guilty than the spectator, but nevertheless, there is, in Michael's ken, a mysterious triad linking all three roles. "Down deep," he thinks, "man is not only an executioner, not only a victim, not only a spectator: he is all three at once." And there is a further complication: in observing the spectator, in trying to understand him, Michael himself risks becoming a spectator. As he puts it: "Who observes the spectator becomes one. In his turn, he will question me. And which of our two lives will weigh heavier in the balance?"

So in the end Michael is unable to hate or judge or even humiliate the spectator. Ironically, the price of this failure is, literally, imprisonment. After Michael leaves the spectator, the latter informs on him, and he is arrested. Hence years after having been liberated from a concentration camp, he again is a prisoner. Thus it may be adduced that Michael's need to return to his hometown stemmed not only from an impulse to confront the spectator but also to satisfy an involuntary inclination to self-victimization. It is as though he must *sacrificially* become a prisoner again in order to placate a sense of guilt for having survived the Holocaust.

Since the alternatives of silence and confrontation of the spectator have not worked, Michael, undergoing the torture of a brutal, relentless interrogation in the local jail, is driven to the point of succumbing to insanity, to a madness "in which anything is permitted, anything is possible."

It is at this critical point in Michael's circumstances that his friendship with Pedro helps to save him from a breakdown. Now he grasps more clearly than ever before the significant differences between his life-style and Pedro's. He looks for a gate that will lead to redemption; and he would like to believe that the universe is inherently founded on order and spiritual laws. By contrast, Pedro has the flexibility to believe that one can find good in evil, that God is both evil and absolution, and that man must have the courage to both listen to and oppose the word of God. Pedro has learned to live with lucidity and grace in the face of ontological uncertainties and ambiguities; and he has come to be grateful for modest expectations and simple pleasures. Unlike Michael, whose impulse is to ascertain the *meaning* of events, it is enough for Pedro to enjoy the concrete, existential immediacy of human existence.

An image of his friend, in the most excruciating moments of his torture, appears before Michael when he resolves not to break down, not to give way to insanity, during the police interrogation. Pedro would have counseled him that madness is no solution; to willingly abandon oneself to madness is to abandon one's humanity. Within the confinement of his cell, Michael imagines the voice of Pedro saying to him: "To see liberty only in madness is wrong; liberation, yes: liberty, no." What is important, then, is to remain human in the face of injustice and cruelty. And yet Michael's resources for holding on are increasingly strained to the breaking point. There are moments when he feels he is "at the end of the line," that he will soon go mad, that he cannot go on alone, that to "stay sane I've got to have someone across from me." He needs to be in a meaningful relationship with another human being.

That someone now appears and Michael is given an opportunity to protect his own sanity and to test the validity of Pedro's teaching by restoring the sanity of his cellmate, a deaf-mute boy. At first, the latter, who had plunged into a psychotic breakdown as a result of brutal treatment by the guards, seems inaccessible to Michael's persistent efforts. But finally the boy begins groping his way back to sanity. Michael's achievement therein supports Pedro's belief that men have the freedom to protest against human suffering by alleviating it. Such commitment, Pedro contends, as does Gyula of *The Accident,* pulls a man away from his own self-involved concerns and directs him toward other human beings.

> If you could have seen yourself, framed in the doorway [Pedro once said to Michael], you would have believed in the richness of existence—as I do—in the possibility of having it and sharing it. It's so simple! You see a musician in the street; you give him a thousand francs instead of ten; he'll believe in God. You see a woman weeping; smile at her tenderly, even if you don't know her; she'll believe in you. You see a forsaken old man; open your heart to him, and he'll believe in himself. You will have surprised them. Thanks to you, they will have trembled, and everything around them will vibrate. Blessed is he capable of surprising and being surprised. (P. 124.)

Indeed, of all the words that Pedro had ever spoken to him and which were to be of crucial importance in his relationship with the deaf-mute boy, Michael recollects these:

> To say "I suffer, therefore I am" is to become the enemy of man. What you must say is "I suffer, therefore, you are." Camus wrote somewhere that to protest against a universe of unhappiness you had to create happiness. That's an arrow pointing the way: it leads to another human being. And not via absurdity. (P. 118.)

So that finally he cannot stand by indifferently while the boy suffers; he feels obliged to help him. This act is in keeping with Michael's resolve to pit himself against those forces which diminish the humanity of men. In helping the other to regain his sanity, Michael's own progression toward madness is checked, and his essential faith in the value of human relationship is shored up. As the book ends, Michael is saying to the boy:

> "What I say to you, pass on to you, little one, I learned from a friend—the only one I had. He's dead, or in prison. He taught me the art and necessity of clinging to humanity, never deserting humanity. The man who tries to be an angel only succeeds in making faces.
>
> "It's in humanity itself that we find our question and the strength to keep it within limits—or on the contrary to make it universal. To flee to a sort of Nirvana— whether through a considered indifference or through a sick apathy—is to oppose humanity in the most absurd, useless, and comfortable manner possible. A man is a man only when he is among men." (P. 177.)

It's harder to remain human than to try to leap beyond humanity—this is the gist of what Michael learns from his experience as a prisoner in Szersencsevaros. Taking one's life or submitting to the oblivion of insanity is no answer to the difficulties of remaining human. Instead, one needs to pit oneself against those forces which diminish a man and to continue asking questions of God and man. Perhaps in consequence of these recognitions, for the first time in a Wiesel novel, the ending contains a ray of light. Unlike *Dawn* and *Night,* which end at night and with images of the protagonist's corpselike face, *The Town Beyond the Wall* ends shortly before the approach of daybreak: "Before him [Michael] the night was receding, as on a mountain before dawn." By extension, one can speculate that some of the night, the suffering, in the protagonist is, if many years after the Holocaust, first beginning to recede.

But if now Michael willingly had accepted the moral obligation to help others, he had not yet found *the* gate. His successor, Gregor, the protagonist of *The Gates of the Forest*, will look for it in a cave within a forest of World War II Hungary, an obscure Roumanian village, in the company of some partisan fighters and finally in a synagogue of postwar Brooklyn.

The Gates of the Forest tests both the limits of disengagement and suffering and the possibilities of fervor. Also, the book dramatizes the protagonist's conflict between yearning for an idyllic, simplified existence and accepting the hard uncertainties and complexities of his actual circumstances. There is still another way in which to describe the central dialectic of the novel: alternately, the protagonist views the world as benign and then as a hostile, malevolent place; or as the narrator of the novel describes Gregor's conflict: "A life-and-death struggle between two angels, the angel of love and the angel of wrath, the angel of promise and the angel of evil." The purpose of what follows is to trace the line of this struggle and to consider its implications.

The Gates of the Forest begins in a cave located within a forest of Transylvania during World War II. Gregor (his real name is Gavriel, but he has assumed a Christian name largely as a symbolic protest against the persecution he suffered as a Jew) has managed to escape the tragic fate of the Jewish community where he had lived. Now he is hiding from the enemy in a forest, one that is emblematic of the purity and unity of creation that existed before the "liberation of the word," the noisome coming of so-called civilized man. The deep silence of the forest coincides with his own need for silence; after his suffering as a Jew during the Nazi occupation, he prefers to be disengaged, disassociated, from the "great, haunted cemeteries" of Europe. In the cities beyond the forest he would feel anxious and dispersed among men who no longer have eyes and ears for one another. In Gregor's words:

> The forest meditates; it listens to voices instead of stifling them. The forest has ears, a heart, and a soul. In the forest simplicity is possible;-simplicity belongs here. And

unity, too. There liberty isn't forced on you like a straightjacket. I am what I choose to be; I am in my choice, in my will to choose. There is no divorce between self and its image, between being and acting. I am the act, the image, one and indivisible. Outside, things are too complicated; too many roads are open, too many voices call and your own is so easily lost. The self crumbles. (P. 221.)

The question that Wiesel poses early in the book is this: Is the forest, as symbolic of a solitary, simplified existence and a withdrawal from other men, a justified escape for a survivor like Gregor? Isn't such isolation a way, as Pedro said to Michael in *The Town Beyond the Wall*, of leaping beyond one's humanity? Isn't it much more difficult to leave the forest and be a man among men in the town, with all its uncertain, complex, and ambiguous weathers? Unmistakably, Wiesel implies that the gates of the forest should ultimately lead back to the gates of the town. Still, the pivotal questions remain: *How* is this change to come about? *Who* is to provide the impetus for it?

Both questions are answered by the coming of the stranger into Gregor's life, a nameless fellow Jew, who has also fled from the Germans and their lackeys, the Hungarians. Gregor invites the other to share the cave with him. The stranger accepts, and at the outset his manner confuses and disturbs Gregor. There are moments when he wonders whether the other is a madman, and at other times whether he is a "messenger" from the dead. For the stranger presents an incredulous report on the destruction of entire Jewish communities, on their deportation to extermination camps, and not, as Gregor had previously supposed, to factories and labor camps. Moreover, what further disturbs Gregor is that the stranger's relationship to him is inconsistent. At first, he seems to be only a dispassionate "messenger," and then shortly he offers himself as a teacher—or perhaps Gregor has unconsciously willed the other to assume this role.

The stranger's teaching is not unlike that of two other "teachers" in Wiesel's novels, Gyula and Pedro. He contends that Gregor's kind of silence (his withdrawal from the world of men) will not do. True, Gregor has suffered, has lost his family and friends, but suffering in silence will help no one.

What is wanted is not tears, not quiet suffering, but rather an active defiance of injustice and despair. One does not feel quite so helpless and despairing when, for example, one can fight off one's sorrow with laughter. Laughter for survivors can be salutary, like the smile of Camus's Sisyphus, who persists at his endless burden of pushing and retrieving the stone. Further, the stranger propagates the view that man must rely solely upon himself for redemption rather than await grace from some outside force, for instance, the coming of the Messiah.

Here the stranger's teaching coincides with that of Gregor's father, who used to say: "The Messiah is that which makes man more human, which takes the element of pride out of generosity, which stretches his soul toward others." Let men be their own Messiahs, urges the stranger. Instead of waiting for redemption in some improbable Messianic future, let men help one another now, in the present. And the most meaningful and efficacious way they can do this is through the grace of friendship:

> "It is to a friend [the stranger says to Gregor] that you communicate.... Is the soul immortal, and if so why are we afraid to die? If God exists, how can we lay claim to freedom, since He is its beginning and its end? What is death, when you come down to it? The closing of a parenthesis, and nothing more? And what about life? In the mouth of a philosopher, these questions may have a false ring, but asked during adolescence or friendship, they have the power to change being: a look burns and ordinary gestures tend to transcend themselves." (P. 27.)

In appreciation for the stranger's teaching, Gregor bestows the gift of his real name, Gavriel (which, translated from Hebrew, means Man of God), on his nameless companion.

Seen as a whole, the function of this sequence in the cave is clear. The protagonist recognizes the limits of a desengaged, insulated way of life and the dangers of chronic inertia and melancholy. Then, too, the influence of the stranger prepares the protagonist for what presently will be his departure from the forest and reentry into the world of men. One may speculate that if the stranger had not appeared, Gregor would have continued to remain in a state of inertia. But when the stranger offers his life (that is, allows himself to be captured by Hungarian soldiers) so that Gregor may be spared, the latter recognizes that the time has come for him to leave the forest. And in the course of his subsequent adventures, Gregor was to have sufficient opportunities for testing the validity of the stranger's teachings.

Shortly after the other's departure, Gregor leaves the cave. It is important to note that he continues to bear the non-Jewish name of Gregor, for he plans to make his way in the places beyond the forest as a incognito Jew.

After leaving the forest, Gregor finds a refuge in the home of a former servant of his family, Maria, who lives in a Roumanian village. Now, although the setting has changed from a cave to that of a rural village, he is still a prisoner in the sense that Jonah was still confined when his location was changed from the hold of a ship to the belly of a whale; in both locations, Jonah was alienated from other men. Maria passes him off as her deaf-mute nephew, so that he will not need to speak and by a faulty Roumanian accent raise the suspicion of the villagers.

It is not easy to maintain an unbroken silence for many hours each day but Gregor, given his solitary existence in the forest, has already served an apprenticeship for this ordeal. Further, his public identity as a deaf-mute is not out of keeping with his inclination to feel guilty for having survived. Because he looks on himself in this way, it is not surprising that the villagers view him in a similar light. That largely is why he is forced to play the unenviable role of a silent Judas Iscariot in the village's annually produced school play.

It is at this point that Gregor breaks his silence. During the course of the play, when he is nearly beaten to death by an audience whose intense anti-Semitic animus comes violently, irrationally, to the surface, Gregor suddenly begins speaking to the villagers in the presumed voice of Judas, saying that they need to see *him* as the victim and not Christ. The symbolic point here is unmistakable: it is the Jew murdered 6,000,000 times who was crucified, and it is of him so sacrificed that the world ought to seek forgiveness.

Escaping from the villagers bent on killing him, Gregor flees to the forest and joins a band of Jewish partisans who are fighting the Germans. This development signals a new turning in the book and in Gregor's changing roles. In the cave he was the Jew in hiding; in Maria's village he was the disguised Jew, and now, in the forest, he is transformed into the fighter. The heroic, admirable leader of this partisan band is a childhood friend of Gregor's, Leib the Lion, who is in the tradition of Jewish fighter stretching from Joshua, Judas Maccabaeus, and Bar-Cochba to the Israeli armies in the War of Independence and the Six-Day War.

But if Gregor holds Leib in reverence, he unwittingly causes his friend's death. The partisans had assumed that the Jews of their respective communities had been sent to labor camps in the East and would .return after the war. When Gregor tells them about what previously he had heard from the stranger concerning the existence of death camps, the partisans are disbelieving. Gregor persuades them that if they wish to question a witness to confirm this incredulous report, the stranger needs to be rescued from the jail to which he was brought following his capture by Hungarian soldiers. It is while involved in the rescue operation of the stranger that Leib is captured and killed. Gregor feels he is guilty of having caused his friend's death; and he openly accuses himself: "I am responsible. He who is not among the victims is with the executioners. This was the meaning of the holocaust: it implicated not only Abraham or his son, but their God as well." This self-accusation is an extension if what both Gregor and earlier Wieselean survivor-protagonists believe— "To live is to betray the death...."

His readiness to blame himself for Leib's death is denounced by a fellow partisan, Yehuda, as an inhuman gesture. The latter suggests that Gregor's attachment to guilt and self-incrimination is a revealing indication of both his need to alienate himself from others and to indulge, uselessly, in further suffering. "You insist upon suffering alone. Such suffering shrinks you, diminishes you." Yehuda then goes on to argue that such self-laceration is hardly a means to a true liberation of the spirit. Instead, what is wanted are human beings constructing bridges to one another, even in the face of the awesome Void. "You say, 'I'm alone.' Someone answers, 'I'm alone too.' There's a shift in the scale of power. A bridge is thrown between the two abysses."

Ideally, then, suffering ought to make us more open, more accessible to others, rather than the reverse; and precisely because human existence is full of so much pain and unhappiness, it is important to give one's best response to the demands of love and friendship. In short, Yehuda speaks to Gregor in the same key that Gyula did to Eliezer and Pedro to Michael. True, earlier the stranger had similarly spoken to Gregor about the meaning of friendship, but the latter had not really been ready then to hear the message.

After the war, Gregor and his wife, Clara, formerly a partisan and Leib's mistress, immigrate to the United States, and they settle in a Brooklyn community. It is essentially a marriage of love, and yet Gregor does not feel he is any closer to the gate he has been searching for; redemption seems as far off as before; he is still in bondage to the griefs of the past, and his day-to-day existence in the realms of normalcy is flat, joyless, routinized.

In a period of severe depression, Gregor makes a pilgrimage-like visit to a Hasidic synagogue in Williamsburg. The worshipers that he enviously observes there are so open and happy that they seem to flow out of themselves with spontaneous singing and dancing. They have no need to wait for the Messiah; a thousand times a day they bring him down to earth with their joyous immersion in the present, in the moment. In their fervor, they body forth the possibilities of a life-style that heretofore, given the tragedy of the Holocaust, Gregor had considered inappropriate.

But how does one attain fervor? he wonders. The Hasidic rabbi of the synagogue, whose followers look up to him as a zaddik, a man of wisdom and saintliness, responds to Gregor's question during the latter's visit. Get out of the solitary self, the rabbi urges; cease being in love with suffering, become one, joyously and in trust, with others.

> At intervals he [the rabbi] pounded the table with his fist. Ferocious and irresistible, he demanded greater enthusiasm and abandon. Don't caress your soul as if it were a body, feeding on kisses. Beat it without humiliating it; whip it without diminishing it; drive it out of your self in order that it may rejoin its source and become one with it in the *Heichal Hanegina,* the sanctuary of melody—it's there I await you in a secret promise. (P. 193.)

But Gregor is not to be easily convinced; he is full of anger and bitterness. "How can anyone believe in God after what has happened?" he challenges the rabbi. And so the argument between them is joined and rages until finally Gregor forces the other to make the admission that God, like man, is often guilty of injustice and cruelty. Still, the rabbi contends, one can defy Him as much by singing and dancing as by shouts of protest or chronic melancholy or suffering or silence.

> "Do you know what the song hides? A dagger, an outcry. Appearances have a depth of their own which has nothing to do with the depth. When you come to our celebrations you'll see how we dance and sing and rejoice. There is joy as well as fury in the hasid's dancing. It's his way of proclaiming. 'You don't want me to dance; too bad, I'll dance anyhow. You've taken away every reason for singing, but I shall sing. I shall sing of the deceit that walks by day and the truth that walks by night, yes, and of the silence of dusk as well. You didn't expect my joy, but here it is; yes, my joy will rise up; it will submerge you.'" (P. 198.)

What is the meaning of human suffering? Gregor further interrogates the rabbi. For if there is no meaning, then God is indeed either dead or malevolent. The rabbi replies that suffering is God's way of testing man.

> For suffering contains the secret of creation and its dimension of eternity; it can be pierced only from the inside. Suffering betters some people and transfigures others. At the end of suffering, of mystery, God awaits us. (P. 201.)

Suffering as a meaningful trial—was this the gate, Gregor wonders, that he had been searching for? And was the God of justice and redemption waiting behind that gate? With the emergence of these questions, the movement of all five novels has come full turn. The archetypal Wieselean protagonist has journeyed a long way from the embittered young man of *Night* who categorically viewed the suffering of victims and survivors as cruelly meaningless.

Thus Gregor's meeting with the rabbi marks another *tikkun*, a turning, in his search for the gate of redemption. This development occurs when, as part of a minyan, he recites Kaddish in a Hasidic synagogue. A Yeshiva boy invites and leads him to this minyan; which is to say, symbolically, that the child within the adult directs the latter back to the source of his childhood faith in God. Gregor's return is not only symbolic; it is *actually* to a familiar place of his boyhood, a synagogue; and significantly, the synagogue is also the setting for the opening pages of the first novel.

Here it is instructive to recall the central settings of the preceding novels. The concentration camp in the middle and ending sections of *Night* is followed by the secret headquarters and cellar execution chamber of the terrorist fighters in *Dawn*. *The Accident* takes place in a hospital. Much of *The Town Beyond the Wall* occurs in a jail. These changing central locations in the first four novels are as so many signposts for charting the stages of the Wieselean hero's journey. He survives the camps and is liberated. But in going underground with the terrorist movement, he is again immolated, this time in an inner prison of self-hate for becoming the executioner. In *The Accident*, at the bottom of his despair, he invites an accident, as though to precipitate and confront the decision of whether to choose life or death. Following his convalescence in the hospital, he undergoes imprisonment in the town beyond the wall. But though behind bars there, he is not the passive, sacrificial victim of Auschwitz and Buchenwald; rather, he opts to actively help his brothers-in-suffering.

Seen in this perspective of place as symbol, the synagogue scene ending *The Gates of the Forest* is telling. For the movement from the synagogue of Eliezer's boyhood in *Night* to the Hasidic synagogue in the last novel suggests that the hero has begun to come full circle in his journey, one marked by the following high points: as a boy, witnessing the mass burning of children, he lost faith in God; as a young man in Palestine he sought to exorcise the Holocaust past by becoming an executioner; as a survivor in New York he attempted suicide to escape from the burden of guilt and suffering; as a prisoner in the town beyond the wall, he discovered the importance of responding to others; and in postwar Brooklyn he was attracted to the possibilities of faith and fervor as a life-style.

During his visit to the Brooklyn synagogue, he finds himself desiring a single identity as a man and Jew. This inclination is signaled in the book's ending by his abandonment of the name Gregor and the reclamation of his real name, Gavriel, an act which indicates that he is ready to *choose* himself as a Jew. In coming to the Hasidic synogogue to recite Kaddish, to pray to God for the souls of his father and Leib, and for "the soul of his childhood," the Wieselean hero returns, if only provisionally, to his boyhood faith, which had been consumed in the flames of Auschwitz. And now, four books later, the older protagonist, Gavriel, reciting Kaddish, proclaims that "great and terrible is the God of the Jews, that his ways are righteous and impenetrable, that he has the right to hide himself, to change face and sides, that he who gives life and light may also take them away." The recitation of this prayer suggests that the cry of Job has become his own. God has remained silent while millions were destroyed during the Holocaust and yet Gavriel, the Jobian survivor, chooses to speak to him—and to wait for a response.

But the only voice he hears is one within himself urging him to love God, saying: "It's not a question of him but of yourself. Your love, rather than his, can save you." It is as though this voice were saying: Stop feeling guilty for having survived. It is not necessary that you pray to God for forgiveness; rather, "forgive" yourself for having survived, bury the dead, choose life, and try to live with fervor.

But there must be struggle, Gavriel realizes; redemption will not simply happen to us by itself and from without. This struggle ought to take place not in cloistered, solitary places of the forest but rather in the streets and houses of the town; that is, one ought not to take easy refuge in a disassociated, hermetic existence; instead, one needs to confront the uncertainties and problems of life in the modern world. This means, among other things, looking with steadiness and compassion at the "thousand faces" of all men: faces of ugliness, hatred, bitterness, torment, chaos, and also those of peacefulness, desire, love.

What is the novel's "last word"? In reciting the Kaddish, Gavriel reserves his final prayer for the soul of his dead friend, Leib.

> The last *Kaddish* would be for him, to ask that the warrior find peace; that the angels, jealous of his strength and, above all, of his purity, cease to persecute him, that he himself cease to cause suffering to those who once loved him and still love him. Yes, the last *Kaddish* would be for him, our messenger to heaven. (P. 226.)

This last moment of the book, then, charts the distance the Wieselean hero has traveled since the time of the first three novels. *Night* ends with the image of Eliezer's corpselike face and *Dawn* concludes with the image of Elisha's tormented reflection in a window facing a dawn of "greyish light the color of stagnant water." *The Accident* ends with an image of ashes—the remains of Eliezer's portrait. By contrast, heaven is the final image in *The Gates of the Forest;* Gavriel prays for the soul of Leib, "our messenger to heaven." What I believe Wiesel, consciously or otherwise, is saying here is that he prays for peace, an end to the suffering of his survivor-protagonist, Eliezer-Elisha-Michael-Gavriel.

Let us now sum up the protagonist's journey through the first five novels. At the foot of the road was the town of his birth and boyhood in Hungary—the innocent days. Then the Germans came: came the long journey in sealed freight cars to "labor camps" in the East, came the crematoria fires, children burning in mass graves and dying on gallows. All through this nightmare of history, the protagonist kept asking the same question: Why does God permit the suffering to go this way? Why doesn't he show mercy to the oppressed? But there was no answer, only a vast silence. And in the vacuum of that awful silence, the protagonist finally turned to accuse Him. His faith had been consumed in the flames of Auschwitz but the anger and bitterness of his accusation against God helped steel him for living through the Holocaust.

He survived and returned from the realm of the dead to the living. And therein is the harsh irony—that instead of continuing to accuse God and man for what had happened, he turned to accusing himself for having survived; he who had been one of the Nazis' vicitms now took upon himself a burden of guilt and shame. It is as though he said to himself: I am alive, so therefore I am guilty; for no one having experienced on his flesh the horrors of absolute evil and oppression should want to go on living in such an impure world. And though continuing to live, he did so, in his own eyes, as a poisoned messenger. He felt that the very sight of his presence disturbed others, incriminated their "innocence." He had survived the camps, survived an attempt at suicide in New York, and now he was spent, empty, adrift without direction.

Because he could not grasp the incomprehensible, what

had been during that season in hell, because he could not explain it to himself, not alone other, he fell into a depressed silence. He had tried, unsuccessfully, to hate the executioners and their accomplices. His attempt at suicide had failed. Language, mere words, did not enable him to speak meaningfully to the living, to those who were not "there." So he was left with the role of the silent, poisoned messenger, despised in his own eyes and disturbing in the eyes of the innocent.

And this towering burden of guilt and shame would have been borne, without diminishment, to the end of his days. But finally a light was born in the darkness, and he saw himself as a brand miraculously plucked from the fire; he *had* endured. Perhaps there was meaning in this singular and astonishing fact.

Then he began to look back with increasing clarity and steadiness at the nightmarish days of the Holocaust. And he saw that not only had there been the victims but also those valiant men who had pitted their pride and dignity against the inhuman, Beside the images of oppression and death he could place the memories of friends—Gyula, Pedro, Leib. The Nazis had been, murder and genocide had been, but so had friendship. Men brought suffering and death to other men, but sometimes they brought the gift and grace of friendship.

Until that point in his journey, haunted by the ghosts of the past, the Wieselean hero had been looking back. And now he came to consider the possibilities of living with fervor in the *present.* In meeting the Hasidic rabbi and his followers, it was as though he were asking them, "Teach me fervor." He had known suffering and death, the loss of faith in God and man, and now he wanted to know a joy akin to their dancing and singing. He had undergone the transmutations of victim, executioner, would-be suicidist, would-be madman, and solitary, and now he wanted peace, rest.

Still, the questioning had not ended, would perhaps never end; the Wieselean hero would go on posing unanswerable questions concerning God, man, and the Holocaust. Unanswerable in the sense that Michael meant when he said to the deaf-mute boy: "The essence of man is to be a question, and the essence of the question is to be without answer... The depth, the meaning, the very salt of man is his constant desire to ask the question ever deeper within himself, to feel even more intimately the existence of an unknowable answer." So the questioning would go on, would not let him rest, but neither had the singing of the Jew ended. And as long as the singing and the questioning went on, the Eternal People would continue resisting and contending and enduring against the Angel of Death.

> The struggle to survive [Gavriel plans to say to his wife] will begin here, in this room, where we are sitting. Whether or not the Messiah comes doesn't matter; we'll manage without him. It is because it is too late that we are commanded to hope. We shall be honest and humble and strong, and then he will come, he will come every day, thousands of times every day. He will have no face, because he will have a thousand faces. The Messiah isn't one man, Clara, he's all men. As long as there are men there will be a Messiah. One day you'll sing, and he will sing in you. (P. 225.)

ELIE WIESEL: BETWEEN HANGMAN AND VICTIM

by Robert Alter

The novels of Elie Wiesel strike me as a singularly impressive instance of how the creative imagination can surprise our expectations of what its limits should be. It is natural enough to wonder whether it is really possible to write about the Holocaust, to use the written word, which by its very nature is committed to order, as a means of representing and assessing absolute moral chaos. With this awesome difficulty in mind, the British critic, A. Alvarez, has suggested that any adequate writing on the Holocaust must be in some way antirealistic, fracturing reality into jumbled splinters, as in fact the Nazi horror fractured the moral world which people used to imagine. The suggestion is plausible, and Alvarez offers one persuasive example for his thesis in the patterned madness of *Blood from the Sky,* a novel by another East-European Jew writing in French, Piotr Rawicz.

The achievement, however, of Elie Wiesel's five published books reminds us of the danger in issuing prescriptions about things of the spirit. He has managed to realize the terrible past imaginatively with growing artistic strength in a narrative form that is consecutive, coherent and, at least on the surface, realistic, in a taut prose that is a model of lucidity and precision. Yet by the very nature of his subject, what we might want to describe as the "realism" of his technique constantly transcends itself, as we are made to feel the pitiful inadequacy of all our commonsense categories of reality. Thus, when the young prisoner in *Night* arrives at Auschwitz, the report he gives us of a flaming ditch filled with the bodies of burning babies is of an event that actually happened at a particular point in history, in our lifetimes. Before the fact of the Holocaust, perhaps only a great visionary poet like Dante could thoroughly imagine such a gruesome reality; after the fact, it still requires a peculiar imaginative courage to abandon all the defenses of common scenes in order to remember and reconstitute in language such a reality. It is ultimately this imaginative courage that endows Wiesel's factually precise writing with a hallucinated more-than-realism: he is able to confront the horror with a nakedly self-exposed honesty rare even among writers who went through the same ordeal.

Wiesel's relation both to his subject and to his craft required that, before he could invent fiction, he should starkly record fact, and so his first book, *Night,* is a terse and terrifying account of the concentration-camp experiences that made him an agonized witness to the death of his innocence, his human self-respect, his father, his God. His innocence, of course, was irrevocably destroyed, like his flesh-and-blood father, but what Wiesel has done in the fiction after *Night* is to try to rediscover grounds for human self-respect, to struggle to imagine a God who is neither dead nor insane, using the same tightly compressed style and the same narrative of ultimate confrontations which were inevitable for that initial record of his actual experiences. Here, for example, is the way his first novel, *Dawn,* begins:

> Somewhere a child began to cry. In the house across the way an old woman closed the shutters. It was hot with all the heat of an autumn evening in Palestine.
>
> Standing near the window I looked out at the transparent twilight whose descent made the city seem silent, motionless, unreal, and very far away. Tomorrow, I thought for the hundredth time, I shall kill a man, and I wondered if the crying child and the woman across the way knew.

There is nothing in this world but the prospect of terrible confrontation, together with the natural reminders of its imminence (sunset, pointing toward the fixed hour of death at dawn) and the symbolic resonators of its implications (the child crying). The closest literary analogy I can think of for Wiesel's imaginative landscapes is the kind of lyric love poetry where all existence is focused in the presence of the lover and the beloved (as in Donne's famous lines, "She's all states, and all princes, I,/Nothing else is."). In Wiesel's case, the world seems to contain only three classes of people, each with its own kind of guilt of complicity: executioners, victims, and spectators at the execution.

If this drastic selectivity in some ways foreshortens the view of reality in his novels, it also generates an extraordinary degree of intensity, at once dramatic and moral. The imponderable keys of life and death are placed in the hands of each of Wiesel's protagonists with the imperative to decide how they should be used: the hero of *Dawn* is a terrorist who has orders to execute a British hostage; in *The Accident,* the protagonist lies in a hospital, hovering—almost, choosing—between life and death; *The Town Beyond the Wall* is the story of a man under torture by secret police, trying to save his friend's life; and the *Gates of the Forest* recounts three wartime episodes in which the hero must save his life—twice while a comrade dies—by hiding or disguise, then a fourth incident, after the war, in which he goes on with the struggle begun in the terror of the war to save his soul.

To describe this focus on finalities in another way, Wiesel's novels, for all the vividness with which they render certain contemporary situations, are more theological parable than realistic fiction: they are written for and about Abrahams on the mountain, Isaacs under the slaughtering knife, and a God who watches but no longer sends His messenger to stay the descending blade. In this kind of parabolic novel our expectations of what people will say, do, or even think are very different from what they would normally be. It is as natural, say, for the patient in *The Accident* to ask his doctor, "Do you believe in God?" as it would be in a more conventional novel for one character to ask another, "Do you smoke?" The protagonist of *The Gates of the Forest,* after meeting a madman, perhaps a divine messenger, in his cave hideout, says to himself, "I think I have lived only for this encounter and this night." And the imagined figure of his grandfather replies, "That, my child, is true of all encounters, of every night." It is a strange truth we are made to feel almost everywhere in Wiesel's fiction of ultimate confrontations.

Since most of the action and thought in Wiesel's novels take place on the broadest level of philosophical or theological generalization, it is entirely appropriate that the argument of the books should repeatedly crystallize in wisdom-statements, whether by one of the characters or by the narrator himself. Sometimes these take the form of extended and impassioned expositions. More often they are memorable aphorisms: about man—"The just man has a thousand truths, and that's his tragedy; the murderer has one alone, and that's his strength"; about God—"The lack of hate between executioner and victim, perhaps this is God"; and their interrelation—"The Jews resemble their God; they're always hiding: the world's not only *Judenrein*, it's *Gottrein* as well."

I suspect the fact the Wiesel works in French makes this sententious method of writing fiction much more natural for him than it could be for an American or British novelist. In this connection, it is interesting to speculate about the reasons for his decision to write his novels in French, a language he did not begin to learn until the age of sixteen, rather than in his native Yiddish or in Hebrew, both of which he writes fluently and eloquently. Perhaps he was motivated in part by the desire to bring his urgent message to a larger audience, but he may also have been attracted to French because of its readily available heritage of stylistic classicism that makes possible the expression of serious emotion with a chaste conciseness quite unlike the effects of pathos and effusion to which Hebrew and Yiddish easily lend themselves. There is a long tradition of aphorism as a major mode of expression in French that goes back to Pascal and La Rochefoucauld and that blends into the novel with some of the nineteenth-century masters, so that the aphoristic style of Wiesel's fiction has ample precedents in the language he has chosen to use. In our own time, moreover, Sartre, Camus, and Malraux have demonstrated in different ways how the French novel could be used to test out or illuminate perplexing and urgent philosophical questions. To these French traditions Wiesel brings a rich knowledge of midrashic, talmudic, and, above all, Hasidic lore, in which aphorism is also very important and where the concise tale is typically used as a revelation of spiritual truth.

The imaginative logic, then, of Wiesel's literary and religious backgrounds explains much of the centrality given not only to the aphorism but also to the figure of the Teacher in his novels. The wisdom taught by the Teacher in his books is, of course, always "existential," never academic, because the figure for Wiesel always derives from the Hasidic spiritual guide—more particularly, from a kabbalistic master of his own childhood whose message was one of redemption, involving the secret knowledge through which man could learn to loose the chains in which the Messiah is bound.

The Teacher first appears in the novels as Kalman the Mystic, but after the Nazis have reduced Kalman to ghastly smoke, his presence returns in a dozen unlikely faces—an eccentric painter, a philosophic smuggler, a soulful partisan, a passionate terrorist. *The Gates of the Forest*, in fact, has at least one teacher for each of its four sections. But is there anything these guides can possibly teach to the Eliezer of *Night* who remains, after all, the protagonist of all the novels—a young man possessed by death, feeling that "To live is to betray the dead"? Wiesel's protagonist is pursued everywhere by the unbearable starkness of dead or deathly eyes—his own eyes as dehumanized victim (the end of *Night*), or as victimizer (the end of *Dawn*) the eyes of the slaughtered kin that were brutally torn from the light (*The Accident* and elsewhere). What the Teachers attempt to do is to exorcise these paralyzing visions without committing the spiritual folly of suggesting that they be forgotten, and this act has general, not merely personal, significance because all of us, to the extent that we have courage to think about the recent past, must be haunted in some way, however intermittently, by these same specters.

The point is worth emphasizing. Some may find it tempting to think of Wiesel simply as a man who has gone through unspeakable horrors and, by means of his writing, is trying to "work it all out," as we like to say in clinical condescension. For Wiesel, however, Auschwitz was not just a personal trauma but a dark revelation of what man, God, and history were all about. He recurs to the broad implications of this revelation again and again in his work; in an essay called "In Defense of the Dead" he states the grim meaning of the death camps with eloquent succinctness: "At Auschwitz not only man died but the idea of man. It wasn't worth much to live in a world where there was nothing else, where the hangman acted as God and judge. For it was its own heart that the world burned at Auschwitz."[1] We are all part of that incendiary world, and Wiesel's writing is intended to remind us repeatedly, painfully, of this fact. Let me hasten to add, though, that his fiction is more than a literary exercise in the

infliction of punishment. Although all four of his novels deal
with victims and refugees of the Holocaust, the books are all
set—with the partial exception of *The Gates of the Forest*—in
the aftermath of the war, for Wiesel's principal concern is to
imagine a humanly possible aftermath, for himself, for all of us.
The exorcism he attempts of the demons of the past is one that
all men now urgently need to carry out, for after all that has
happened since 1933 it is not easy to reconceive humanity in
any configuration other than the fatal triangle of executioner,
victim, and spectator.

It is almost misleading to try to paraphrase the terms in
which this exorcism is undertaken in the novels because any
possible "message" in Wiesel's fiction is meant—like the
charismatic teaching of the Hasidic masters—to be experienced as much as it is comprehended, through the tensions
and flexions of particular personalities pounded and wrenched
by particular experiences. This is why the aphorisms carry
conviction, and this is why, I think, as Wiesel has moved
toward a kind of affirmation in his two most recent novels, he
has also needed a more elaborate fictional strategy, a fuller
world of people and events, to give weight and credibility to
whatever affirmations are intimated.

The positive statement of the last two novels is memor-
ably summed up by Pedro, the principal Teacher in *The Town
Beyond the Wall:* "To say, 'I suffer, therefore I am' is to become
the enemy of man. What you must say is, 'I suffer, therefore
you are.'" Out of context, this may sound a little like the
familiar formula of love and the brotherhood of man that is
offered as an easy anodyne for all the world's ills by certain
contemporary writers, Wiesel's novel, however, concludes
with a harrowing illustration of the awful difficulties in
applying Pedro's maxim to harsh reality. The hero of the
novel is locked in a prison cell for an indefinite period with a
completely brutalized, mute idiot boy. (The cell here, like the
cave at the beginning of *The Gates of the Forest* and the cellar in
Dawn, becomes the whole world.) The protagonist determines to defy the utter hopelessness of his imprisonment by
devoting all his energies to an attempt to teach the brutalized
idiot some semblance of a human response. The Talmud
speaks of man's partnership with God in the work of creation,
but here the prisoner must pray to God not to be against him

"this time" as he himself, with his pitiful human powers, "resumes the creation of the world from the void."

This is not only courageous, Wiesel makes clear; it is also mad. The idiot continues to stare blankly while his fellow prisoner shouts, cajoles, pleads, exhorts, prophesies of the time when this maimed creature will enter into the wholeness of community with other men. The entire scene is absurd, outrageous, and very moving. In the kind of world we live in, the novel suggests, one has to be mad in order to be truly sane; if God has betrayed His creation, man has to be crazy enough to assume God's responsibilities, even with the knowledge that he is only man.

The same notion of a fateful exchange of roles between man and God is expressed with further complications in Wiesel's most recent novel, *The Gates of the Forest*. Since this book is in a sense a culmination, even a kind of tentative, uneasy resolution, of his earlier work, an account of its general imaginative scheme may reveal something of the spiritual enterprise his writing represents. The book's theme is role-playing in the most deadly serious sense: the struggle over and with the names—in the Bible this term implies "essential nature"—that man attaches to himself, the words he assigns himself to speak. In the epidemic madness of Final Solutions, Wiesel suggests, words themselves have been twisted into a hideous reversal of their primary function as instruments of creation: "Words kill. At the beginning there is always the word. *Fire!* a lieutenant was calling out somewhere, and a line of men and women tumbled into a ditch," In the sinister jumble of such a world, man no longer knows who he is or who God is, and so Wiesel's protagonist begins, like Jacob in Genesis, by struggling with a mysterious stranger for his name.

But his predicament differs in one crucial respect from that of the biblical figure: the stranger has deliberately abandoned his name in the war, and the protagonist, instead of winning a name from his adversary and friend, ends by giving him his own—Gavriel, which signifies "man of God." The ambiguity of this transference is the central one of the novel. Does the man of God really exist, wonders the hero who now takes the Gentile name Gregor, or has Gavriel been only a creature of his own naming, his own creation? The entire relationship between divine and human has become profoundly confused. Late in the novel, when the Jacob motif is recalled in another wrestling of souls, between Gregor and a Hasidic rabbi, Gregor asks, "Which one of us is Jacob, and which the angel?" and the rabbi himself must answer, "I don't know." Perhaps, the novel argues, man has to be able to exchange roles with God, if God has so completely abdicated His responsibilities; perhaps men must become, individually, the Messiah, if the Messiah has so failed to live up to the name of Consoler that tradition assigns him.

   The Gates of the Forest establishes an impressive narrative equivalent for this sense of reversed positions and dubious identities by presenting much of its most critical action under the aspect of conscious playacting. In the background of Gregor's personal ordeal, while he hides out from the Fascists in the Transylvanian hill country, European history is seen in glimpses as an incredible, unreal play in which machine gunners, given their cues by comic-opera officers, methodically topple line after line of human beings like bizarre dolls. In the foreground, Gregor's two central experiences in the war after his initial encounter with Gavriel both involve playing a part until the actor becomes the part. The first of these episodes concludes in a stunning dramatic action: Gregor, pretending to be a deaf-mute Christian, is made to play the role of Judas in a passion play put on by the schoolchildren of a little Hungarian village. At the climax of the play, audience and actors merge in an orgy of no longer pretended hatred for the betrayer of Christ, and the dumb sufferer saves his life only at the last moment by prostrating his attackers with sudden speech, a terrible indictment after silence kept too long.

   If role-playing of this sort, in which murderous history is reenacted, can invite man to be less than human, there are other parts to be played which—however ambiguously—may teach him to become more fittingly himself. In Gregor's next experience, he and a girl named Clara enter a Hungarian town, pretending to be innocent young lovers, in order to spy for a band of partisans. Gregor's acted love soon becomes quite genuine, but Clara has other attachments; ironically, when they finally marry after the war, she will undermine his affection for her by making him play in her mind the role of her dead lover, Leib.

   By means of these dramatizations, these repeated revelations of the fluctuating gap between part and player, action and identity, Wiesel has managed to create a fictional world in which both the terrifying traps and the slender possibilities for hope in life after the Holocaust are sharply illuminated. His arresting aphorisms resonate more fully here than in his earlier novels because they have greater reverberations in the pattern of the action itself. "What, then, is man?" asks the narrator, echoing the Psalmist, but also echoing Gregor's whole relentless struggle with an elusive man whom he has given a name—"Hope turned to dust. But ... the opposite is equally true, What is man? Dust turned to hope."

This striking summary of ultimate contradictions, which expresses so much of Wiesel's spiritual world, is reminiscent of a teaching of the Hasidic master, Simha Bunam of Pzhysha, who used to say that every man should have two pockets, one in which to put a slip of paper with the rabbinic dictum, "For my sake the world was created," and the other to carry Abraham's confession of humility before God, "I am dust and ashes." The transmutation that occurs in Wiesel's restatement of the parodox is instructive. In the Hasidic teaching, both man's awesome importance and his nothingness are conceived in terms of his stance before the creator. In Wiesel, on the other hand, the theological center has shifted to the human spirit: it is pathetically finite man who is the source of miraculous aspiration, of regeneration, in a world where all life is inevitably transient. We may tend to be suspicious of affirmations, for it is often in their affirmative moments that even writers of considerable integrity yield to the temptation of offering a facile and superficial counterfeit of wisdom. In Wiesel, however, one senses that the affirmations are hard-earned, and, indeed, by incorporating as they do their own threatened negations, they may even be hard to assimilate. What is true of the affirmations is true of Wiesel's books in general, which are easy to read but difficult to assimilate. For they are the stages of his own way both from and toward faith, and, at this point in history, that way could not be easy, either to walk or to imagine.

1. In this one instance, the translation from the French is mine.

WIESEL AND THE ABSURD

by Josephine Knopp

Elie Wiesel, journalist and novelist of the Holocaust, claims to owe his writing career to three years of imprisonment in Nazi concentration camps, starting at the age of fourteen. He relates in his quasi-autobiographical works that in the Hungarian *shtetl* of his early years he had been completely immersed in Talmudic studies (in the time-honored manner of intelligent Jewish boys), presumably preparing for life as a Talmudic scholar. His world was that of orthodox Judaism, governed in every detail by Jewish law, outside the mainstream of European culture.

To the young Wiesel the notion of an "absurd" universe would have been a completely alien one. Indeed, the world of orthodox Judaism would appear to allow no place in it for notions of the absurd in the contemporary, existential sense. For the traditional Jewish view holds that life's structure and meaning are fully explained and indeed derive from the divinely granted Torah. Yet, this view of Judaism, while accurate on the most basic level, is simplistic, ignoring, as it does, the well-established Jewish tradition of challenging God by questioning His ways. While Job is the most obvious (and perhaps the best) example to cite in this connection, it should not be forgotten that other prominent figures of the Old Testament, including Abraham, Moses, and Jeremiah, rebel against God and hold Him responsible for the injustice of the world.

As witness to the Holocaust, Elie Wiesel, remaining firmly within this Judaic tradition of protest, cries out against the destruction of European Jewry, against God's failure to intercede on behalf of His creatures. Wiesel's first five novels, in fact, can be meaningfully read as a sustained, developing revolt against God from within a Jewish context. Jewish tradition provides not only adequate precedents for such revolt, but the legal and moral sanction as well, in the unique covenant with God into which the Jewish people entered: "We are to protect His Torah, and He, in turn, assumes responsibility for Israel's presence in the world. Thus, when our spirituality — the Torah — was in danger, we used force in protecting it; but when our physical existence was threatened, we simply reminded God of His duties and promises deriving from the covenant."[1] In effect, the covenant brings God and man into a moral partnership, with each of the two parties having a clearly defined responsibility to the other.[2]

Against this background the reality of Auschwitz confronts the Jew with a dilemma, an "absurdity" which cannot be dismissed easily and which stubbornly refuses to dissipate of its own accord. "In faithfulness to Judaism ... [the] Jew must refuse to disconnect God from the holocaust."[3] Since the Jewish God is "a God who is Lord of actual history, its external events included," it is an inescapable conclusion that "Auschwitz is not an accident ... because of the fact tht God is part of it."[4] Thus, the continued validity of the convenant itself is called into serious question. Clearly, any recognition that the covenant might no longer be operative would strike a devastating blow at the very foundations of Judaism and leave the theologically serious Jew isolated, to struggle in an unaccustomed loneliness with an indifferent, or worse, hostile universe. After Auschwitz, he is joined to the French existentialists in being confronted with the absurdity of the universe, an absurdity engendered and given substance by the Holocaust and signaling the breakdown of the covenant. The only possible response that remains within the framework of Judaism is denunciation of God and a demand that He fulfill His contractual obligation.

This is the religious and moral context within which Wiesel attempts to apprehend and assimilate the events of the Holocaust. It would appear to be an underlying purpose of Wiesel's creative efforts to reconcile Auschwitz with Judaism, to confront and perhaps wring meaning from the absurd, which emerges as the true antagonist in his fiction. In this respect Wiesel is on common ground with other Jewish writers of the Holocaust, notably Andre Schwarz-Bart and Nelly Sachs, whose poetry, according to her own description, is "always intent upon raising the unspeakable to a transcendental plane, in order to make it tolerable."[5]

A less obvious and therefore more interesting analogy may be drawn with Albert Camus, who, according to Maurice Friedman, "sees his art itself as a dialogue with the Absurd, a dialogue from which emerges not only values but hope and joy."[6] While, as we shall observe, the art of Wiesel may be similarly described, the contrasts between the two writers may be as revealing as the similarities. In sharp distinction to Wiesel, for whom the absurd is the breakdown of the accustomed order in God's world, the dissolution of a long established relationship between man and God, for Camus no such order and relationship ever existed, since Camus is, quite simply, an atheist. Indeed, in the thinking of Camus the absence of a Higher Authority in the world seems to be connected with the roots of man's absurd condition, for Camus describes the absurd as arising from man's realization that he can have no direct knowledge of the world, that he can make no contract with absolute truths and values. "The meaning of life,"Camus writes, "is the most urgent of questions," yet this meaning eludes the human being.[7] Thus, "man stands face to face with the irrational. He feels within him his longing for happiness and for reason. The absurd is born of this confrontation between the human need and the unreasonable silence of the world."[8] Since it is certain that human life is transitory and its meaning (if any) apparently unfathomable, Camus concludes that "there is but one truly serious philosophical problem, and that is suicide. Judging whether life is or is not worth living amounts to answering the fundamental question of philosophy."[9]

Wiesel too has seriously considered this problem in his novel, *The Accident,* whose protagonist-narrator is almost killed in an "accident" that is an apparent attempt at suicide. With this act Wiesel's rebellion against the God of Judaism, begun passionately in the setting of Nazi concentration camps in the autobiographical *Night* and continued on a more detached, philosophical plane in his second novel, *Dawn,* reaches a climax. For the sacredness of life, as God's gift to mankind, is basic to Judaism and in fact arguably the most basic tenet of the Jewish faith. In the Jewish view it is not for man to judge "whether life is or is not worth living"; only the God of Israel, a Creator and Giver of Life is to determine when life is to end. In Wiesel's peculiarly Jewish context, therefore, the suicide attempt takes on added significance as a kind of ultimate defiance of God, explainable only on the basis of a recognition, in reaction to Auschwitz, that God encompasses evil as well as good, that in violating His covenant with man, God has not only withdrawn His protection but has left man free of the restraints of His laws and commandments.[10]

Wiesel's hero has thus come to share the attitude which characterizes Camus' protagonist, Meursault, at the beginning of *The Stranger*—a sense of the absurdity of the world and the pointlessness of human existence. In contrast to Meursault, however, Wiesel's character is obsessed by the relationship of man and God. It is of great significance that although Eliezer, the young protagonist of *Night*, bitterly and repeatedly denounces God, "who chose us from among the races to be tortured day and night," he remains a Jew and never loses his belief in God's presence in the world: "I did not deny God's existence, but I doubted His absolute justice" (*N*, pp. 73, 53). Meursault appears to be without a past, living in a kind of timeless present, devoid of history and human attachments; the hero of *The Accident*, by contrast, when urged to forget the horrors of his past and find happiness in the present, can only answer, "I am my past. If it's buried, I'm buried with it" (*A*, p. 62). Characteristically, Meursault leaves unexplored the genesis of the indifference toward life that he displays in the striking and effective opening of *The Stranger*, "Mother died today. Or, maybe, yesterday; I can't be sure,"[11] while the narrator of *The Accident* is at great pains to explain his desire to die, to make understood "the tragic fate of those who came back, left over, living-dead" (*A*, p. 75). Wiesel's survivor questions incessantly, though expecting no answers, aware that the existence of answers is itself in question.

On the other hand, the narrator of *The Accident* shares Meursault's essential passivity. His suicide attempt is, after all, *nearly* an accident; he does not actively attempt self-destruction, but grasps the opportunity that presents itself by failing to avoid the on-rushing taxicab: "The cab, I had seen it coming.... I could have avoided it" (*A*, p. 117). To him applies equally Germaine Brée's insight into the character of Meursault: "The very essence of *l'absurde* in his case is that out of indifference he linked forces with violence and death, not with love and life."[12]

Like Meursault, the protagonist of *The Accident* refuses to deny the absurd; he avoids what Camus has termed "philosophical suicide," that is, the attitude of existential philosophies which *a priori* reject the idea that life has some transcendental meaning and then, by a sudden "leap of faith," find such meaning, abandon revolt, become reconciled.[13] Confronting the absurd has led to the narrator's attempted suicide, and physical recovery does not bring with it spiritual solace. Despite the efforts of his friend, Gyula, and Dr. Russel, the physician who saved his life after the accident, he continues to be tormented by his past, guilty for having survived the concentration camps where so many others perished. Through Gyula and Dr. Russel, Wiesel counters the survivor's hopelessness and obsession with the dead with a sense of the beauty and preciousness of life and the recognition of an obligation to the living. Both advocate deeds rather than faith as a response to futility. Dr. Russel confesses to a belief in God, "but not in the operating room. There I only count on myself" (*A*, p.68). He finds in the narrator's indifference toward life a puzzle to be understood and an enemy to be combatted: "Anyone who rejects life is a threat to him and to everything he stands for in this world ..." (*A*, p. 71). Gyula, too, rests his ultimate faith in man rather than God ("Maybe God is dead, but man is alive" [*A*, p. 117]) and demands of man that he "keep moving, searching, weighing, holding out his hand, offering himself, inventing himself" (*A*, p. 118). The message of *The Accident*, transmitted through Dr. Russel and Gyula, is essentially the same as that conveyed by Meursault—that man, like Sisyphus, can find fulfillment (if not meaning) in confronting his fate with lucidity rather than denial, in not hesitating "to draw the inevitable conclusions from a fundamental absurdity," in struggle itself.[14] Yet, in *The Accident* (as in *The Stranger*), lucidity is unaccompanied by meaningful action that might lead to such fulfillment for the protagonist. Dr. Russel's daily struggle to save human life leaves Wiesel's narrator unmoved, if not unimpressed, while Gyula's destruction of the portrait he has painted of the narrator, a symoblic attack upon past horrors, breaks through the protagonist's indifference only insofar as it moves him to tears. Nevertheless, this limited reaction is the first sign that the survivor may someday be able to count himself among the living again.

The passivity of the narrator of *The Accident* gives way to the positive action of Michael, protagonist of Wiesel's succeeding novel, *The Town Beyond the Wall*. Michael is also a survivor of the Nazi death camps and he too is obsessed by the memory of those who died. Yet his longing to return to the town in Hungary in which he was born and raised is the opposite of indifference; it is, in fact, a passion for clarity, a desire to confront and understand, within the limits of human possibility, the catastrophe which befell him, his family, the Jewish community. While at first only vaguely aware of his reasons for returning, a sudden, violent memory at the place where the old synagogue of his town once stood reveals the precise purpose for which he has made the trip: the "need to understand . . . the others—the Other—those who watched us depart for the unknown; those who observed us, without emotion, while we became objects—living sticks of wood" (*T*. p. 159).

Michael confronts the absurdity of the Holocaust by focusing upon the spectator, the indifferent observer, who, though neither executioner nor victim, is inextricably bound up with the event. The later face-to-face meeting with this man, however, forces Michael into an awareness of the role in the disaster played by the victims themselves. Expressing "a shocked feeling that I was a spectator at some sort of game—a game I didn't understand: a game you had all begun playing, you on one side, the Germans and the police on the other," the onlooker makes a telling point: "A few policemen—not more than ten—led you all to the slaughterhouse: why didn't you seize their arms?" (*T*, pp. 168, 170). Michael is forced to concede the point; the directness of his own action is in marked contrast to the passivity of those victims of that earlier time, who "should have known . . . could have known" their ultimate fate but refused to listen to those who had seen and knew (*T*, p. 168).

We may conjecture that those unresisting Jews were awaiting until the end the intervention of God, who would save them as He had saved their ancestors fleeing from the Pharaoh, that they would rather face death than acknowledge the breakdown of the covenant, the indifference of the universe. This steadfast trust in God, in the face of impending disaster, places these victims of the Nazi extermination close in spirit to Father Paneloux of *The Plague*, who refuses to accept medical attention when he contracts the disease. The priest's death is thus as suicidal as are the deaths of Wiesel's Jewish victims. The underlying cause is the same in both cases—the inability or unwillingness to surrender faith, the inability to cope with an irreducible absurdity, the refusal to acknowledge the possibility of evil within God.

In contrast, Michael is able to make this acknowledgment and, in so doing, is freed to take positive action, to follow the advice offered by his friend Pedro: "Camus wrote somewhere that to protest against a universe of unhappiness you had to create happiness. That's an arrow pointing the way: it leads to another human being" (*T*, p. 127). Indeed, Michael's ultimate triumph over the tortures and loneliness of imprisonment comes about, not through prayer, which he rejects in spite of the danger of perdition, but by extending his help "to another human being," the demented young prisoner whose life he saves, whose mind he struggles to bring out of its catatonic state. The struggle to cure the boy saves Michael because it is a meaningful protest against the world's indifference, "rooted in the uncertain soil of humanity" and, as such, an antidote to clinical madness (*T*, p. 183). As Byron Sherwin has pointed out, Michael does in fact display a kind of madness in *Town Beyond the Wall*, the "moral madness" (in the sense of A.J. Heschel) of the ancient Hebrew prophets, which "entails remaining human and retaining a concern for others in a world in which the social norm is hate and indifference."[15] It is in this sense that Sherwin interprets the novel's epigraph from Dostoevsky: "I have a plan: to go mad."

Moral madness reappears as an important force in Wiesel's succeeding novel, *The Gates of the Forest*. At the beginning of the work it is not Gregor, the young protagonist, but Gavriel, his philosopher-teacher, who displays moral madness in reacting to the horrors of the war: "I'm listening to the war and I'm laughing" (*G*, p.17). Gavriel clings to this position in the face of his own death; exposing himself to capture in order to save Gregor, he bursts suddenly into overwhelming laughter at the moment he is taken prisoner by the German soldiers. With Gavriel's capture (and certain death) the theme of madness is carried forward in the person of Maria, who "had decided to struggle . . . against the monstrous machine of war" by hiding Gregor at risk to her own life, and by the Hasidic Rebbe, who advocates song, dance, prayer, and joy in the face of the Holocaust: "The man who goes singing to his death is the brother of the man who goes to death fighting" (*G*, pp. 71, 196).

The moral madman is closely linked in spirit to the "absurd man" in the sense of Camus; both are able to face the world's absurdity unflinchingly, with aversion, perhaps, but without denial. Whereas the absurd man may succeed in doing this on the basis of a rational decision, executed by force of will, the moral madman, like the Hebrew prophets, often acts upon inner compulsion, unable to do otherwise.[16] The end result is the same in either case—that genuine confrontation with the absurd advocated in *The Myth of Sisyphus*. Camus' thoughts on the necessity of such confrontation is reflected in Pedro's message: "Remaining human—in spite of all temptations and humiliations—is the only way to hold your own against the Other" (*T*, p. 183), and in the actions of the moral madmen of *The Gates of the Forest;* it is reflected as well in the emergence of Michael as a healer reminiscent of Dr. Rieux of *The Plague,* who finds in saving human life a potent counter to the despair latent in absurdity (*T*, p. 183). (Of course, Wiesel's Dr. Russel is also strongly remindful of Dr. Rieux.) Thus, with Rieux (and Russel), Michael stands in direct opposition to that divinely inspired passivity in the face of death displayed by the Jewish victims of the Holocaust and by Father Paneloux, who feels that in fighting the plague he may well be thwarting the will of God.

In the same way that Father Paneloux's confrontation with the plague is overlaid with difficulties stemming from faith, Wiesel's confrontation with the absurd is complicated (as compared with that of Camus) by his adherence to Judaism. However, Paneloux's resolution of the problem through suicide is not the answer for Wiesel, who finds his solution instead in protest, not merely against absurdity, but against God Himself. The nature of this protest has been described by

Wiesel: "The Jew, in my view, may rise against God, provided he remains within God. One can be a very good Jew, observe all all *Mitzvot*, study Talmud—and yet be against God" (*J*, p. 299). The apparent contradiction in Wiesel's position is in fact explainable on the basis of the covenant. For him the object of protest against God is not nihilism, not denial of God, but the very opposite—the re-establishment of God's order in a world which has witnessed the destruction of order. Indeed, through Michael, Wiesel confesses his inability to repudiate God: "I want to blaspheme, and I can't quite manage it. I go up against Him, I shake my fist, I froth with rage, but it's still a way of telling Him that He's there, that He exists . . . that denial itself is an offering to His grandeur" (*T*, p. 123).

Though Wiesel clings to God in the face of injustice, his position cannot be termed philosophical suicide, in the sense in which Camus understands that phrase. On the contrary, Wiesel is a perfect example of Camus' "absurd man," striving for clarity whatever the consequences, recognizing the complicity of God in the evil perpetrated by man, in spite of the shattering effect of such recognition: "The student of the Talmud, the child that I was, had been consumed in the flames" (*N*, p. 46). For Wiesel, thus, there is no "leap of faith" but rather what may be termed a leap *away* from faith, although it is not successfully realized. The boy of *Night*, who vows never to "forget those flames which consumed my faith forever," gives way to the man of *Gates of the Forest*, who understands that "God's final victory . . . lies in man's inability to reject Him" and has "only one purpose: not to cause others to suffer" (*N*, p. 45; *G*, pp. 42, 194). Thus Thody's description of Camus' intellectual development applies equally well to Wiesel's: "He passes from a violent, personal and intolerant revolt . . . to a revolt which seeks essentially moderation, tolerance and communion with other men."[17] Ivan Karamazov believes that without God all things are possible; Wiesel shares with us his discovery that all things are possible even with God and therein lies his unique contribution to our understanding of the human condition.

1. Elie Wiesel, "Jewish Values in the Post-Holocaust Future," *Judaism*, XVI (Summer 1967), 281; further parenthetical references will be preceded

by *J*. Other Wiesel works cited in the essay, with their abbreviations, are as follows: *N—Night*, trans. Stella Rodway (New York: Hill and Wang, 1960); *A—The Accident*, trans. Anne Borchardt (New York: Hill and Wang, 1962); *T—Town Beyond the Wall*, trans. Stephen Becker (New York: Avon Books, 1964); *G—Gates of the Forest*, trans. Frances Frenaye (New York: Avon Books, 1967).

2. Harold Schulweiss, "Man and God: The Moral Partnership," *Jewish Heritage Reader* (New York: Kaplinger Publishing, 1968), pp. 118-21.

3. Emil Fackenheim, *God's Presence in History* (New York: New York Univ. Press, 1968), p. 76.

4. *Ibid.*, p. 68.

5. Nelly Sachs, Notes to "Eli" in *Zeichen im Sand: Die Szenischen Dichtungen der Nelly Sachs* (Frankfurt am Main: Deutsche Verlags-Anstalt, 1962), p. 345. Translation mine.

6. Maurice Friedman, *To Deny Our Nothingness* (New York: Dell, 1967), p. 338.

7. Albert Camus, *The Myth of Sisyphus* (New York: Random House, 1955), p. 4.

8. *Ibid.*, p. 21.

9. *Ibid.*, p. 3.

10. Byron Sherwin, "Elie Wiesel and Jewish Theology," *Judaism*, XVIII (Winter 1969), 46.

11. Albert Camus, *The Stranger* (New York: Random House, 1946), p. 1.

12. Germaine Brée, *Camus* (New York: Harcourt Brace and World, 1964), p. 117.

13. Albert Camus, *The Myth of Sisyphus*, pp. 21ff.

14. Jean-Paul Sartre, "An Explication of *The Stranger*," *Camus: A Collection of Critical Essays*, ed. Germaine Brée (New Jersey: Prentice-Hall, 1962), p. 109.

15. Byron Sherwin, "Elie Wiesel on Madness," *Central Conference American Rabbis Journal* (June 1972), 27.

16. A.J. Heschel, *The Prophets*, II (New York: Harper, 1962, 1971). See especially pp. 223-26.

17. Philip Thody, *Albert Camus: A Study of His Work* (New York: Gove Press, 1957), p. 72.

ELIE WIESEL: NEO-HASIDISM

by Lothar Kahn

On the surface, Elie Wiesel's Jewish attitudes resemble those of Josué Jehouda. Wiesel, too, is an integral Jew for whom the outside world has a low literary existence value. Both are products of ghetto environments and a strictly Judaic education. Both began with Hasidism and evolved further in that direction. Both used the novel as a tool for religious-spiritual expression and not as an end in itself. But where one looks in vain for many original formulations in Jehouda, Wiesel's books abound with them. Also Wiesel is a highly skilled and moving writer, a talent not shared by Jehouda.

Wiesel has been considered the chief novelist of the holocaust. But it was only in *Night* that he disclosed the horrors of Auschwitz as he had personally experienced them. In other novels, the hero, a former inmate, is mercilessly pursued by past memories. They shape his attitudes toward all later experience. But Wiesel's novels of horror are more searching and penetrating than other writings on the subject. He has approached the holocaust mainly from a moral standpoint, leaving legalistic and political debates to others. He has dealt with Auschwitz, not only on the level of Man, but also that of God.

Wiesel's six books to date have marked him as the messenger of the Jewish dead to the living. The mystic Wiesel appears to have intrepreted his survival as imposing two obligations: first, to tell the ugly and unvarnished story of the dead, and to plead for understanding of the unheroic manner in which they perished; second, to attempt to fathom the unfathomable reasons for which they died, to comprehend the human and divine madness behind the deed. Finally, he has unwittingly assumed the role of prophet, cautioning against another Auschwitz, linking the burning ovens to burning Hiroshima, recognizing the infectiousness of evil and destruction, and the callousness of the witnesses, the comfortably uninvolved. But Wiesel is not only the representative of the dead to the living. He is also their ambassador to God. In this capacity, Wiesel has ceaselessly interrogated the Divinity, now begging Him for enlightenment, now castigating Him for his silence, now in despair turning away from Him, or seeking Him out more than ever.

This writer has considered most of the questions suggested by the holocaust. What is the meaning of absolute evil? How can any faith survive in this confrontation? How could men remain so uninvolved in the misery of others? To what low of animal living can Man descend as a result of untellable suffering? What are the implications for human progress, the human future? Finally, what did the tragedy teach about the state of Jews, their destiny, their guilt and promise? These considerations have lent Wiesel's work an importance far beyond the boundaries of world Jewry, this despite the omnipresence of Hasidic tales, Cabbalistic allusions and Talmudic sayings. Besides being the keenest interpreter of the most bewildering deeds of all times, Wiesel also proffers hope of becoming one of the most authentic and constructive Jewish writers of our century. For he has not been contented with merely posing questions; he has searched for answers within Jewish tradition and found at least some in Hasidism.

Wiesel was born in a Transylvanian village near the Rumanian border—a village which keeps reappearing in some form in each of his novels. His father, a rationalist, seemed skeptical of traditional Judaism and urged the youthful Eliezer to look westward for humanist values. His mother, on the other hand, adhered to traditional modes, inclined toward Hasidism, and was instrumental in securing for her son a thoroughly Jewish upbringing. Wiesel appears to have been more fortunate than the other writers in his religious teachers; he has repeatedly paid tribute to them. Several of these teachers leaned toward mysticism, which in a Western sophisticated garb still marks the mature writer of today.

Then came the great break. The war had seemed remote to Hungarian Jews despite the proximity of the Nazis. But overnight the latter insisted on the final solution for unsuspecting Jews. In 1944, with the Russians within thirty miles of their city, with booming guns clearly heard, they were yet rounded up—Father, Mother, children. They were kept in an alternately hopeful and despairing uncertainty, and finally shipped off in a cattle-train, destination unknown. *Night,* Wiesel's first book—and one of stunning power, an effect achieved by restraint and utter sparseness of style—records the heartbreaking months of agony, horror, and guilt. Not the least of his lingering memories was of a little boy who had been hanged, and was dangling, still not wholly dead, from the gallows; another was of the valiant attempts to keep alive his aging and weakened father only, in the end, secretly to wish for his death and see this wish granted. Finally, the towering guilt over the death wish, the gnawing guilt of surviving, the knowledge of having descended to the brutality of sub-human existence. Again and again, Elie has returned to these themes: the dying father, the lost youth, the burden of survival, and the road to spiritual recovery; finally the search for meaning after total emptiness.

Wiesel was alone after the war. While still an adolescent, he found his way to Paris, a city he grew to love. He quickly acquired a mastery of French—the language in which he prefers to write. He studied philosophy at the Sorbonne. Keeping faith with a death-camp vow and struggle, Wiesel left for Israel. From the strife-torn country he reported on the evolving struggle for independence. Thus began a journalistic career which eventually brought him to New York. For the past eight years, he has served as United States and U.N. correspondent for an Israel daily.

These various locales which have been focal points in Wiesel's life also constitute the physical settings for his novels. In the tradition of exile and flight, his characters roam the earth's surface—from Hungary to Paris, from Paris to New York, from New York to Israel and opposite directions. Wiesel has been an impassioned traveler, and has significantly been drawn to the myth of the Wandering Jew. But wherever his heroes are, they are tormented by the ugly memories of the past, the inability to cope with them, the realization that this past—in new and vile forms—is ever-present and that the negative in various shapes—Hiroshima, Communists prisons, etc.—has demonstrated a virulent capacity to renew itself.

Dawn begins in a Palestinian terrorist hideout, with quick mental returns to Paris and the death camps. The mood is somber as the young hero, recently released from Auschwitz, is faced with the grim assignment of executing an innocent English officer as a retaliatory measure. During the night preceding the execution, the Jewish hero searches his conscience for any and all legitimate reasons that will enable him to do his hateful duty. He is acutely aware that he is departing from the traditions of his people, which admitted suffering and rejected violence. The hero would like to hate his victim, but finds that hatred doesn't come easy "... because my people have never known to how to hate. Their tragedy throughout the centuries has stemmed from their inability to hate those who have humiliated and from time to time exterminated them. Now our only chance lies in hating you, in learning the necessity and the art of hate. Otherwise ... our future will only be an extension of the past, and the Messiah will wait indefinitely for his deliverance."

The still very fresh memory of Jews being tamely led to slaughter finally justifies in the hero's mind the legitimacy of his task and conquers the old aversion to violence. Even rabbis had now sanctioned terrorism in the light of recent events. Upon his admission to the terrorist group the hero was sufficiently a victim of wartime Jewish passivity to think "that the mission of the Jews was to represent the trembling of history rather than the wind which made it tremble." As the hero is gradually propelled to action he becomes increasingly aware of the moral sacrifice it represents. The promise made by Elie in *Night*, that he will turn to Zion if ever he becomes free, is fulfilled in *Dawn*.

Dawn is thus inseparably tied to *Night* and *The Accident* (the French title *Le Jour* ["Day"] should have been retained in the English version) is attached to both. Now in New York, the hero, who has become a foreign correspondent, suffers a severe automobile accident that for weeks keeps him tottering on the verge of death. As he ponders over the accident and discusses it with his physician and mistress, he comes to realize that the accident had been no accident, that he had tried to relieve himself of the unbearable weight of guilt. The burden of memory, of living with ghosts, had become too heavy. The journalist-hero recognizes that his articles are those of a man at the end of his rope and that the youth sliced out of his life has turned into an insurmountable handicap of living. He knows that all he touches bears the stamp of death, that even his mistress is compelled to fight the dead through him. His own suffering and the memory of it has opened unbreachable gaps in his relations with others. "Men reject the sufferer, unless they see a God in him." The accident occurred at a moment of supreme conflict, just after he had promised his mistress to forget the past because it precluded any possibility of love.

The hero's physician stands for the principle of life. Where his patient is powerfully attracted to death, the physician is certain of man's limitless capacity for living, of the ultimate victory over doom and death. Day follows night with the hero's final realization that the past must be chased "with a whip if necessary." He accepts the notion that the dead must leave the living in peace and that the guilt for living must be ruthlessly discarded. He has learned that it is man's duty to make suffering cease, not to keep it alive. Despite the glimmer of hope brought on by the day, the hero has no illusions about the obstacles ahead. Forgetting will be a hard task, even as he has found a moral basis and psychological determination to perform it.

Indeed, *Town Beyond the Wall* leaves no doubt that the hero has not forgotten. He has, however, emerged from the night, seen the dawn and benefited from the day. The reliving of his haunting past drives him in an act of physical—and metaphysical—madness to the *City of Luck,* as Wiesel ironically calls the town of his birth. Here he searches for the Other, whose eyes have pursued him throughout his tragic peregrinations. They are the eyes of the Witness, the man who had peered from behind the curtain windows, had seen the Jews rounded up, old and young, herded together in the marketplace, thirsty for water, crowded like cattle into the wagon of death. The other had calmly and dispassionately watched the perpetration of dastardly deeds. The hero is drawn back to face this Other, a man without seeming guilt or shame. In a passage of unusual power, Wiesel assails the witness psychology and with it sides with existential commitment and the notion of human community.

But is not the silent, unconcerned witness also the silent, seemingly unconcerned, God who also watched and allowed things to happen? And now, on the hero's return to the home-

town, is not the Witness-God still sullenly silent and responsible for denouncing him to the new masters of Hungary?

Yet now the hero's reaction has changed. He no longer
addresses the Witness or God through reasoned language,
through questions and reproaches. He has given up on that.
He now acts. Through a frantic deed of loyalty to a human, a
crucial act of affirmation, Wiesel offers the very symbol of
rehabilitation. The forces which had hitherto been expended
in the struggle for physical and spiritual survival and self-
restoration are now channeled into frenzied service to another.
In the jail of the *City of Luck,* Wiesel's hero joins the human
race even as he languishes in jail awaiting probable death.

The Gates of the Forest once more returns the hero to his
Hungarian youth. To escape deportation he is now hiding in a
mountain cave. One night he is visited by a strange man whose
stories and laughter have an unsettling, if not hypnotic, effect
on the youngster. Their hideout is accidentally discovered and
the older man ostensibly sacrifices himself for the youngster
by surrendering to the police. But the hero, who has given him
his own name of Gavriel, is obsessed with the memory of the
stranger. In the months of underground existence in the village
of their former maid, who has sheltered him and given him a
Christian identity, the hero thinks he recognizes Gavriel at a
village passion play. Again Gavriel rescues him without
clearly revealing himself, as the villagers out of religious fervor
nearly kill the hero playing the role of Judas. Once more, years
later, he believes he is confronting Gavriel, only this time at a
Hasidic festival in Brooklyn. But who is Gavriel? Is he, too,
God, who has watched over him, guarded him through the
tribulations of a perilous existence? Or is Gavriel the Messiah
about whom he has told some fascinating and philosophically
significant tales? (As Wiesel describes him below.) Or perhaps
he is the symbol of the ghosts of the past whose power must
finally be broken if they are not be a permanently crippling
force in living. The excitingly told episodes of the young
hero's adventures lead him to the acceptance of life as it is,
with hope being a modest but necessary component. The
hero's entente with life has become realistic:

> Whether or not the Messiah comes doesn't matter; we'll
> manage without him. It is because it is too late that we are
> commanded to hope. We shall be honest and humble and

strong, and then he will come, he will come every day, thousands of times every day. He will have no face, because he will have a thousand faces. The Messiah isn't one man, Clara, he's all men.

In the final pages the hero is found in the synagogue, reciting the Kaddish, "concentrating on every sentence, every word, every syllable of praise." He can now pray calmly for the souls of the dead, for his father, his friends, even himself. Why for himself?

... that the angels, jealous of his strength and, above all, of his purity, cease to persecute him, that he himself cease to cause suffering to those who once loved him and still love him. Yes, the last *Kaddish* would be for him, our messenaer to heaven.

The glimmer of unexpected hope in *Accident*, the frantic doings and affirmations in *Town Beyond the Wall*, have been transformed by the end of his latest novel into a quiet and more mature faith. The hero appears to abandon the useless dialogue, the hopeless quest for all-embracing answers, the mad, mad searchings, and perhaps even the guilt and guilt-fixing patterns of earlier years. Although he has now learned the lesson taught him by Pedro, the most intriguing character in *Town* that "You suffer—therefore I am," the hero is not entirely in the clear. The questions have deepened, but the answers forthcoming are still shrouded in fog and uncertainty. Other Wiesel novels are likely to proffer new approaches to existence in a world still contaminated by the stench of burning flesh. Yet the direction of salvation has been indicated. It lies in the commitment to humanity and justice on the one hand and the joy in living and God on the other. Under the aegis of Hasidism, Wiesel is still attempting the near insurmountable task, "to turn a tremendous amount of despair into a chant, into a prayer."

His all-encompassing effort to comprehend the evil of the past has kept Wiesel from expressing himself specifically on contemporary Jewish issues. What views he has voiced have had their foundation in the holocaust and are perhaps weak superstructures.

Wiesel has made it plain—though never directly or specifically—that the anti-Semitism of the holocaust was merely different in intensity and scope from that of earlier varieties. In *Gates of the Forest*, the hero depicts his Hungarian childhood as filled with assaults by other children on Jewish youths. In various articles in *Le Chant des Morts*, he comments bitterly on European anti-Semitism and sees significance in Hitler's choice of Poland as the site of the extermination camps. Wiesel also seems to suggest religion as the prime basis of anti-Semitism although he never dwells on the theory. The anti-Semitic attacks he describes are invariably followed by shouts of "Christ-Killer." In *Gates*, Wiesel answers the charge through his own treatment of the Judas theme, hinting that the passion of Christ has been dwarfed by that of the Jews, a passion mercilessly repeated throughout the centuries.

Similarly Wiesel's vision of Jewish history has the holocaust as its vantage point. He cannot forget or forgive that all doors were closed to Jews. The Evian Conference had made it plain to the Nazis that no one wanted the publicly lamented Jews and that they could safely proceed with the Final Solution. He believes Eichmann's recorded statement that even if he had agreed to sell Jews for a fixed amount, there would have been no buyers. Jews simply were not popular and were dispensable, marginally human elements in the Christian world of the Diaspora. Wiesel's resentments may be gleaned from an occasional remark on the subject, but nowhere is Christianity or even Germany a prime target of protest. The permanent and mysterious significance of the holocaust alone has preoccupied Wiesel, not its transient facets rooted in time and place.

Like others hurt by the sharp edges of anti-Semitism, Wiesel was drawn to Zionism from the first. The thought of a Jewish home was a comfort to him in the dark days of the crematoria. Wiesel welcomed the establishment of a Jewish home, has lived in Israel and remained a correspondent for one of its major dailies. In a mood half playful and half serious, Wiesel has recently said that the coming of the Jewish state when it did was in part a misfortune, It provided the outside world with a quick palliative for its guilty conscience when a lengthy wrestling with this conscience would have yielded the greater long-range moral benefit.

But unlike most Jews acutely aware of anti-Semitism, Wiesel has never attributed Jewish survival to the stresses and

insecurities of the Jewish condition. While he concedes that
Judaism has flourished under stress, he reminds Jews that this
stress was imposed, not chosen. He leans almost to the
opposite view that Jews managed to oppose persecutions and
stress an affirmation of life and in fact the sanctity of life.

More that any other writer Wiesel is entirely wrapped up
in Jewish tradition. The outside world, he confesses, barely
existed for him in his Hungarian youth. It appears to occupy
even now an insignificant role. He may feel that enough
writers are feeding on the Western Christian tradition without
a Jewish writer interpreting the same experience. Little
surprise, therefore, that in his ceaseless investigation into the
holocaust, Wiesel has been singularly unconcerned with the
executioners and all the more with their victims. To be sure, he
has displayed a lively interest in the moral apathy of the
witnesses to the executions, whom he seems to condemn more
than the executioners themselves. But again it is not the
practical, temporal dissociation of the witnesses which prompts
his remarks, but his own growing realization of the responsibility of one human to another.

The double moral imperative that history must not repeat
and that Man cannot be a silent witness to injustice has driven
Wiesel out of his tower of mystical speculation to enmesh
himself in the destiny of Russian Jewry. In this one area of
external relations, Wiesel's voice has been heard loudly and
clearly and in characteristically Wiesel language. Thus he has
called Russian Jews the "Jew of silence." On a visit to Russia,
Wiesel was struck by the remarkable vitality of Russian Jews
four decades after the Revolution and despite determined
efforts to eradicate any group characteristics and loyalty. He
was equally astounded that Russian Jewish youngsters,
Communists like all others their age, could yet sing and dance
and rejoice in Hebrew and Yiddish on a Jewish holiday.
Wiesel has called for a determined effort on the part of world
Jewry to use its total influence in behalf of even limited Jewish
survival in the Soviet Union.

Wiesel's attitudes toward Jewish external problems are
only vaguely defined. His attitudes toward the Jewish heritage
is not. He worships at the shrine of Jewish literary traditions
which have served him more that any other Jewish writer as
the source for creative endeavor. He continues to read Talmud

with regularity and, especially in his last two novels, has employed its sayings, parables and tales to release the development of plot and action. The Talmud is for him the very symbol ot the Jewish people. Burned countless times by non-believers, it has yet managed to survive and overcome. But it represents more than part of Jewish history. It contains the will and dedication to live, which Wiesel—so long in the shadow of death—has come to regard as the essence of Judaism.

But no facet of the Jewish tradition has lured Wiesel more than the Hasidic. Just as he is a perennial student of Talmud, he has become a frequent visitor to the Hasidim of Williamsburg. The significance of Hasidism for this Auschwitz graduate finds expression in this impassioned statement by the Hasidic Rebbe in *Gates of the Forest:*

> The man who goes singing to death is the brother of the man who goes to death fighting. A song on the lips is worth a dagger in the hand. I take this song and make it mine. Do you know what the song hides? A dagger, an outcry. Appearances have depth of their own which has nothing to do with the depth. When you come to our celebrations you'll see how we dance and sing and rejoice. There is joy as well as fury in the hasid's dancing. It's his way of proclaiming. "You don't want me to dance; too bad, I'll dance anyhow. You've taken away every reason for singing, but I shall sing. I shall sing of the deceit that walks by day and the truth that walks by night, yes, and of the silence of dusk as well. You didn't expect my joy, but here it is; yes, my joy will rise up; it will submerge you."

It is not only the Hasid's stubborn affirmation of life that attracts Wiesel, but also his tales. He has been intrigued with their curious blend of realism and suggestions of transcendence which he has transformed into significant sections of his own books.

Wiesel's language is suffused with phrases and images from Hebraic literature, especially its mystical segments. For example certain expressions recur with particular frequency. These Wiesel endows with special attributes. Thus, on the folklore of death: Death has no hair—it has only legs. A dying man listens only to his stomach. There are girls who like to make love only to men obsessed with death. Dead souls have more to say than living ones. God is in the graves to make men and women warm. The sea makes one think of death. Death and life are juxtaposed. Following his accident, the hero of that novel comments:

> I ... thought of myself as dead. I thought I was dead and that in a dream I imagined myself alive. I knew I no longer existed, that my real self stayed there, that my present self had nothing in common with my other self, the real one.

Even life doesn't want to live. For life is really fascinated with death.

Invariably the lore surrounding these words is modified by Wiesel's own aphoristic style. To use another high-frequency word, suffering. Here the man Wiesel and the experiences of brutal reality break through the net of Jewish lore and mysticism. But even there his words retain their aphoristic potency and essentially biblical quality. Suffering does not lead to saintliness. It brings out the lowest and most cowardly in man. There is a phase of suffering beyond which man becomes a brute and is pulled hopelessly away from other humans. Suffering dehumanizes and makes moral contact impossible.

But lore and man are reunited in the highest frequency word of all, God. Wiesel has been called a God-besotted writer and one critic commented that it is as natural for a Wieselian character to ask, "Do you believe in God?" as it is for most mortals to inquire, "Do you smoke?" He speculates ceaselessly about His intent and purpose, always within the context of Judaic lore. At times He is a God of chaos and impotence, sometimes capable of committing the most unforgettable of crimes—to kill without reason. But perhaps God is condemned to eternal solitude and compulsively amuses Himself by using Man as a toy. But he always surprises by extending signs of friendship, as when he speaks in dreams. The existence of this God is tied to ours. The obsession with Him never ceases, being funneled every few pages into new speculative moods.

Wiesel's Jewish sources have, of course, suffered the influence of some Western sophisticated philosophical ideas. Slightly detectable are the influences of Camus and Sartre and perhaps that of Dostoyevski. Jewishly he has been under the wing of Abraham J. Heschel more than any other contemporary thinker. Add the personal experience of the holocaust and two of Wiesel's primary themes, madness as lucidity and silence as true communication, which are the slightly expectable compounds of this rather odd concoction.

Dostoyesvski's quote, "I have a plan to go mad," serves as the motto for *Town Beyond the Wall.* The hero strives for a metaphysical madness which would enable him to understand what normal lucidity veils from him. In several novels it is the *mad* man or woman to whom God reveals himself and who perceives most clearly the true character of events. In *Night* it is the town madman who has escaped from captivity to warn his unsuspecting fellow Jews, only to be cast aside as insane by the rational fools. In the cattle-train to Birkenau a mother, beserk with grief over separation from her husband, sees fire in her trances and Cassandra-like she prophesies their doom in the ovens. Again and again the insane, the drunks, the discarded have grace, justice and truth on their side. "Lucidity," writes Wiesel in *The Accident,* "is fate's victory, not man's. It is an act of freedom that carries within itself the negation of freedom. Man must keep moving, searching, weighing, holding out his hand, offering himself." In *Town,* the hero's father explains why he seeks out the company of Mad Moishe:

> Moishe—I speak of the real Moishe, the one who hides behind the Madman—is a great man. He is far-seeing. He sees worlds that remain inaccessible to us. His madness is only a wall, erected to protect us: to see what Moishe's bloodshot eyes see would be dangerous.

Wiesel has stated that madness began to interest him because it was madness that swept through the world from 1939 to 1945, resulting in what Buber has called "The Eclipse of God." Similarly, his concern with silence has its roots in the same period which taught him the horrible failure of language, its inability to express this eclipse, to explain the mystery of the holocaust, to lend itself to such crimes as labeling selection and resettlement the worst crimes in history. Wiesel regarded Arthur Miller's *Incident at Vichy* a major failure because of its refusal to employ the maximum of silence, and its audacity to assume that such horrendous events lend themselves to the use of words. Wiesel is acutely conscious that he himself has been forced to employ words to present his ideas and has thus partly failed in his protest against language. But he has consciously attempted "to inject as much silence in his books as possible, a silence between and within his words."

Wiesel has carried the experience of the holocaust from a simple yet overpowering documentary report in *Night* through the agonies of readjusting to a life that has become incomprehensible as well as insufferable. In having his hero travel the long road back to psychological and moral integration, Wiesel has undertaken the most ambitious and difficult assignment of interpreting the whole trauma of the 1940s and its aftermath. In the process he has supplied twentieth-century Jewry—and indeed contemporary man—with exemplary, yet realistic, prescriptions of hope and determination. This hope and determination achieve meaning and purpose only through the involvement of man in the destiny of others, in action and commitment that favor justice and humanity, in the joy of living. Streamlined Hasidism, as reflected in Buber and perhaps even more in Heschel, provides more meaningful answers to life than the rational line pursued by earlier thinkers. Wiesel has succeeded in blending Jewish philosophy, mythology and historical experience. In this respect he must be placed alongside two other practitioners of Jewish fiction in the front ranks of the art. One of these is Andre Schwarz-Bart whom Wiesel overshadows as a weaver of ideas, but whom he cannot match in warmth and humanity; the other, the much older Isaac Bashevis Singer, who employs many ingredients similar to Wiesel's, but whose mixture appears less varied even as his narrative skill is superior. Among the top American Jewish writers, Wiesel bears a greater resemblance to Malamud than to either Bellow or Roth.

There are flaws in Wiesel's novels. Often the action of the story does not directly lead to the philosophical conclusions of the end. (*The Accident* is perhaps the most seriously flawed in this respect.) His work also bears the heavy introspective stamp of many twentieth-century French novels which unquestionably have greatly influenced him. If Wiesel's work has caught on in America only with select few, it is because the intellectual novel is still rare in this country and the intellectual hero trying to solve religious-spiritual problems is even less common. In Elie Wiesel we may well have the brightest young hope on the Jewish literary horizon.

THE HOLOCAUST IN THE STORIES OF ELIE WIESEL

by Thomas A. Idinopulos

The stories, essays, and reportage of Elie Wiesel have been dominated to date by a single theme: the Holocaust. His writings are not, however, contributions to the historical and psychological study of the death camps seeking answers to the questions *How?* and *Why?* For Wiesel the destruction of six million men, women, and children, methodically and without passion, is a terrifying mystery before which one's reason is silenced. Facts can be discovered and explanations given, but the act of "making sense" is somehow incommensurable with the catastrophe.[1] The enormity of the evil, suggested in the very word—*holocaust*—forces Wiesel beyond explantions to judgments that one must call *theological.* For a fire lit by men with purpose of consuming men strikes at the very heart of creation; and it compels the survivor to ask not only whether God rules the universe but whether he deserves to rule. It is in a way Job's question that Wiesel raises in his stories, the question of divine justice or the morality of God; but he also raises the question at the heart of mediaeval Jewish mysticism, whether God truly defeated Satan in the primeval struggle—a question inescapable for one contemplating Job in the light of Auschwitz.[2]

Wiesel's childhood faith in the goodness and promise of God was forever shattered when as a young boy he was deported along with his family from their native Transylvania to Auschwitz. Arriving at Auschwitz Wiesel learned what Dostoevsky in his own time knew, that the sin against the child is the only unforgivable sin, for it indicts not only man but man's creator. Echoing Dostoevsky, he writes: "A Child who dies becomes the center of the universe: stars and

meadows die with him." In one long train ride, Wiesel had
been transported from the only world he had known, that of a
young Jew growing up, devoutly studying Talmud by day,
the Cabbala by night, to a new world which he describes
in these stark lines:

> Never shall I forget that night, the first night in camp,
> which has turned my life into one long night, seven times
> cursed and seven times sealed. Never shall I forget that
> smoke. Never shall I forget the little faces of the children,
> whose bodies I saw turned into wreaths of smoke
> beneath a silent blue sky.
>
> Never shall I forget those flames which consumed my
> faith forever.
>
> Never shall I forget that nocturnal silence which de-
> prived me, for all eternity, of the desire to live. Never
> shall I forget those moments which murdered my God
> and my soul and turned my dreams to dust. Never shall I
> forget these things, even if I am condemned to live as
> long as God himself. Never.[3]

The question of God is one strand in Wiesel's response to
the Holocaust. Woven tightly with it is a second: the memory
of the Holocaust, felt as an agonizing obligation on the part of
the survivor. The hero of Wiesel's early stories is ashamed at
having survived the dead. He yearns to crawl back into the
grave. He cannot regard his life as any less absurd than the fire
that turned into smoke his father, mother, and sister. He has
survived, but it is a survival he can no more come to terms with
than the wholly meaningless deaths visited on his family and
the millions of others. His link with the past is found in the refrain,
"Never shall I forget." He says of himself, "I was now just a
messenger of the dead among the living."[4] This is Wiesel's
own confession. In remembering the dead through his stories,
Wiesel gives them honor; letting them speak again, he cheats
the death factories of what would be their final victory, the
silencing of each soul in the abstractness of the number
6,000,000. "The act of writing," he says, "is for me often
nothing more than the secret or conscious desire to carve
words on a tombstone: to the memory of a town forever
vanished, to the memory of a childhood in exile, to the
memory of all those I loved and who, before I could tell them I
loved them, went away."[5]

Wiesel begins to remember in his memoir, *Night,* when he tells the story of Sighet, his home town in Hungary, and recalls Moche the Beadle of the synagogue, and Kalman, the Hasid who initiated him in the mysteries of the Cabbala. What gives his writing its power is that the act of recollection is suffused with a sense of that deep mystery—how in one long night a small world of Jews, their lives and their history over centuries, could become transformed into a column of white smoke. It is the juxtaposition of the Holocaust with the sweetness of a child's memory of growing up that produces in *Night,* and in the stories that followed, a curious blend of beauty and suffering.

Story-telling is the medium of remembering for Wiesel. The meaning he discovers in the art of story-telling and its relation to his own life constitutes a third strand in his response to the Holocaust. In telling the story the dead are honored and the survivor can affirm his own life. The Hasidic saying which serves as prologue to his novel *The Gates of the Forest* could well be taken as prologue to Wiesel's whole authorship:

> When the great Rabbi Israel Baal Shem-Tov saw misfortune threatening the Jews it was his custom to go into a certain part of the forest to meditate. There he would light a fire, say a special prayer, and the miracle would be accomplished and the misfortune averted.

> Later, when his disciple, the celebrated Magid of Mezritch, had occasion, for the same reason, to intercede with heaven, he would go to the same place in the forest and say: "Master of the Universe, listen! I do not know how to light the fire, but I am still able to say the prayer," and again the miracle would be accomplished.

> Still later, Rabbi Moshe-Leib of Sasov, in order to save his people once more, would go into the forest and say: "I do not know how to light a fire, I do not know the prayer, but I know the place and this must be sufficient." It was sufficient and the miracle was accomplished.

> Then it fell to Rabbi Israel of Rizhyn to overcome misfortune. Sitting in his armchair, his head in his hands, he spoke to God: "I am unable to light the fire and I do not know the prayer; I cannot even find the place in the forest. All I can do is to tell the story, and this must be sufficient." And it was sufficient.

God made man because he loves stories.[6]

The evil of the Holocaust is impenetrable, but as a story-teller Wiesel can create a meaning where there was none before. And, as the Hasidic legend suggests, the art of the story is the telling of it. In telling his story, Wiesel is the artist who, to use Joseph Conrad's words, "speaks to our capacity for delight and wonder, to the sense of mystery surrounding our lives; to our sense of pity and beauty and pain."[7]

The alternative to art is madness. Madmen people Wiesel's stories, for it is in madness that one comes closest to perceiving the actual meaning of the Holocaust.[8] Wiesel suggests that there is a bond of madness which unites victims, survivors, and even executioners. In one story, after the Germans have machine-gunned all the Jews of a small village in the Carpathian mountains, the officer in charge discovers that one Jew has escaped the slaughter, that he is standing before his killers continuing to sing the song all the Jews were singing during the massacre. The officer tries unsuccessfully to kill this lone survivor; finally in desperation he falls to his knees before him, recognizing that in some fantastic way victim has become conqueror, and he says,

> You're humiliating me, you're taking your revenge. One day you'll regret it. You'll speak, but your words will fall on deaf ears. Some will laugh at you, others will try to redeem themselves through you. You'll try to reveal what should remain hidden, you'll try to incite people to learn from the past and rebel, but they will refuse to believe you. They will not listen to you. In the end you'll curse me for having spared you. You'll curse me because you'll possess the truth, you already do; but it's the truth of a madman.[9]

The question of God, the obligation to remember the past, and the importance of story-telling are intertwined in Wiesel's effort to create a meaning, a "legend" as he calls it, for all the people destroyed in the Holocaust. They are the motifs of all his stories, beginning with his memoir *Night*. However, in observing the succession of stories beginning with *Night*, one recognizes a development of sensibility in Wiesel's hero, a vision of escaping the nightmare of the past that becomes fully articulated in Wiesel's masterpiece, *The Gates of the Forest*.

Wiesel concludes his memoir with his liberation from Buchenwald. Looking at himself in the mirror for the first time since leaving the ghetto in Hungary, he says, "From the depths of the mirror, a corpse gazed back to me. The look in his eyes, as they stared into mine, has never left me." Here Wiesel expresses his feeling of being haunted by the past, of belonging more to the dead than the living; it is the feeling that defines the central character in his stories *Dawn, The Accident,* and *The Town Beyond the Wall.*

Each of these stories has as its hero a survivor of the death camps who is struggling to discover in the past some meaning that will fulfill his obligation to the dead and thus justify his survival. In *Dawn* the hero, Elisha, has gone to Palestine after his release from a concentration camp to join an underground struggling to liberate Palestine from British control. Elisha learns that the death of his father in Buchenwald cannot be avenged when he is assigned the task of killing a British officer in reprisal for the execution of a Jewish agent. He recognizes that the ghost of the past cannot be exorcised by another death; rather, when he becomes an executioner, his dead reproach *him* for being a murder. The story ends when Elisha, confronted by the terrible ambiguity of living through his memories, realizes that he has found no way of overcoming the past.

It is in *The Town Beyond the Wall* that Wiesel expresses most deeply his feeling that memory has chained him to a ghost-filled past. Here the hero, now called Michael, has convinced himself that if he returns to his home town in Hungary and confronts the past, then somehow the ghost of the past will be exorcised. Michael both succeeds and fails in his mission. He returns to discover that a town which willingly emptied itself of all its Jews has erased the memory. No one there can remember the day in which the Jews were torn from their homes and deported by cattle car to their deaths. Where there is no memory there is no past, no pity, no sense of shame or of loss, no recognition of guilt. Michael eventually recognizes that the return to his home town is not a return to a past whose meaning he can recover. He sees that on the day that he, his family, and all the other Jews were rounded up in the synagogue and put on a train for Auschwitz, on that day the town of Szerencsevaros ceased to exist for Jews, just as Jews ceased to exist for the good citizens who continued to live out their lives in Szerencsevaros.

Though the journey to discover the meaning of the past has been a failure, it has made it possible to honor the memory of the dead, to repay a debt to the past. This occurs when Michael seeks out a man whom he remembers as watching at his window with indifference, each day for a week, the town's Jews being herded into the synagogue for deportation. Michael wants to look into this man's face, to talk to him, to understand how a man could remain indifferent to what he saw. The man is found, and Michael accuses him.

> People of your kind scuttle along the margins of existence. Far from men, from their struggles, which you no doubt consider stupid and senseless. You tell yourself that it's the only way to survive, to keep your head above water. You're afraid of drowning, so you never embark. You huddle on the beach, at the edge of the sea you fear so much, even to its spray. Let the ships sail without you! Whatever their flag—Communist, Nazi, Tartar, what difference does it make? You tell yourself, "To link my life to other men's would be to diminish it, to set limits; so why do it?" You cling to your life. It's precious to you. You won't offer it to history or to country or to God. If living in peace means evolving in nothingness, you accept the nothingness. The Jews in the courtyard of the synagogue? Nothing. The shrieks of women gone mad in the cattle cars? Nothing. The silence of thirsty children? Nothing. All that's a game, you tell yourself. A movie! Fiction: seen and forgotten. I tell you, you're a machine for the fabrication of nothingness.

And he concludes:

> The dead Jews, the women gone mad, the mute children —I'm their messenger. And I tell you they haven't forgotton you. Someday they'll come marching, trampling you, spitting in your face. And at their shouts of contempt you'll pray God to deafen you.[10]

Having spoken his accusation, Michael realizes that, to the extent it can be paid, he has paid his debt to the past. Honoring the memory of the dead, he has begun to earn the right to live. And for the first time in his stories Wiesel has his character speak as a healed man:

Suddenly I had no further desire to speak or listen. I was weary, as after a battle fought without conviction. I had come, I had seen, I had delivered the message; the wheel had come full circle. The act was consummated. Now I shall go. I shall return to the life they call normal. The past will have been exorcised. I'll live, I'll work, I'll love. I'll take a wife, I'll father a son, I'll fight to protect his future, his future happiness. The task is accomplished. No more concealed wrath, no more disguises. No more double life, lived on two levels. Now I am whole.[11]

The hero of *The Accident* is a journalist for an Israeli newspaper assigned to the United Nations. One day he is critically injured by an automobile when crossing Times Square with a young woman. Throughout his stay in the hospital he resists the efforts of his doctors to save him. Unlike Elisha, he seems to know that his only chance for life lies in putting an end to his suffering through accepting the love offered him by Kathleen, the young woman, and the friendship of Gyula, an Hungarian painter. But he is drawn to his suffering as a guilty man to his accuser. He cannot escape the past, because it is more real for him than anything in the present. The novel ends with the revelation that he might have avoided the accident but made no effort to do so.

Wiesel has said that the question which the Holocaust raises about man and his relation to God cannot be answered.[12] With the appearance of *The Gates of the Forest* one is persuaded that Wiesel has at least discovered ways to live with the question. The hero of the story, Gregor, is a boy of seventeen, hiding out from the Nazis after his family has been deported from their town in Transylvania. The story consists of four episodes, chronicling the period in which Gregor achieves self-discovery. In each of the episodes Gregor encounters persons who act to save his life; but more significantly, relationships of need, affection, friendship, comradeship, and love are formed with human beings—relationships that heal the wounds of the past, making it possible for him to live forward again.

Through Gregor, Wiesel expresses his belief that the past cannot and should not be forgotten. But the past is dangerous, for it can consume a person, destroying any chance of life. The effort must be made again and again to make out of memory a *witness* to the past, which is to bring the past into the present moment by exposing oneself to the actions, feelings, and thoughts of other human beings. Gregor comes to learn this beginning in the spring when he shares a cave with another young Jew who is also in hiding, and who has lost not only family and home, but strangely, also his name. Gregor gives his own Jewish name of Gavriel to his friend, for in the author's mind Gavriel has come to Gregor as an angelic messenger bringing news of the slaughter of Jews, but bringing as well the message of survival and the promise of new life. The giving of a name is in Wiesel's stories a symbol of human communion. Where *The Town Beyond the Wall* ends with this symbol, *The Gates of the Forest* begins with it. Gavriel fulfills his promise, for the sequence ends with Gavriel sacrificing himself to the police in order to effect the escape of Gregor.

Gavriel's friendship and courage have saved Gregor from the demons in the forest which lie in wait for innocent young Jewish boys. Here the forest is Wiesel's symbol for the experience of the Holocaust. Gavriel's act of freeing Gregor from this madness is paralleled throughout Wiesel's stories. In *The Accident* Gyula, the painter, seeks to free the survivor from the suffering which is driving him mad. Similarly Pedro in *The Town Beyond the Wall* liberates Michael as he struggles in the last scene of that story to unchain a young boy from the silence which is the symbol of his madness.

In the episode of summer, Gregor has taken refuge in the house of Maria, an old Christian woman who was once a servant in his father's house but now lives in her own village across the mountain border in Rumania. Maria knows that she can succeed in protecting Gregor only by concealing his identity as a Jew. She proposes that he pose as her nephew, the child of her sister who left the village some twenty years ago. To safeguard the deception Gregor must learn the rituals and beliefs of Christianity, but Maria is still anxious and persuades him to pose as a deaf-mute lest his voice and manner betray his real identity. Gregor willingly engages in the masquerade. He succeeds so brilliantly that in a short time the villagers regard him with that special affection reserved for those in whom one sees the working of God's hand. It seems that Gregor's "mother" had a reputation (in her youth) as the village whore; thus Gregor's "affliction" as a deaf-mute is interpreted by the superstitious villagers as God's punishment of the mother through the son. The villagers pour out their hearts and confess their inner secrets before this divinely stricken lad who, they believe, can neither speak nor hear.

The ruse is exposed when Gregor plays the part of Judas in the Easter passion play which the villagers perform. Gregor has been chosen for the part because he is so obviously innocent of any sin, bearing as he does the stigmata of his own mother's wickedness, so that he alone in the village has the inner security which frees him to take the role of the "Christ-killer." The irony that Wiesel has created is searing: the Jew-turned-Christian, in order now to remain alive, must pose before a Christian audience as the most detestable of all Jews.

The play is performed wretchedly before an indifferent audience. But when Judas finally makes his appearance on stage to confront Christ, new feeling seizes the peasants. Their boredom turns to hostility focused on the person of Christ's betrayer. "Judas! Traitor! . . . Judas! You did it for money!" is heard in the audience. "You betrayed the Son of God! . . . You killed the Savior!" In a few brief moments the figure of Judas, the Christ-killer, has obscured in their minds their beloved deaf-mute, Gregor. The script had called for a verbal denunciation of Judas, a clear vindication of the forces of righteousness; but the actors, sensing the possibility of a dramatic success where before there had been only tedium, heartily join the audience in a common attack on Judas. Now real blows are rained down on Gregor, and his face is quickly bloodied. Unknown to all, the Jew is now to suffer the real fate of the Jew. Wiesel describes Gregor's feelings as he accepts his punishment and then brings it suddenly to a halt.

> As the attack grew more violent Gregor discovered that he was stronger than they; they were suffering and he was not. The scene had the unreal, oppressive quality of a nightmare. The pain, there, on him, in him, an alien presence, was that of a nightmare. He felt the pain, but at the same time he knew that when he chose he could stop it. . . .
>
> Gregor spread his legs in order to stand firm upon the stage and slowly, very slowly, he raised his right arm. The other actors, believing he had decided to defend himself, were ready to throw him down and trample him.

One man in the audience picked up a chair and was going to use it. He had to act quickly to forestall him. Every second, every breath, every gesture counted. Time was pressing. A thousand veils were rent: the Prophets emerged from the past and the Messiah from the future. Quickly! Something had to happen. Gregor breathed deeply, and his voice rang out firmly as he spoke to the audience: "Men and women of this village, listen to me!"

In their amazement they froze, incredulous, as if death had surprised them in the midst of battle. Projected out of time they were like wax figures, grotesque and idiotic, without destiny or soul, clay creatures, damned in the service of the devil. Their upraised arms hung in the air, their mouths were half open with tongues protruding and features swollen; the slightest breath would have knocked them over and returned them to dust. All breathing ceased. They were afraid of discovering themselves alive and responsible. The priest was bent over as if he were about to fall on his stomach; he seemed to have lost his eyelids. Then, their faces drained of hate gave way to animal fear. The silence was heavy with blood. Suddenly an old man recovered sufficiently to throw himself upon the floor and to cry out in terror, "Merciful God, have pity on us!"

And he burst into sobs.

And another, imitating him, exclaimed, "Merciful God, forgive us our sins!"

And a third, "A miracle! A miracle, brothers! Pray to Our Lord to have pity on us, for we are miserable creatures."

"Yes, yes, yes! A miracle, a miracle before our eyes! Our dear Gregor is no longer dumb; he is speaking! Our own beloved Gregor! God had made him speak! Look and see for yourselves: God has accomplished a miracle before our eyes."[13]

A scene of macabre humor is now played out. The villagers are stunned by what they believe to be a miracle wrought by God before them. Gregor seizes the moment and compels his fellow villagers to confess fervently that they made a mistake, that their Gregor is not the hated Judas. He then commands them to ask forgiveness for their cruelty not from Christ but from Judas himself, for it was finally Judas, not Christ, whom they wronged. Even the priest is willing to admit that their guilt is before Judas not Christ. "Say after me," Gregor commands them, "'Judas is innocent and we humbly implore his forgiveness.'"

Then Gregor stuns them again. He announces his true identity. He is not the son of the village whore; not their precious deaf-mute. He is in fact a Jew from a village across the mountains who has been hiding from the killers of Jews. Now, Wiesel writes, Gregor

> was silent and there was a smile, not of triumph, but of pity on his face. The peasants opened their mouths wide in astonishment. This was the last thing that they had expected and it was too much for them. The priest collapsed onto his chair, and the villagers stared at the stage without comprehending. In all their minds there was a single thought: we are the victims of a Jew who holds us in his hands. If he goes on making these confessions, the earth will swallow us up.

> The old man who a few minutes before had called him a saint was the first to regain his composure. Brandishing his fists threateningly, he cried out, "Liar! Dirty liar! You've deceived us, you've betrayed our trust, you've made fun of innocent people, and you shall pay for it!"[14]

Out of the traditional drama of Christ's suffering and death Wiesel has constructed a parable of the existence of the Jew ever since the death of Jesus. History has reversed the roles. Judas, the Christ-killer, has become the victim; and Christ, in the form of Christian civilization, has become the Jew-killer. Since the death of Christ, the Jew is presented with the most degrading alternative: To survive he must renounce or conceal his identity as a Jew; to affirm his identity he must be prepared to suffer. Confronted always with this alternative the Jew could not help but feel "set apart." By the twisted ironies of history, it appears that the biblical writers really spoke the truth: The record of Jewish history shows that God did in fact choose his people; and that the Jew has paid in blood the price of his election.

Wiesel, like the theologian Richard L. Rubenstein,[15] recognizes that it is not in eschatology but rather in history that the Jew is to seek the basis of his unity with other Jews, living and dead. The solidarity of Jewish people is based on the simplest and most courageous of human cats: the communication of one Jew to another that he is a Jew, and thus shares his identity. In *Legends of Our Time* Wiesel tells the story of The Jew from Saragossa. On a holiday in Spain, in the famous city of the Basques, the narrator of this story engages a native to act as his guide. Upon discovering that the tourist is a Jew who knows the Hebrew language, the guide asks a special favor. Would he come to his room that evening and read to him the words on a treasured piece of paper that has been in his family for generations? The language is foreign to him, it may be Hebrew, but no one in his family that he can remember has ever been able to understand its meaning. That evening the tourist succeeds in deciphering to the Spaniard this testament of his ancestor, who, it turns out, was a Spanish Jew living in the time of the Exile.

> I, Moses, son of Abraham, forced to break all ties with my people and my faith, leave these lines to the children of my children, and theirs, in order that on the day when Israel will be able to walk again, its head high under the sun, without fear and without remorse, they will know where their roots lie. Written at Saragossa, this ninth day of the month of *Av,* in the year of punishment and exile.[16]

The Spaniard learns that he is a Jew, a descendant of the Marranos, those who disguised their identity five hundred years before to escape persecution and death in Spain. As the legend of Rabbi Israel of Rizhyn states, the telling of the story is sufficient to avoid disaster. The dead have succeeded in telling their story to the living. A Jew from the fifteenth century has brought to birth a Jew from the twentieth century.[17]

The Gates of the Forest moves through the fall, during which time Gregor is part of an underground resistance group of young Jews, and it concludes with a winter episode years later when, the war having ended, Gregor has emigrated to America. Gregor is now married to Clara, the sweetheart of a childhood friend, with whom he was reunited in the forest but who died at the hands of the Fascists. In this last episode Gregor has an exchange with a Hasidic Rabbi in which the fundamental question of his life is posed.

Gregor challenges the Rabbi to defend his belief in the righteousness of God in light of the slaughter of his people, Israel. The Rabbi, torn by the challenge, replies:

> So be it! . . . He's guilty; do you think I don't know it? That I have no eyes to see, no ears to hear? That my heart doesn't revolt? That I have no desire to beat my head against the wall and shout like a madman, to give rein to my sorrow and disappointment? Yes, he is guilty. He has become the ally of evil, of death, of murder, but the problem is still not solved. I ask you a question and dare you answer: 'What is there left for us to do?'[18]

What indeed is there left to do? This is the question which Gregor must face if he is to live with his memories and not be robbed of life because of them. Gregor has lost faith in the God of Israel as young Elie Wiesel himself in the memoir *Night* confesses that he lost faith in the God of his childhood. But the Rabbi leads Gregor to the truth that if he is not to put his faith in the God of Israel then he must not deny faith in the community of Israel.

Wiesel seems to be saying that if there is meaning left in the God of the Jews, it must be found in Jewishness.[19] And, paradoxically, the road to Jewishness lies through community that is inextricably sacred and human. In the prayers of celebration, praise, and lamentation, the Jew *as Jew* responds most humanly to the mysteries of good and evil, and in that response heals the wounds inflicted on him by man in the sight of a helpless God. In a sense God died for Wiesel at Auschwitz, but if after Auschwitz the Jew is to affirm his identity through solidarity with other Jews, he must affirm God, the ground of solidarity. As the Jew cannot be Jew without God, so Wiesel, echoing the mystical teachings of the Cabbala, holds that God cannot be God without the Jew and all the other creatures of his creation. Wiesel speaks of this mutuality as the faith by which man liberates God from his own imprisonment. The life of one is incomplete without the other, though the story of their common existence is filled as much with strife as with love. Referring to this bond, Wiesel writes in the epilogue to *The Town Beyond the Wall:*

> As the liberation of the one was bound to the liberation of the other, they renewed the ancient dialogue whose

echoes come to us in the night, charged with hatred, with remorse, and most of all, with infinite yearning.

God remains guilty, but one must forgive God his sin if God and man are to continue to live again with each other; and for the Jew, there is no alternative.

The Rabbi knows this; Gregor will learn it. For in response to Gregor's indictment of God's immorality, the Rabbi asks, "Do you want me to stop praying and start shouting? Is that what you're after?" "Yes," whispered Gregor. And the Rabbi replies:

> "Who says that power comes from a shout, an outcry rather than from a prayer? From anger rather than compassion? Where do you find certainties when you claim to have denied them? The man who goes to death death is the brother of the man who goes to death fighting. A song on the lips is worth a dagger in the hand. I take this song and make it mine. Do you know what the song hides? A dagger, an outcry. Appearances have a depth of their own which has nothing to do with the depth. When you come to our celebrations you'll see how we dance and sing and rejoice. There is joy as well as fury in the *hasid's* dancing. It's his way of proclaiming, 'You don't want me to dance; too bad, I'll dance anyhow. You've taken away every reason for singing, but I shall sing, I shall sing of the deceit that walks by day and the truth that walks by night, yes, and of the silence of dusk as well. You didn't expect my joy, but here it is; yes, my joy will rise up; it will submerge you,'"[20]

Gregor does finally come to identify with a small group of Hasidic Jews in Brooklyn led by the rabbi, and he is drawn to the affirmation he recognizes in their celebration.

> The celebration was at its height. It seemed as if it would never come to an end. The *hasidim* were dancing, vertically, as if not moving from their place, but forcing the rhythm down into the earth. What did it matter if the walls gave way except to show that no enclosure was large enough to contain their fervor? They sang; and the song gave them life and caused the sap to well up in them and bind them together. Ten times, fifty times, they repeated the same phrase, taken from the Psalms or some other portion of Scripture, and every time the fire would be renewed again with primordial passion: yes, once God

and man were one, then their unity was broken; ever since they have sought each other, pursued each other, and before each other have proclaimed themselves invincible. As long as the song and dance go on, they are.[21]

Gregor has seen the truth of the Hasidic affirmation for his own life. The ghosts of Auschwitz and Buchenwald are as real as the corpses; but it is the ghosts alone that harm the living if the living allow them One cannot live the past. Gregor has learned this; Clara has not. She has married Gregor but she wishes to exist only the memory of her dead lover, Gregor's friend, Leib. She regards her suffering as faithfulness, and to share her suffering with another is faithlessness. But Gregor knows that if she does not share it, she will be possessed by the dead as he was himself possessed so very long. Resolving to continue struggling to win Clara back to a life with him and not with a dead man, he says to himself:

> "Knowing then that all of us have our ghosts ... They come and go at will, breaking open doors, never shutting them tight; they bear different names. We mustn't let ourselves be seduced by their promises ... "Yes, Clara, they'll continue to haunt us, but we must fight them. It will be a bitter, austere, obstinate battle. The struggle to survive will begin here, in this room, where we are sitting. Whether or not the Messiah comes doesn't matter; we'll manage without him. It is because it is too late that we are commanded to hope. We shall be honest and humble and strong, and then he will come, he will come every day, thousands of times every day. He will have no face, because he will have a thousand faces. The Messiah isn't one man, Clara, he's all men. As long as there are men there will be a Messiah. One day you'll sing, and he will sing in you. Then for the last time, I'll want to cry. I shall cry. Without shame."[22]

It is with this humanistic vision of the meaninglessness of God without man, of God's dependence on man, that Wiesel's story draws to its close.

In the next moment Gregor recites the *Kaddish*, praying for the souls of his father and of his departed friend Leib, and praying too for the soul of God and for his own soul. In the sacred words of this prayer he senses for the first time the possibility of meaning. Wiesel writes:

> [Gregor] recited [the *Kaddish*] slowly, concentrating on every sentence, every word, every syllable of praise. His voice trembled, timid, like that of the orphan suddenly made aware of the relationship between death and eternity, between eternity and the word.[23]

Through Gregor, Wiesel expresses his acceptance of the Hasidic wisdom that men can survive the disasters of their lives through the experiences of other human beings, encountering meanings in whose depths one feels perhaps for the first time the presence of sacredness. In the recitation of the Kaddish, the traditional prayer for the dead, Wiesel finds it possible to live with the memory of his father's death at Buchenwald,[24] and he comes to know again that God *is*, and that it is possible to live without hating him.

But the prayer is inseparable from the story; after telling the story so many times, the wound has healed, memories which once haunted have now begun to nurture the living.

1.   "I cannot believe that an entire generation of fathers and sons could vanish into the abyss without creating, by their very disappearance, a mystery which exceeds and overwhelms us. I still do not understand what happened, or how, or why. All the words in all the mouths of the philosophers and psychologists are not worth the silent tears of that child and his mother, who live their own death twice. What can be done? In my calculations, all the figures always add up to the same number: six million." Elie Wiesel, *Legends of Our Time* (New York: Avon Books, 1970), pp. 222-223.
2.   For a treatment of the influence of cabbalistic teachings on Wiesel see Byron L. Sherwin, "Elie Wiesel and Jewish Theology," *Judaism* (Winter, 1969), pp. 39-52. While it is plain from his stories that Wiesel doubts the power of God over evil, it is far from clear that he holds the "gnostic" belief that there is a second divine principle, a god-of-evil, as has been suggested by Seymour Cain in his article, "The Questions and Answers After Auschwitz," *Judaism*, (Summer, 1971), p. 274.
3.   Elie Wiesel, *Night*, translated from the French by Stella Rodway (New York: Avon Books, 1970), p. 44.

4. Elie Wiesel, *The Accident*, translated from the French by Anne Borchardt (New York: Avon Books, 1962), p. 49.

5. Wiesel, *Legends of Our Time*, p. 26.

6. Elie Wiesel, *The Gates of the Forest*, translated from the French by Frances Frenage (New York: Avon Books, 1966).

7. Quoted by Gerald Green, *The Artists of Terezin* (New York, 1969), p. 159.

8. Moche the Beadle in *Night* witnesses the slaying of Jews by Nazis, returns to tell the story, and is taken as a madman by all the Jews of Sighet. Elsewhere Wiesel writes, "These days honest men can do only one thing: go mad! Spit on logic, intelligence, sacrosanct reason! That's what you have to do, that's the way to stay human, to keep your wholeness!" ... "God loves madmen. They're the only ones he allows near him." *The Town Beyond the Wall*, translated from the French by Stephen Barker (New York: Avon Books, 1964), pp. 20, 24.

9. Elie Wiesel, *A Beggar in Jerusalem*, translated from the French by Lily Edelman and the author (New York: Random House, 1970), p. 80.

10. Wiesel, *The Town Beyond The Wall*, pp. 172-173.

11. Ibid., p. 118.

12. *Legends of Our Time*, p. 222.

13. Wiesel, *The Gates of the Forest*, pp, 112,113-114.

14. Ibid., p. 118.

15. Richard L. Rubenstein, *After Auschwitz* (Indianapolis, 1967).

16. Wiesel, *Legends of Our Time*, p. 97.

17. Thomas Lask has incisively observed that the use of history to create meaning for the contemporary event is a form which Wiesel has developed in his stories. "The written law and oral tradition support, explain and expand the 20th century event. Describing a Kol Nidre service in the camp for the Day of Atonement in *Legends of Our Time,* Wiesel recalls one legend that says that at that hour the dead rise from their graves and come to pray with the living. Looking about him in the barracks, he realizes that the legend is true, Auschwitz confirmed it." Thomas Lask, a review of *One Generation After* by Elie Wiesel, *The New York Times,* December 15, 1970.

18. Wiesel, *The Gates of the Forest*, p. 196.

19. It is the failure to recognize the centrality of Jewishness in Wiesel's stories that mars Maurice Friedman's analysis. The argument that Wiesel's hero is the "Job of Auschwitz" who "trusts and contends" with God has point, but it is overstated when Friedman interprets this motif according to the existentialist doctrine of moral responsibility before evil as expressed by Camus. The rebellion against the Absurd waged by Dr. Rieux, the hero of Camus' *The Plague,* is not parallel with Wiesel's struggles to learn to live with the memories of all those whom he knew and loved in the Jewish community in Sighet. Wiesel's "contention" with God occurs within an acutely Jewish sensibility where one can be angry with, pity, and even pray for God, but never reject God in favor of an ethical universal, rebellion against the absurd, as Rieux did. Maurice Friedman, "Elie Wiesel: The Job of Auschwitz," unpublished paper delivered at the national meeting of the American Academy of Religion, New York, October, 1970.

20.   Ibid.
21.   Ibid., p. 187.
22.   Ibid., p. 223.
23.   Ibid.
24.   Wiesel's account of his father's death in *Night* and *Legends of Our Time* conveys in its restraint, in its lack of physical horror, the depth of suffering of the son who witnessed and cannot cease remembering. It is not death per se which causes Wiesel suffering but the humiliation of those who died. This is perceptively noted by Thomas Lask (loc. Cit.): "There is surprisingly little physical horror in [Wiesel's] books. It is the mind that is outraged, the spirit that is degraded. When an emaciated father gives his bowl of soup to his starving son, when a naked mother covers her child's body with her own against the expected spray of bullets, pain and death pale before the suffering and humiliation in these events."

ELIE WIESEL AND JEWISH THEOLOGY

by Byron L. Sherwin

As for God, I did speak about Him. I do little else in my books. It's my problem, and His, too.

ELIE WIESEL[1]

Elisha—Prophet or Heretic?

Whenever Israel Friedman, the rabbi of Ryzhn, was faced with misfortune, he would sit in his armchair, his head in his hands, and speak to God: "I am unable to light the fire which the Baal Shem lit to awaken Your mercy. I do not know the Besht's prayer invoked by my great-grandfather, the Maggid of Mesrich, when he would intercede with Heaven for his people. All I can do is tell the story of how the Baal Shem would go to a certain part of the forest (perhaps to the gates of the forest), where he would meditate, light a fire, say a special prayer—and a miracle would occur. But as for me, the story alone must suffice as my prayer."[2]

Elie Wiesel's stories are his prayers. All his stories are one story; all his prayers are one prayer: "Why was God's prayer not answered?" And what does God pray? "May My attribute of mercy suppress My anger; may it prevail over My other attributes" (*Berachot* 7a).

The Holocaust is evidence that God's prayer was not answered, that the perennial prayer of the Jew was not answered.[3]

Has Wiesel's prayer been answered?

Like Levi Yitzchak's, Wiesel's prayer is a *Kaddish*. Levi Yitzchak's *Kaddish* is a challenge and a praise. Wiesel's *Kaddish* is a mourner's *Kaddish* which indicts while it affirms.

The Berditchever learned his tactics from Honi: "'I will not move from this place until Heaven answers.' If Honi had not been successful, Shimeon ben Shetach would have excqmmunicated him for apostasy" (*Taanith* 19a, 23a). Unlike Honi and like the Berditchever, Wiesel has not been answered, and to some, perhaps even to himself, he walks the thin line between faith and heresy. The hero of *Dawn* bears the name Elisha — also the name of the prophet of resurrection (II Kings 13:21, *Hullin* 7b, *Sanhedrin* 47a) — and of ben Abuya (Aher), the excommunicate heretic (*Hagiga* 14b-15a).[4]

The ultimate evil in Christianity is the death of God on the cross. This evil was, however, justified by the resurrection which brought redemption and a good far surpassing the evil. The ultimate evil in Judaism, the Holocaust, has seen no resurrection. Perhaps this is why Wiesel names the hero after Elisha the prophet.

To the neo-Maimonidean mind, Wiesel might not be Elisha the prophet but Elisha the heretic. But it can easily be shown that he is firmly within a tradition which finds its sources in Biblical theology and which develops throughout Jewish literature, notably Kabbalistic writings. Wiesel's blasphemy is a traditional, uniquely Jewish blasphemy. It is based on disappointment, not rejection, inspired by sympathy and love of God:[5]

> You are blaspheming, he repeated gently, as if he were envious, as if he would have liked to blaspheme as well. "God's victory, my son, lies in man's inability to reject Him. You think you're cursing Him, but your curse is praise; you think you're fighting Him, but all you do is to open yourself to Him; you think you're crying out your hatred and rebellion, but all you're doing is telling Him how much you need His support and forgiveness."

Wiesel holds membership in the fellowship of those reconstructionists of faith who have arisen amongst traditional Jewish blasphemers after each major tragedy in Jewish history. After the destruction of the Temple, the Talmud was committed to writing. After the expulsion from Spain, the Kabbalah flourished in an attempt to explain what had occurred. Wiesel is the *Tanna Kama* (master-teacher) of the new Talmud, trying to explain why God's prayers, as well as man's, remain unanswered. He is the *Ari,* the "Lion" of our generation: he roars at God, he purrs at God. Perhaps it would be more correct to say that he is writing a new Bible. For the Holocaust claims Wiesel: though it is the antithesis of Sinai, it is its equal in significance. This new Bible would have as its major theme not God's disappointment with man but man's disappointment with God.

The tradition of Jewish protestantism was begun by Abraham: "Shall the Judge of all the earth not do justice?" (*Genesis* 18:25)—and developed by the prophets: "Wherefore does the way of the wicked prosper?"—"Lord, how long shall I cry and Thou wilt not hear, even cry out unto Thee of violence and Thou wilt not save . . . The wicked encompass the righteous, wrong judgment proceedeth . . . Wherefore holdest Thou Thy tongue when the wicked devoureth the man that is more righteous than he?" (*Habakkuk* 1:1-3) This, Harold Schulweis writes, "is the unprecedented struggle between man and God in which the Jew asserts nothing less than his moral equality with his Father."[6] It is carried on by the Talmudic sages: "'Who is like unto Thee among the mighty (*elim*), O Lord?' (*Exodus* 15:11). Said Rabbi Ishmael: 'Read rather: "Who is like unto Thee among the silent (*elmim*), O Lord"—seeing the suffering of His children and remaining silent?'" (*Mechilta*, ed. Horowitz, p. 142) Wiesel joins this tradition of calling God to justice, which expresses the Jew's perennial struggle to believe in God in spite of Him.

If God's trials of the pious are in some way an expression of His love (*Bereshith Rabbah* 54:1), then the faithfuls' trials of God are also an expression of their love. The moral challenge to God does not manifest arrogance but profound disappointment in a loving parent. It is an encounter which assumes a deep intimacy with the Divine. As in the lawsuit of the Berditchever against God, for example, Wiesel, too, prays to God to aid him in his unbelief.[7] The trial itself is harsh and legal, but its purpose is not to chastise the defendant but to express the advocate's desire that He at least offer a plea on His own behalf.[8]

Only once in Wiesel is such a plea heard—God's answer is an answer which speaks with silence.[9] The answers come but are not understood.[10] In a way Wiesel is apprehensive of the answer. He yearns to "know God" and is afraid to do so. Here, too, Wiesel is Elisha. He is entering the Garden (*pardes*) of forbidden knowledge, aware that this may bring insanity or apostasy (see *Hagiga* 14b): "You can love God but you cannot look at him. . . . If man could contemplate the face of God, he would stop loving Him.[11]

But Wiesel, having seen God in the face without His

mask,[12] continues to love Him in disappointment. Despite all his yearning for God and for an answer, he must condemn God for the most unforgivable crime—useless murder. Man can live with a cruel God, who creates men to murder them,[13] who chooses a people to have them slain on a sacrificial altar,[14] but he cannot live in a world without God. Better to be insane, better to blaspheme, than to be without God.[15]

The Sin of Imitato Dei

Second to Wiesel's indictment of God is his accusation of man. Man was created in the image of God, inheriting the cruelty of his Creator.[16] Wiesel, like Camus, insists that that no one has escaped the guilt; no one is clean.[17] As Sartre puts it, everyone shares in the crime of the twentieth-century "rummage sale, the liquidation of the human species ... by the cruel enemy who has sown from time immemorial ... to destroy him, that hairless, evil, flesh-eating beast—man himself."[18]

> The inhabitants of Solom didn't kill children before their mother's eyes. The citizens of Gemorrah went in for vice, not for death. Our generation is worse than theirs. It's the generation of the guilty. We all have to share in the crime, even if we combat it; there's no escape from the trap.[19]

> I feel ashamed as a human being living in this century. I am ashamed to think that I belong to a civilization which has done what it has done. And I do not speak of the Germans. I speak of everybody else.[20]

Man, like God, is indicted for one crime—being a spectator, being indifferent.[21] Our worst sin is not that of criminal activity but of nonactivity, of apathy, indifference. "Evil is human, weakness is human, indifference is not."[22] It is incomprehensible how humans find it so easy to be inhuman:[23]

> I pinched my face. Was I still alive? Was I awake? I could not believe it. How could it be possible for them to burn people, children, and for the world to keep silent?

The spectator is an "it"[24]; only thou's have a claim upon being human.[25]

Wiesel's question and quest while the crime was being perpetrated remained his question after the war. Then the search for an answer began.

This, this was the thing I had wanted to understand ever since the war. Nothing else. How a human being can remain indifferent.[26]

The answer has not been found because the question is being relived. The question for Wiesel is not: Where were the Germans?—but: Where was man? The even deeper question is: Where was the Jew then? Where is the Jew today? Does the Jew, like his God, insist on always hiding?[27]

The deepest and most incomprehensible tragedy for Wiesel is the failure of the Jew, the unprecedented failure of one Jew to care for another. We are indicted with the claim: "The Jewish brain has killed the Jewish heart."[28] The meaning of the Holocaust and its lesson are the cost of indifference:

The injustice perpetrated in an unknown land concerns me; I am responsible. He who is not among the victims is with the executioners. This was the meaning of the Holocaust; it implicated not only Abraham or his son but their God as well.[29]

We are each warned: "God wouldn't judge you by your deeds, but by what you haven't dared to do."[30]

Classical Kabbalah and Wiesel's Theology

The assumptions underlying the problem of theodicy in Western theology are: God is good; God is all powerful; evil is real. Most attempts to treat theodicy have sought either to deny or to modify one or more of these premises. In the philosophical schools, generally speaking, the attempt was made to deny that evil is real. It was argued that what is called evil is a negation, a background for good, and thus not an entity in itself,[31] or it was asserted that evil is illusory or only subjective, and understood in a larger, more objective panorama, it would prove not to be evil at all.[32]

But the Holocaust proves to be a disteleological surd.[33] All traditional philosophical accounts of evil are rejected by Wiesel as not valid explanations of the tragedy in Europe. From the Kabbalah, however, some glimmer of an answer is obtained. Wiesel expresses a distaste for the dogmatic rigor of classical philosophy and for the enthronement of reason: "On your way throughout life you'll meet men who cling to reason, but reason gropes like a blind man with a white cane

...."[34] He turns away from philosophy toward Kabbalah with a fervor reminiscent of Rabbi Moses of Burgos who, when he heard philosophers praise, would angrily say:[35] "You ought to know that these philosophers, whose wisdom you are praising, end where we [mystics] begin." So Wiesel, too, denies all three premises in the unique manner of Kabbalistic discourse.

Is God Good? The chief answer that Biblical faith offered to the problem of evil was that God's ways are higher than man's and, therefore, incomprehensible to him (*Isaiah* 55:8; *Job* 36, 38). Rabbinic thought and some of the philosophers, such as Saadya, introduced what may be termed "the argument for eschatological verification"—justice in the after-life.[36] For Rabbi Akiba, sufferings were accepted in love for their soul-cleansing power. For his contemporary, Elisha ben Abuya, apostasy was the only answer. With the flowering of Kabbalistic thought in the early Middle Ages, when Gnostic and neo-Platonic influences were strongest, a revolutionary idea entered Jewish thought: God is not absolutely good; there is an element of evil *within* God.

But though the Bible, to a great extent, had eliminated the demonic element of God in its theology, this was not completely purged (for example, *Exodus* 4:24). That the demonic must be accepted as a basic element in religious experience was again recognized by Rudolph Otto and William James, for example. The notion that evil was a creation of God is present in *Job* 2:10 and *Isaiah* 45:7. Some Rabbinic literature, however, sought to oppose this notion, and the effect is evident in the morning liturgy.[37]

Non-mystical Jewish literature tends to lack the notion of flow, development and becoming of Kabbalistic literature. In Kabbalah nothing is static, everything is becoming. In non-mystical thinking God is a Being: in Kabbalah, He is Becoming.[38] Here the purging of the evil element in the Godhead is a central scene in the divine drama.

In the *Sefer Ha-Bahir,* the oldest Kabbalistic text, which Scholem places in the late twelfth century, the notion of an evil element in the divine appears thus:[39]

> The foregoing comes to teach us that there is in God an attribute (or a "principle") that is called evil, and it lies in the north of God, as it is written: "Out of the north the

evil shall break forth upon all the inhabitants of the land"
(*Jeremiah* 1:14).

Though retaining this notion, the *Zohar* detoxicates it somewhat
by removing evil from the focus of the Godhead and instead
invokes the idea of a process of emanation. Evil in the *Zohar* is no
longer an attribute of God, but the emanation if an attribute—
the emanation of stern justice, *gevurah*.[40] The *Zohar* pur-
posefully assigns evil to the lowest parts of the Godhead, the
"lower, distant faces" (II, 86b-87a). Rather than stressing the
theme of the evil element in God, it appears to stress the need
for the divine element in evil to maintain the latter's very
existence. Thus the *Zohar*, and later also the Baal Shem Tov,
stressed the needed presence of the divine within evil in order
that its existence be sustained, while the philosophers insisted
that the presence of evil signified the absence of the divine. Evil
for the *Zohar*, then, merely exists for the purpose of bringing
about good (II, 163a).

The expulsion of the Jews from Spain encouraged new
speculations on the problem of theodicy. It would seem that the
place of the evil element in God was reasserted by Luria. The
apologetics of the *Zohar* were side-stepped in reaction to the
historical tragedy which had befallen Sephardic Jewry. Luria's
teachings, as preserved by Hayim Vital, appear to suggest a
small but real element of evil in God, from which He
is consistently purging Himself internally.

Part of the Lurianic process of catharsis is the "breaking
of the vessels."[41] The quantity of evil in God is compared by
Vital to a ship's cargo of ink dumped into the sea. It is a small,
unintelligible, but present element. The cosmic tragedy of the
shattering of the "vessels" is the "necessary evil" in the act of
creation. The purpose of this evil ultimately derives from God
and becomes disclosed in *tzimtzum*, the process of divine
contracting.[42]

Three notions emerge from the Lurianic account of
creation: 1) the evil element in God; 2) the necessary existence
of evil in the universe as a byproduct of the creative process;
and 3) the notion sometimes asserted that a flaw in the process
caused more than the minimum necessary amount of evil to be
generated. All three notions have a place in the writings
of Wiesel.

Wiesel's presentation of the notion of the presence of evil in God is biting. If it is blasphemy, it is traditional blasphemy.[43] The notion of evil as a necessary by-product of creation,[44] Wiesel combines with the idea of God's mistake in creation: "After creating the universe, says the Cabalah, God smashed his tools. Why? To avoid repeating himself."[45]

Is God omnipotent? Is evil real? The mystical emanation of the *sefirot* is theosophy, not theology. It tells the story of a development within the Godhead. The emanations are the finite manifestations of the Infinite (*En Sof*). The distance between the incomprehensible, infinite nameless God of Maimonides and the finite world of four material elements is bridged by finite manifestations of divinity and of creation. The problem of evil is thus perhaps best understood as the existential expression of a central theological issue of which it is a necessary corollary—that is, the challenge to theism to account not only for the existence of evil but for the existence of anything at all other than God.[46] Therefore, any attempt to explain the existence of the finite is also an attempt to explain the problem of evil. From the view of finite man the finite appears real and absolute, but for the Infinite Mind, the finite, including time and space, are only apparent, "accidental" dimensions of existence.[47] The relationship between the problem of evil and the existence of the finite suggests the presence of an evil element within the Godhead, once finiteness is derived from it.

Wiesel, in suggesting a notion of finitude and evil within God, thus follows a respected, well-trodden path in Jewish theology. Perhaps it is our nineteenth-century *haskalah,* neo-Maimonidean attitude which Wiesel affronts; perhaps it is our jolly-old-man-in-heaven-God-idea attacked so harshly by Wiesel that makes us shiver. But perhaps the God of Abraham Azuli, Isaac Luria, Israel Baal Shem, Moses de Leon, Aaron of Starojjele—the God of Wiesel—is closer to being the God of the Jews than the neo-Kantian system of synthetic *a priori's* amongst which the Master of the World seems to have disappeared.[48]

Wiesel has been criticized for obscuring his meaning with continuous paradoxes. In doing this he writes not so much as a novelist but as a Kabbalist. The *Zohar* speaks in paradoxes as its way of rejecting the narrowness of a philosophical system built upon Aristotelean logic. Why waste time debating God's ability to make round squares and to make "A" be "not—A"? For God both can exist simultaneously.[49] The infinite God can exist simultaneously with the finite God; the omnipotent God of spiritual activity can exist simultaneously with the impotent God dependent upon human action; the God who brings redemption can also be the God who awaits redemption.

Rabbi Akiba's insistence that God's presence in the world is determined by the deeds of man and the suggestion that there is a lack of complete divine omnipotence is the thesis of Jewish theology. Rabbi Ishmael's calling God to account is the anti-thesis. Though the synthesis is yet to be found, the movement of the dialectic in Wiesel is the latest manifestation of a perennial theological dilemma.

As no question can be asked of the infinite, silent God— the *En Sof*—the Unmoved Mover, before whom all man's profoundest questions are only expressions of his pitiful finiteness, Wiesel turns his attention to the manifested God of appearances, who appears to man in "vestments." Expecting no response from the Unmoved Mover of the Godhead, Wiesel turns to the Most Moved, that aspect of the Godhead which in a way shares in our finiteness. The turning is made especially toward the *Shekhinah*, the "indwelling" presence of God in the world, who, like man, has no substance of its own and is only the reflection of the divine powers above. This is the aspect of God which yearns for man, the aspect of the Divine in need of man and in search of the human attribute of infinity—active concern.[50]

Rabbi Akiba suggested that the fate of God in the world is effected by the fate of man.[51] When man is imprisoned, God joins him. Both share in the redemption from slavery which is yet to come. Man occasionally is complacent with his slavery, but God awaits redemption.

The major purpose of man's existence according to the *Zohar* is to give "strength to God" (II, 33a). The *Zohar* also contains the idea that *zeevug* (union) would bring redemption to God and the world through uniting all primordially dispersed elements of divine and material entities. Through man's action, which thus gains a cosmic significance—having an effect on the internal state of the Godhead itself—either redemption, unification, or a sharper disunity and dispersion of the forces occur.[52]

Perhaps the central idea of Kabbalah is this ability, indeed this destiny of man to play a central role in the life of God. Hegel suggests that world history is God's autobiography.[53] The Kabbalah disagrees: world history is God's biography as written by God and man; God supplies the letters—man writes the sentences.

Wiesel expresses this idea of the interdependence between man and God. The freedom of God, the liberation of the divine "sparks," is man's task. "God is imprisoned. Man must free Him. That is the best guarded secret since the creation."[54] The criminals of the world, the forces of evil, know this secret. It is for that reason that they seek imprisonment. For once in prison they can kill God.[55]

God awaits redemption from His confinement. He awaited it in Auschwitz, and He awaits it today as He dwells among the Jews in Russia.[56] The truest Jews share in the plight of God. The truest Jews are those who await the redemption of God and of man.[57] The genuine Jew not only awaits the Messiah but is the Messiah.[58]

Man's suffering gains meaning when it is for a thou, whether the thou be human or divine. The "other" attains his existence through our suffering for him. To the human thou Wiesel suggests: I suffer—therefore you are.[59] Even the existence of God is in a way determined by human suffering:[60]

> A teacher explained to his pupils: Do you know what the eternity of God is? It is we. By dancing on fire, by suffering death man creates the eternity of his creator— he offers it to Him and justifies it.

Freedom

The legend with which Wiesel concludes *The Town Beyond the Wall,* in which man and God change places, expresses the interdependence of human and divine fate and freedom. The corollaries which Wiesel develops from this legend are that man assumes a degree of freedom and infinity surpassing that of the imprisoned God, and that from man's adopted role it follows that God is dependent upon man to assert His existence and reality, which are dependent upon human activity and suffering.

Like Sartre, Wiesel sees a man as condemned to freedom. Sartre's man is free to bring himself into existence. For Wiesel man's freedom brings God into existence. For Sartre man is totally free because there is no God. For Wiesel man is free only in order to free God from His confinement. For Sartre man is totally responsible to himself because there is no God.[61] For Wiesel man is totally responsible to a God whom he must free: Blessed be man who frees Him who is in captivity.

Man is given freedom of action, while this is denied to God.[62] "Freedom is given only to man, God is not free."[63] How is this freedom given to man? Through suffering.[64] The meaning of suffering is its ability to elevate man above God, to secure His redemption from confinement. Suffering and evil are inherent in the processes of redemption as well as of creation.

Wiesel restates the Kabbalistic notion that the internal unity of the Godhead is to be equated with redemption. Unity, the "collection of the sparks," restoring the primordial unity of the divine forces in the cosmos, stressed in Lurianic thinking, is reiterated by Wiesel:[65]

> Once I asked my teacher, Kalman the cabalist, the following question: For what purpose did God create man? I understand that man needs God. But what need of man has God? ... The holy books teach us, he said, that if man were conscious of his power, he would lose his faith or his reason. For man carries within him a role which transcends him. God needs to be ONE ... man who is nothing but a handful of earth is capable of reuniting time and its source and of giving back to God his own image.[66]

How God Is Dead

Not only is God's redemption dependent upon man, but so, in a way, is His existence and presence in the world. Wiesel often speaks of God's dying,[67] but he as often denies being a "God is dead" advocate. "God cannot die; He is immortal"— His immortality and His eternity are assured by man's suffering.[68] God is not dead; He is buried alive[69] by man's indifference. Since the destruction of the Temple, the *Shekhinah* has been limited to four cubits. Man, too, is ultimately limited to four cubits—his grave. The God who dies in Wiesel's writings has the face of a child, a face of innocence, helplessness, victimized by human brutality and indifference.[70] God only dies insofar as the image He shares with man, the stamp of divinity, has been erased by apathy—erased from God, erased from man. Only the redemption will herald the return of the image.[71]

The "God is dead" movement, consisting of comfortable American theologians who gained their theological training contemporaneously with Auschwitz, makes its claim after Auschwitz. Wiesel, the messenger of the dead,[72] who gained his theological training in Auschwitz, spends his life thirsting for and seeking the God he lost at Auschwitz. With the loss of innocence the search is difficult, but the farther God hides the greater is Wiesel's yearning. Or as Hasidim would say: "Once one knows that God is hidden, He is no longer really hidden." Wiesel is God-intoxicated. His yearning is fierce. He asks the same question asked by the "God is dead" theologians: "After what has happened to us, how can you believe in God?" While for them the question alone suffices, Wiesel requires an answer: "With an understanding smile on his lips the Rebbe answered: How can you *not* believe in God after what has happened?"[73]

Perhaps Wiesel is the *rebbe*. Perhaps he is our *rebbe*. Perhaps not, for he has been called the "high priest of our generation."[74] If so, was he not made ritually impure by the corpses at Auschwitz? No. Like God, he is a priest who was purified by fire (*Sanhedrin* 39a).

Though he tells only of God's continued dying, never of His being dead, those who argue for Wiesel's membership in the "God is dead" club nevertheless always quote an episode in *Night* as their evidence. This episode does not, however, express a "post-modern" theology. It only expresses man's insistence upon seeking to rid himself of his Creator's imprint. It does not express the message of a "new theology" but of an old *Gemara*:

> But the third rope was sitll moving, being so light the child was still alive ... For more than half an hour he stayed there struggling between life and death, dying in slow agony under our eyes. And we had to look him full in the face. He was still alive when I passed in front of him. His tongue was still red, his eyes were not yet glazed. Behind me I heard the same man asking: Where is God now? And I heard a voice within me answer him: Where is He? Here He is—He is hanging here on the

gallows.[75] Rabbi Meir said: A parable was stated: To what is the matter comparable? To two twin brothers who lived in one city. One was appointed king and the other took to highway robbery. At the king's command they hanged him. But all who saw him explained: The King is hanged! (*Sanhedrin* 46b)

When man becomes a criminal the image of God swings to its death. The sign of God upon man is his only claim to the possibility of being human. Once the sign is removed, man becomes a *Golem,* dust in essence and recklessly destructive in practice.

Waiting for Dawn at the Gates

A progression from deep pessimism toward a somber but firm optimism is discernible in the chronological development of Wiesel's writings.[76] His earliest work, *Night,* presents a world without mercy, without humanity, without God. It is a world of night and abandonment of responsibility.[77]

This motif, so widely expressed in contemporary existentialist literature, is as old as the Bible.[78] While the Rabbis also compared this world to night,[79] this deep pessimism serves as a minor theme, overlaid by the fervent hope for the future expressed by the Prophets and later by the Rabbis.

Wiesel's second work—*Dawn*—begins the end of night. A glimmer of hope is presented. The meaning of the establishment of the State of Israel begins the end of absolute pessimism for the survivor of tragedy. *Le Jour* is mistakenly translated as *Accident;* it should be called "Day." With the assertion that life has meaning, Wiesel states the assumption to be expounded in his following work, *The Town Beyond the Wall.* In this work meaning in life is understood as found in one's caring for another, in suffering for another, and in preventing another from suffering: I suffer—therefore you are. These ideas are explored more completely in the *Gates of the Forest,* Wiesel's latest novel.[80] Here Wiesel is optimistic. As long as there is man, there is hope. "What is man—dust turned into hope."[81] The theme of care and suffering is expanded. Suffering endows man with the fortitude to work, even in spite of God, for redemption.[82] Remembrance of former suffering and new faith are needed to prevent a reoccurrence of old suffering; the meaning of suffering is to prevent more suffering. The goal of suffering is to ennoble.

Israel waits to whisper the secret of suffering and the secret of survival to mankind. In the face of nuclear holocaust, the suffering of Israel may be a beacon-light to warn mankind of the price of indifference (see *Isaiah* 49:6). Said the Besht: *tzarah* (suffering) brings *tzohar* (light). The flames of the crematoria do have a purpose; they are a light to the nations.

Wiesel, in the last analysis, is a hopeful worshiper, not a blasphemer. Like Ibn Gabirol, in fleeing from God, he actually flees toward God (*Kether Malkhut*). He is a novelist and a Kabbalist. In Kabbalah nothing occurs by chance. There is meaning in all hints. Perhaps there is meaning in Wiesel's number at Auschwitz (as he reports in *Night*) having been 7713. In *Gematria*, adding up the sum of the digits, this equals 18—*Hai*—Life. Emerging from a planet of death, Wiesel affirms life.

1. Elie Wiesel, "Jewish Values in the Post-Holocaust Future: A Symposium," JUDAISM, Summer 1967, p. 298.
2. Elie Wiesel, *The Gates of the Forest*, New York 1966, "Prologue."
3. "Useless prayers, useless tears. The intercession had done no good. God has closed his eyes and let it all happen." (Elie Wiesel, "The Last Return," *Commentary*, March 1965.)
4. Milton Steinberg, in his novel *As a Driven Leaf* (New York 1939), a fictional biography of Aher, suggests the apparent meaningless deaths of Rabbi Meir's sons as the impetus for Aher's apostasy. The source for the account of the deaths seems to be *Midrash Mishle* 31:10, Buber edition, pp. 49b-50a; in Steinberg, pp. 130-134.
5. *The Gates of the Forest*, p. 33.
6. Harold Schulweis, "Man and God: The Moral Partnership," *The Jewish Heritage Reader*, ed. Lily Edelman, New York 1965, p. 118.
7. Elie Wiesel, *The Town Beyond the Wall*, New York 1964, pp. 44, 47-48.
8. *Ibid.*, pp. 48, 149ff.; Elie Wiesel, *Dawn*, New York 1961, p. 66; Elie Wiesel, *Night*, New York 1960, p. 73.
9. Elie Wiesel, *The Accident*, New York 1962, p. 72.
10. *Night*, p. 16.
11. *The Accident*, p. 11; see motto of *The Town Beyond the Wall*; also, *Night*, p. 73.

12. *The Accident*, p. 116.
13. *The Gates of the Forest*, pp. 134, 190.
14. *Night*, p. 73.
15. *The Town Beyond the Wall*, p. 165.
16. *Dawn*, p. 18.
17. Albert Camus, *The Fall*, New York 1956.
18. Jean-Paul Sartre, *The Condemned of Altona*, New York 1961, p. 177.
19. Elie Wiesel, "A Witness Speaks," *Conservative Judaism*, Vol. 21, No. 3, p. 42.
20. *Ibid.*, p. 43.
21. "The Last Return," *op. cit.*, p. 49.
22. *The Town Beyond the Wall*, p. 177.
23. *Night*, p. 42; see *Dawn*, p. 29.
24. *The Town Beyond the Wall*, pp. 160-161.
25. *Ibd.*, p. 150.
26. *Ibid.*, p. 149.
27. "A Witness Speaks," *op. cit.*, pp. 43, 47; Elie Wiesel, *The Jews of Silence*, New York 1967, pp. 70, 71, 102, 103; "Jewish Values in the Post-Holocaust Future," *op. cit.*, pp. 282-283.
28. *The Jews of Silence*, p. 103.
29. *The Gates of the Forest*, p. 166.
30. Jean-Paul Sartre, *op. cit.*, p. 140.
31. RaDaK on *Isaiah* 45:7; Geddes MacGregor, *An Introduction to Philosophy of Religion*, Boston 1959, chapter 47; Isaac Husik, *A History of Medieval Jewish Philosophy*, Philadelphia 1958, p. 288.
32. Louis Jacobs, *We Have Reason to Believe*, London 1961, chapter 5 ("The Problem of Pain"), p. 44ff.
33. Geddes MacGregor, *op. cit.*, chapter 38, p. 360 ff.
34. *The Gates of the Forest*, p. 11.
35. Quoted in Gershom Scholem, *Major Trends in Jewish Mysticism*, New York 1941, p. 24.
36. Julius Guttman, *Philosophies of Judaism*, New York 1964, p. 71; *Three Jewish Philosophers*, ed, Alexander Altmann, Philadelphia 1960, chapter on "Saadya," p. 139 ff.
37. Ben Zion Bokser, trans., *The Prayer Book*, New York 1957, note, p. 128.
38. See Hans Joanas, "Immortality and the Modern Temper," *Harvard Theological Review*, January 1962, pp. 1-20.
39. Margoliot ed. #162; see #38. Scholem always quotes not Margoliot but the Leipzig 1923 edition.
40. See Isaac Tishbi, *Mishnat Ha-Zohar*, Volume I, Jerusalem 1949, p. 223 ff.
41. Hayim Vital, *Etz Hayyim*, Gate #1.
42. See also Isaac Tishbi, *Torat ha-ra v'ha-klipot b'kabbalat ha-Ari*, Jerusalem, 1942.
43. Compare Nikos Kazantzakis, who explores these themes of God's cruelty and evil attribute in his books, especially *The Last Temptation of Christ*, New York 1960; and *Saint Francis*, New York 1962. See also, *The Gates of the Forest*, pp. 21, 129.

44. *The Gates of the Forest*, p. 201.
45. *The Town Beyond the Wall*, p. 114; see also, *The Gates of the Forest*, p. 21.
46. Louis Jacobs, *Seeker of Unity: The Life and Works of Aaron of Starosselje*, New York 1966, pp. 93, 98; see p. 60 for Maharan's view.
47. *Ibid.*, p. 27.
48. Hugo Bergman, *Faith and Reason*, New York 1961, p. 41: "When [Hermann] Cohen still lived in Marburg, he once explained to an old Jew the idea of God which he had developed in his ethics. The old man listened attentively, but when Cohen had finished, he asked him: 'But where is the *bore olom*, the creator of the world?' Cohen did not reply a single word, but there were tears in his eyes."
49. Louis Jacobs, *Seeker of Unity, op. cit.*, p. 102 ff. Descartes also had this notion; see his 1630 letter to Mersenne.
50. See Abraham J. Heschel, "The Mystical Element in Judaism," in Volume II of *The Jews*, ed. Louis Finkelstein, New York 1949, p. 936 ff.
51. *Exodus Rabbah* 15:12; *Sukkah* 4:5.
52. Abraham J. Heschel, *The Theology of Ancient Judaism* (Hebrew), London 1962, I, p. 96 ff.
53. Sidney Hook, *From Hegel to Marx*, Ann Arbor 1962, p. 36.
54. *The Town Beyond the Wall*, p. 10.
55. *Ibid.*, p. 135.
56. *The Jews of Silence*, p. 4.
57. *Ibid.*, p. 94.
58. *The Gates of the Forest*, p. 225.
59. *The Town Beyond the Wall*, p. 118.
60. "The Last Return," *op. cit.*, p. 47.
61. Cf. Jean-Paul Sartre, *The Condemned of Altona, op. cit.*, p. 165.
62. *The Town Beyond the Wall*, see especially pp. 10, 94, 179 ff.; *Night*, p.
63. *The Town Beyond the Wall*, p. 94.
64. *Night*, p. 74; *The Town Beyond the Wall*, p. 10.
65. *The Accident*, p. 42.
66. *The Town Beyond the Wall*, p. 79.
67. *The Town Beyond the Wall*, p. 67; *Dawn*, p. 61; *Night*, p. 73; *The Accident*, p. 32: *The Gates of the Forest*, p. 129.
68. "The Last Return," *op. cit.*, p. 47; *The Accident*, p. 32.
69. *The Accident*, p. 32.
70. *Dawn*, p. 48; *Night*, p. 73; *The Gates of the Forest*, p. 82.
71. *The Accident*, p. 42.
72. *Ibid.*, p. 45.
73. *The Gates of the Forest*, p. 194.
74. Steven S. Swarzschild, "Toward Jewish Religious Unity: A Symposium," JUDAISM, Spring 1966, p. 157.
75. *Night*, p. 71.
76. Jack Riemer, "Elie Wiesel: Messenger of the Dead," *Torch*, Fall 1967.
77. *Night*, p. 81.
78. Abraham J. Heschel, *The Insecurity of Freedom*, New York 1966, p. 147, note 5.

79. "In this world of war and suffering, evil inclination, Satan and the angel of death hold sway" (*Midrash Vyoshah, Beth Midrash*, ed. Jellinek, Part 3, p. 55). "This world is compared to night" (*Baba Metzia* 83b and *Pesachim* 2b).

80. The theme of suffering and redemption forms the key part of the structure of Wiesel's "Messiah concept." That notion is quite complex and is expanded in his latest book, *The Beggars of Jerusalem* (French), published too late for inclusion in this essay.

81. *The Gates of the Forest*, p. 87.

82. Cf. "Jewish Values in the Post-Holocaust Future," *op. cit.*, p. 299.

WHAT IS A JEW?

Interview of Elie Wiesel

by Harry James Cargas

Could I begin our conversation by asking you what it means to be a Jew today?

That is one of the hardest questions to answer, as you know. Recently, Israel, the whole country, was in turmoil because of that question: who is a Jew? Who is a Jew, I don't know. But what is a Jew I could tell you, because I know what a Jew should do in order to be Jewish. He must assume his Jewishness. He must assume his collective conscience, he must assume his past with its sorrows and joys. Tell the tale. In other words, he must bear witness.

In that sense is it any different from what any other man must do?

Not at all. Someone who is a Jew is to me as important as someone who is not a Jew. It is a matter of truth and lie. If a Jew refuses to be a Jew, he refuses to be a man. What I want from a Catholic is to be a good Catholic. What I want from a Communist is to be an authentic Communist and not a salon Communist. What I want from a Jew is to be an authentic Jew. I give what I have, and I appeal to you in what you have the best and what makes you what you are. So a Jew to me is no different, really, not in this respect. It is his specificity, his authenticity, that makes him Jewish.

Yet there is the element in his past, the suffering, the persecuted Jews, that makes him different, and I want to ask about the value of that past suffering for the Jew of today.

Suffering is alien to Judaism. The Jew never wanted to suffer. It was imposed upon him from the outside, but he accepted it.

He accepted it in a kind of refuge, and he made out of it a message of hope. Again that is what makes him Jewish.

Other people believe in suffering as an end; take for instance in the Buddhist religion. Suffering is very important. It is part of it; it is a road of salvation. Not in Judaism. In Judaism suffering is impure. In the Bible, for instance, you know—in the Talmud—a man who chooses suffering, a Nasaim, is guilty, because life is sacred, and only life is sacred, and only what makes a man human is good. What takes him away from it is not good. So suffering has become a part of our past, unfortunately. And it has also become part of our mystery; what did we do in order to deserve it? Often I think about it: 2000 years—why? Why just us, always us, more than the others or different than the others? I have no answer to that. What I do know is that 2000 years we were not contaminated by it. Suffering did not change us. Sometimes we identified with it, but never with those who gave it to us.

In recent history Jews did experience the Holocaust in Europe: the six million deaths. What kind of a framework do you put this in?

It is beyond all frameworks. In all of my works—I've written ten books, as you know—they all have to do with the Holocaust, but never directly, except for the first book, *Night*. All of them go around it. Because I have the feeling almost of sin when I speak about it. What happened twenty-five years ago was so unique; even within the framework of our own history, it is unique. It never happened before. It can be compared to no other event. The victim was another victim, and the executioner another executioner. It was a mutation on a cosmic scale and it always implies more than man—it implies God, it implies history, it implies metaphysics. We deal in terms of absolutes. So I don't really know what it is. Sometimes I wonder did it happen; even today, did it really happen?

So I think we are helpless. The feeling that it gave us, really, is a feeling of helplessness. We don't know how to tackle with the subject. And yet it is here. It is a permanent present. I wrote a book called *The Town Beyond the Wall*, which is a novel. I described in imaginary terms my hometown before all this took place. And I tried to deal with man's relation to God, because God is always there. When man talks to man, somehow, God is there. And it was written in the third person, which is rare in my books, but if you ask 99 percent of the people who read the book they will tell tell you it is written in the first person. And to me it was a discovery; it pleased me very much, because I was so much there, although it was pure fiction. And the same goes for the Holocaust. I never really write about the Holocaust. Yet, ask people who read (and there are a few) and they will tell you that I write nothing but about the Holocaust.

You have said that sometimes you wondered if it really happened. It seems to me that from a certain point of view it would be dangerous for the non-Jew to wonder that. Doesn't he have to be conscious of this having actually taken place so that it will not take place again?

I think that is one idea he must now realize and accept, because he was on the other side. When the chips were down, very few non-Jews came to the aid of the Jews during the Holocaust—which for us was an eyeopener with sad—not angry but sad—connotations. We were very sad. This is man. Therefore we try to remind, we try to speak, we try to tell the tale. Most of my readers are non-Jews, and I think I do establish a kind of rapport, a kind of dialogue with non-Jews, like with Mauriac. Why do they read what I try to offer them is—the sincere Christian knows that what died in Auschwitz was not the Jewish people but Christianity.

John the XXIII was one of the greatest men I have known. I have met him. He's one of the most humanistic persons that I have ever met. John the XXIII understood it. He did feel guilty, although he personally tried to help more than anyone else in his church. What he did for the Jews—we considered him as a saint—yet he felt guilty, and that's what made him really so great. He understood, also, that Auschwitz represented a failure, a defeat for 2000 years of Christian civilization. Because, just think about it: The commandoes were the worst of the criminals. They were the killers—not the Christians of the gas chambers, but they were the killers in the Ukraine, in Poland. They were shooting thousands and thousands of Jews—entire communities, with machine guns, directly. There was a direct contact. And they had Ph.D.s and some of them were theologians, and some of them, many of them, went to the priest, to confession and so forth. So John the

XXIII understood it; Mauriac understood it: that what happened in Auschwitz, with this kind of mutation, marked an end to orthodox Christianity. And therefore he opened the doors. And therefore he liberalized the church. That explains Vatican II, the ecumenical movement.

Let me ask then, about the role in history of the Six Million. So many people said they ought to have actively resisted when they didn't. Do you find this a good judgment?

Whose are those who ask these questions? How do they dare, really? I don't. When I think of these people: abandoned, betrayed, forgotten, forlorn, deceived, who am I to judge them? Who am I to question their motivation? What does that mean: resist? How could they resist? With what? There was in London and in Moscow and in Washington a desk for every people, an organization to help everybody; there were arms for the Poles and Czechs and the Lithuanians. But who really cared about the Jews? Who tried to send arms, who tried messengers, who tried to send any help at all? Who tried to warn the Jews not to go to the camps?

I come from Hungary. In March, April, that was the beginning for us. In March and in April, there was not a single leader or a single public official in London and Stockholm and Switzerland and America who don't know what Auschwitz meant. They knew it from '42. There are books out about it. There were documents, there were diagrams, everything, all details. The only ones who didn't know were the Jews in Hungary. When we came to Auschwitz, I remember, I was still young, very young. I remember we saw "Auschwitz" on the railway station and we asked each other, "What is it?" In March-April, 1944 we still believed that Auschwitz is the name of a peaceful railway station somewhere in Poland. We never could have imagined that hundreds and thousands of men and women and children could be massacred and reduced to ash and the world would keep silent. We couldn't have believed it.

So how can today, twenty-five years after the event, some people even dare to come and say that they should have resisted? With what? And for what? For what ideals? I don't know. Sometimes I try to imagine what did they feel when they went to the mass grave. What did they feel when they went to their death? And I am sure, because I saw some of them going, that they felt no bitterness, no hate. There was never any hate involved. They didn't even feel anger or sadness. I think they felt pity. Pity not for themselves, pity for mankind that will survive their death. If this is mankind, the hell with it.

This has to be carefully phrased because it could seem an irreverent question, and I don't mean it that way, but is there some sense in which it could be said that those who perished in this Holocaust triumphed and their executioners were defeated?

No. I think the word "triumph," unfortunately, does not apply to anything relevant to the Holocaust. There was no triumph. I think Man was defeated there. The Jew in some way came out in a better way, because he is used to suffering and because of historic situations that he has known. It happened that he was not the executioner, he was the victim. And in those times it was better to be victim than executioner. But no one triumphed. It was triumph for nobody—for man or for God either. Therefore we have this strange, strange feeling of helplessness of which we spoke before. But something went wrong with creation. Maybe the angel of Death, to use a cabbalistic expression, substituted himself for God then.

Can we turn for a moment to some of your writings specifically? One critic at least has recognized that a Jew in your books is a metaphor for man. Would you accept that judgment?

Absolutely. What I try to do is to speak for man, but as a Jew. I make no distinction and I certainly make no restriction. A Jew is not someone who is in a ghetto, or is a privileged person to be Jewish, against someone else. Not at all. It is *with* someone else. Except he offers his experiences, he offers his knowledge, his soul to someone else.

In your books, the notion of silence plays an important role. Characters in your novels assume silence for long periods. Could you tell us a little bit about your ideas on this silence?

I have many obsessions, as you know. There are certain key sentences or key expressions in my mythology, in my universe. One of them is the eyes. The other one is silence. Why? Because of my upbringing. As a child I was studying the Talmud, but mainly mysticism. My master was a mystic. And silence, in mysticism, is very important. It's the essential. What you don't say is important. For instance, I wondered many times: within our tradition we know what God said at Sinai. But there are certain silences between word and word. How was this silence transmitted? This is the silence that I tried to put in my work, and I tried to link it to the silence, the silence of Sinai. There is a healthy silence, Sinai, and an unhealthy silence, the Deluge or the chaos before the Creation. There is a political silence which is criminal: today to be silent when so many injustices are being performed and perpetuated: in Russia against the Jews; in Vietnam against the Vietnamese; in all kinds of countries against minorities. To be silent about it is criminal.

On the other hand, there is a different silence which is penetrated, inspired. When you want to say something and you don't say it. You want to say thank you, but you don't say it. The thank you is there. The feeling of gratitude is there. When I hear a beautiful trio by Beethoven or Mozart, I feel gratitude towards Beethoven and Mozart, and I keep quiet, and then I feel that I share, I participate in the playing with my silence. So silence is, of course, a universe of silence. And you can say about it what you can say about life and about death and about God. And the totality of what you say will not make up completely what there is to be said about it.

Another part of your mythology is an idea on something that is almost opposite, and that is laughter.

Yes.

How do we reconcile this in your work?

Of course, you realize when I say laughter I don't mean comedy. Laughter as defiance. I'll give you an example in Abraham, Isaac, and Jacob, our ancestors, our forefathers. Isaac in Hebrew means Itzhak, he who will laugh. And I was always wondering, why did he get such a silly name? Why would he laugh? And I worked on it very, very hard. The whole holocaust, the binding of Isaac, was always mystifying to me and terrorizing to me. I worked on it many months to write an essay on that, and I came to a very poetic conclusion that in this word, in this name, in this episode could be contained our history. Isaac, the most tragic figure of our history. He has seen his father almost become killer. He has seen his God who ordered his father to betray him. He has seen the knife. He was the first survivor, after all. So of course he will always be traumatized by that experience, but yet he will be able to laugh.

So laughter becomes a defiance. A defiance and a victory. The only way to be victorious over God is to laugh, not at Him, but with Him. Laughter is also a sort of anguish. In times of my despair, I was wondering what was the purpose really, what's all the purpose of God doing all these things or permitting all these things? Why did he create a world only to make it suffer? And I could hear a kind of laughter and I was afraid maybe it's his laughter. Maybe he simply created man to laugh at him. So laughter again has all the possibilities in my tales to open all the avenues and explore all the hypotheses of God and Man, and man and Man.

Another distinguishing feature of your work is a kind of fusion of different times into one— the almost lack of distinction between what is happening to a particular Jew in a novel now and what happened to his grandfather or even someone centuries ago. Could you explain why you do that?

When you write you are the last writer and the first. That means every word should be the first word you have ever written and the last. Meaning you take upon yourself all the books that were written before you, whether you have read them or not. They become part of your book, except you go one step forward. So for me when I write time doesn't exist because writing, *a priori,* means a defiance of time. You impose *your* time, or your concept of time upon the reader. Therefore it's creation, and when you create you are like God and God is about time. So for me to write today about the present means to include the past. I could, I'm sure, one day, describe the trial of Isaac and Abraham in modern terms, in contemporary terminology. It still would be the same tale.

You have been called a prophet, you have been called a mythologizer. What are you?

I am no prophet; I am no mythologizer. I really see myself as a witness. I bear witness and my form is a form of tales, of story-telling. Prophets.... I'm a prophet of the past. My mythology is a mythology of the present but I bring in the past. But mainly, what I try to do, really, is to reach out, mainly to the young people and tell them, "Look what happened, listen. It's not that awful; it's not to be sad about it. It's a privilege and a curse at the same time, to live today and to have your age. So listen to my tales and spread them."

Can your message be listened to and spread equally by all men? I want to ask about Christians but I want to ask about Arabs, too.

Absolutely. Not being an Israeli I don't have, fortunately or unfortunately, the same problems that they have. I have many contacts with Arabs. I was very moved, a couple of months ago in some university, where I spoke. There were Arab students there, and one of them came up and told me how much they read my books. For me it was very important because, again, I don't want to divide people. I want to bring people together from all sides: Buddhists and Arabs and Europeans and Americans. Because, again, a witness is what? A witness is a link. A link between the event and the other person who has not participated in it. A witness is a link between past and present, between man and Man, and man and God. Being a witness I would like to be that link between the Arabs and the Jews, and the Jews and the Christians, and the Jews among themselves Again, I was in Paris some months ago, and I was invited officially to go and visit all the Arab countries. I will accept it and will go there because I am glad that the Arabs see my work in that light: that I am not trying to oppose them or to spread hate to them. Far from me, that idea. There is enough hate anyway in the world.

WIESEL'S THEORY OF THE HOLOCAUST

by Michael Berenbaum

Elie Wiesel's position with respect to the Holocaust is contradictory and paradoxical, and this paradox is central to his theological position. On the one hand, throughout his essays Wiesel attempts to defend the mystery of the Holocaust from the encroachments of objective analysis. He is distrubed by the cold objectivity of Hannah Arendt's historical analysis and by the limits of Bruno Bettelheim's psychological explanation,[1] above all, Wiesel is disturbed by the sense of detachment from the events which he finds in the analyses of Arendt, Bettelheim, and perhaps Hilberg[2] and by what he senses to be their judgment of the victims. In response, Wiesel asserts the essential mystery of the Holocaust and the inability of modern people and contemporary analysis to grasp fully the nature of the events.

On the other hand, Wiesel's novels reveal the weakness, as well as the strength, of people under the strain of extraordinary conditions, and Wiesel's tone is often highly critical. In fact, Bettelheim could point to Wiesel's novels, and most particularly to his memoir *Night,* to substantiate some of his own claims. In reality Wiesel's defense of the mystery of the Holocaust is but another confession of the void. Wiesel's assertion of the mystery preserves for the reader the holiness of the victims precisely at the point that Wiesel's writings underscore the compromises which were made. Wiesel's differences with Arendt and Bettelheim closely resemble the differences outlined between Wiesel and Rubenstein; namely, that like most of the American Jewish community, Wiesel is uncomfortable with the use of analytic language, the abandonment of the mythic, symbolic system of traditional Judaism.

Wiesel is troubled by the use of language that does not preserve the complexity of the original experience and that ignores its nuances and ambiguities. Furthermore, Wiesel sees the collapse of one world view and chronicles its demise while he feels acute discomfort when others, who share his perceptions but do not openly manifest his pain, confront him with the reality they both perceive. Finally, some speculative reasons will be offered as to why Wiesel's position finds a responsive audience in the American Jew.

A

The Holocaust in Wiesel's Novels and Memoir and Bruno Bettelheim's Theory of the Holocaust: *The Informed Heart* and the Pained Soul

Bruno Bettelheim has been unrelenting in his critique of the "business as usual" attitude of the Jewish community during the Holocaust.[3] His choice of the Frank family as the example *par excellence* of this attitude was bound to endear him to no one though it intensified the impact of his analysis. Bettelheim argues that the Jewish community failed to heed all of the warnings of impending doom and hence did not effectively mitigate their fate. Bettelheim criticized the Frank family for not separating in order to make their capture more difficult, for not making adequate escape provisions in their hideout, and for not pursuing the type of survival education which would have been so necessary had any member of the family escaped incarceration. Bettelheim furthermore argues that contemporary humanity has continuously refused to deal with the reality of the camps, for that reality would seriously damage their narcissistic pride in the accomplishments of modern civilization.[4] Jews cannot afford to delude themselves in this way for they have tragically experienced the peril of denial. As to the reasons why Jews did not revolt while in the camps, Bettelheim argues that the Jews were trapped by their intense emotions. In order to effectively control the rage that they felt toward the Nazis, the Jews exaggerated the Nazi threat to the point where it immobilized them. They were caught in a web of repression which was partly of their own making.[5]

Bettelheim has been severely criticized for his insensitivity to the agony of the Jews and for his emphasis on survival at any price.[6] However, Wiesel has not been criticized for his blatant expression of similar Jewish misperceptions and inaction. Bettelheim and Wiesel share similar perceptions though they speak from different perspectives. Bettelheim expresses his perceptions in analytic language which maintains a sense of objective distance,[7] (and at least for his critics the posture of judgment) while Wiesel speaks in the first person and recreates the experience in rich subjectivity.

Elie Wiesel has claimed that he has written directly of the Holocaust only in *Night*,[8] and it is in his memoir *Night* that Wiesel expresses his greatest impatience with the "business as usual" attitude which predominated his community. Wiesel wrote that in the spring of 1944, "people were interested in everything—in strategy, in diplomacy, in politics, in Zionism —but not in their own fate."[9] In his description of Sighet, he commented that even after the Nazis had arrived and the verdict had been pronounced, "the Jews of Sighet continued to smile."[10] Wiesel's imagery reflects his impatience with skepticism with which his warning is greeted. In *Night* the character is Moshe the beadle.[11] In an "Evening Guest" the character is Elijah who brings evil tidings of doom rather than good tidings of the coming Messiah.[12] The messages are never heeded. Wiesel, like Bettelheim, is critical of the Jewish community's failure to confront the reality and act accordingly.

Just as Bettelheim points to Anne Frank's education as an example of dysfunctional denial, Wiesel portrays characters whose education is similarly inappropriate to their situation. Both Eliezer in *Night* and Michael in *The Town Beyond the Wall*[13] are not trained to confront their situation. Eliezer was trained for eternity as history abruptly intruded into his life. Michael was saved from the madness of the mystical orchard only to enter the madness of the camps. Only Gavriel Gregor in *The Gates of the Forest* confronted the reality of extermination, and he ends up in the forest among the partisans. He survives through a combination if luck and audacity and through his initial refusal to delude himself.

The degree of self-delusion is even a shock to the inmates who can no longer accept the blindness of the outside world. In *Night* Wiesel describes the impatience with which the new arrivals at Auschwitz were greeted.[14] The inmates cannot believe that the world does not yet know and that people can still be arriving complacently for their own cremation. Wiesel continues to be critical of the Jews' repression of their fate. He described his family's decision not to uproot themselves and emigrate to Palestine and then immediately described the observance of Passover which commemorates the Israelites' departure from Egypt in the middle of the night without sufficient time for their bread to rise. Just prior to the description if the Passover seder, Shlomo Wiesel comments:

> "I'm too old, my son ... I'm too old to start a new life. I'm too old to start from scratch again ..."[15]

Ironically, Shlomo Wiesel renounces the possibility of a new life just as he celebrates the festival of spring. On the seventh day of Passover, Jews commemorate the saving at the sea and the "Song of the Sea"[16] is chanted in the synagogue. According to Wiesel's description in *Night*, it was precisely on the seventh day that the Jewish leaders of Sighet were arrested. The remembrance of God's saving presence and the faith that God will continue to save His people falsely consoled the people and contributed to their illusions. The race toward death had begun, yet Wiesel observed:

> The general opinion was that we were going to remain in the ghetto until the end of the war, until the arrival of the Red Army. Then everything would be as before. *It was neither German nor Jew who ruled the ghetto—it was illusion.*[17] (italics added)

Foremost among the illusions was the illusion if time.

Throughout Wiesel's novels and short stories a character continually reappears who has been to the camps and seen their reality and returns to the world of the living only to be frustrated by the victims for various other reasons. For example, the young arrivals at the camps wish to revolt, yet their elders reply, "One must never lose faith even when the sword hangs over your head. That's the teaching of our sages."[18] Wiesel's tone here emphasizes the delusionary and debilitating nature of their faith.

Lucy Dawidowicz in *The War Against the Jews* approaches Jewish behavior during the Holocaust from the perspective of Jewish sources.[19] She spoke of the importance of Jewish tradition which emphasized the justice and goodness of what happened and taught that all must be accepted as good from God. The Jews saw themselves as co-workers with God and hence they responded with activity to impending danger developing the virtues "of self discipline, prudence, moderation, foregoing present gratification for eventual benefit."[20] They found ways of circumventing discrimination and deflecting persecution. It was these methods that the Jews practiced during the Holocaust. Jewish policy had a double thrust. Internal Jewish policy was aimed at bolstering morale, outwardly alleviating hardship, and mullifying persecution.[21] Although Dawidowicz does not deal with the concentration camp situation except for but the briefest references, the policies of the Jewish organizations are accurately described though not evaluated by her. The early Wiesel, the author of *Night,* felt that the bolstering of morale was a costly self-deception for the Jews while Bettelheim could easily see in Dawidowicz's descriptive documentation of the persistence of a business as usual attitude among the Jews. As Dawidowicz clearly shows, the nomos of the community re-established itself again quite quickly despite the anomic situation.

Wiesel does not shrink from exposing or at least uplifting aspects of the victims' behavior and refuses to unequivocally heroize the victims. In *Night* Wiesel describes the moments of anomie in which each man battled on his own for survival. The moments were the ones in which fathers betrayed sons and sons fathers. Rabbi Eliahou's son ran away[22] from his father, and Eliezer resented the burden of his father's presence and briefly betrayed him.[23] Wiesel continually underscores the price paid for survival both in terms of what has been called survivors' guilt and in terms of the knowledge of one's limited humanity. Wiesel describes his raction to the death of his father:

> I did not weep, and it pained me that I could not weep. But I had no more tears. And, in the depths of my being, in the recesses of my weakened conscience, could I have searched it, I might perhaps have found something like— free at last.[24]

Eliezer was freed of the burden of his father, but he was also bereft of his father's love. During the next months he lived as if in a haze without reason and without hope, consumed by his own guilt and the memory of betrayal. The tale of *Night* is a tale of fratricide and patricide as well as a tale of filial love and devotion. The moments of betrayal predominate, but there are also moments of triumph, moments when the young boy chooses death over betrayal,[25] or when the condemned man proclaims "Long live liberty! A curse on Germany! A curse …"[26] The complexity of the picture that Wiesel presents forces the reader to confront the nuances of meaning, meaning that Wiesel fears might be lost in abstractions.

B

The Holocaust in the Essays of Elie Wiesel

While Wiesel's novels portray Jewish behavior in all its complexity without distorting the moments of human collapse or of human triumph, his essays present Jewish behavior in a rather different light. In fairness to Wiesel, it must be stated that his essays are written in response (and often in polemic response) to portrayals of Jewish behavior which Wiesel perceives as insensitive to the anguish of the human situation. In his essays Wiesel is usually quite defensive about the victims' behavior and is highly critical toward the behavior of the world, including world Jewry.

Wiesel's defensive posture often sounds apologetic. The reader is informed that the Jews did not rebel "to punish us, to prepare a vengeance for us for later."[27] While in his memoir *Night* Wiesel depicts the affirmations of faith by the elders in response to the young men's cries for revolt, in his essays Wiesel presents a different response. The young men continue to demand revolt:

> Even if you are right … even if what you say is true, that doesn't change the situation. Let us prove our courage and our dignity, let us show these murderers and the world that Jews know how to die like free men, not like hunched-up invalids.[28]

However, the elder's reply no longer speaks of faith but of condemnation of all mankind. One old man replied: "As a lesson, I like that … But they don't deserve it."[29] In addition, even Sighet's unpreparedness and unresponsiveness to the danger at hand is cast in a new light in Wiesel's essays. Wiesel argues that the Jews of Sighet listened to the radio and heard foreign broadcasts but that none of these broadcasts warned them of their fate.[30] Their ignorance is no longer treated as a failure to confront reality but as proof of the world's guilt.

I wish to emphasize the fact that I write of Wiesel's defensiveness without any pejorative implication. The world's neglect of the Jew's fate and the Jew's resistance to facing that fate are both parts of the historical reality. However, in his essays Wiesel chooses to concentrate on the world's responsibility. There is, however, one major danger in Wiesel's defensiveness and that is that it may deprecate some of the valuable insights into Jewish behavior and the human condition which are now available in analytic writings.

One of the major functions of Wiesel's treatment of the Holocaust presented in his essays, as opposed to his memoir and novels, is the effective engenderment of guilt. In his final two essays of *Legends of Our Time,* "The Guilt We Share" and "A Plea for the Dead," Wiesel explores the phenomena of guilt. In "The Guilt We Share" Wiesel uses guilt to spur Jewish action, to explain Jewish behavior, and to undermine the moral credibility of the Western world. No one emerges from the Holocaust without a stain of guilt. The Allies are castigated for their refusal to bomb the camps. America is rebuked for its failure to intervene, neutral countries are criticized for their neutrality, and world Jewry is faulted for its relative indifference and inaction. Wiesel's expectations for world Jewry are enormous and although he has a genuine right to feel betrayed, his hopes are inflated by the mythic power he attributes to solidarity. He writes:

> The American Jewish community never made adequate use of its political and financial powers; *certainly it did not move heaven and earth, as it should have.*[31] (italics added)

A belief in the mythic powers of solidarity should not obscure the perception of class differences and conflicting loyalties which contributed to Jewish inaction. However, Wiesel may sense that the universalization of Jewish guilt can be a successful strategy for overcoming these differences in cases which require concerted Jewish efforts such as the state of Israel and Soviet Jewry.

Wiesel also used guilt in another context as an explanation

for Jewish compliance. Wiesel claims that in the camps the Jews did not revolt because they were consumed by their own guilt as survivors. The victims realized that to be alive was to be guilty for to be alive meant that you were "the cause, perhaps the condition, of someone else's death."[32] To live was to compromise, and to revolt would have meant a betrayal of the dead.

> To die struggling would have meant a betrayal of those who had gone to their death submissive and silent. The only way was to follow in their footsteps, die their kind of death—only then could the living make peace with those who had already gone.[33]

Fidelity to the dead meant following in their footsteps. Throughout his essay Wiesel uses guilt to defend the victims, to castigate the bystanders, and to deny everyone the right to judge.

As has been previously mentioned, Wiesel is angered by the tones of self-assurance which permeate objective considerations of the Holocaust. He is concerned that the Jews may be held responsible for their own deaths and that the responsibility of the Nazis will thus be diminished. He is also furious at the imposition of degrading motives to the actions of the dead.

What then, is Wiesel's plea for the dead? On the one hand, Wiesel argues for silence. He fears that reflection after the experience may distort or diminish the experience. Yet all of his work and his commitment to the task of witness reflects his own inability to remain silent so that silence is emphatically not the final response. Wiesel suggests that one must assume a specific attitude toward the Holocaust and that within the framework of that attitude one is permitted to ask certain questions. He seems to compare the Holocaust to the Talmudic description of *Pardes,* the mystical orchard where the punishment of the innocent is contemplated. One must not enter the orchard too easily for one runs the risk of madness, loss of innocence, and death, yet only by entering the orchard and identifying with the pain of the victims does one earn the right to question. Prior to the identification with the victims, silence is demanded. Otherwise, the memory of the dead and the mystery of the experience might be eclipsed. Wiesel recounts a conversation he held with one of the judges at the Eichmann trial. He asked the judge if he understood the Holocaust, and the judge replied:

> "No, not at all ... There is in all this a portion which will always remain a mystery; a kind of forbidden zone, inaccessible to reason ... Who knows, perhaps that's the gift which God, in a moment of grace, gave to man: it prevents him from understanding everything, thus saving him from madness, or from suicide."[34]

For Wiesel the Holocaust is a mystery which should be protected from the process of demystification. The analytic writings of the historian, the critical tones which assimilate and evaluate facts, threaten to destroy the mystery and rob it of its power. In a sense, the historian and the social scientist go beyond the void by participating in a conceptual universe which, though not necessarily insensitive to the pain of lost meaning, possesses a vocabulary far removed from the domain of metaphysics and ontology and hence from the void which Wiesel so intensely describes.

For Wiesel "the revolt of the believer is not that of the renegade."[35] He asks:

> Can you compare ... the tragedy of the believer to that of the non-believer! The real tragedy, the real drama, is the drama of the believer.[36]

The real dimensions upon which Wiesel demands a response are the metaphysical and the ontological dimensions. The media which best captures the dimensions of pain and ambiguity is the tale with its open-ended reality. The reason Wiesel rejects all answers is because on the metaphysical and ontological levels his experience is profoundly that of the void. The void is best expressed by the question that remains a question in quest of an answer.

One of Wiesel's more recent essays on the Holocaust shows yet another dimension of his lowering of expectation and also indicates his own solidarity with the survivors as he once felt his place was with the dead. While his earlier essay was entitled "A Plea for the Dead" his more recent essay was entitled "A Plea for the Survivors." He moved to the world of the living who, like Isaac, had experienced death and returned. Wiesel's plea ironically is quoted approvingly by Bettelheim in his article on surviving. Wiesel bemoans the cheapening of the Holocaust and the loss of humility: "As the subject becomes popularized, so it ceased to be sacrosant or rather was stripped of its mystery. People lost their awe."[37] Like Bettelheim, Wiesel sees himself in a community of people who have survived and who are increasingly despondent not merely that their experience is being misused, but by their own inability to fully explain their experience and by contemporary fascinnation with the killers. Both realize that survivors won't be around much longer and both fear that the survivor is the only one who knows.

C

Ontology and History: Wiesel and Arendt

Although Wiesel appears to resent Hannah Arendt's work on the Holocaust, a comparison between Arendt's approach and Wiesel's will clarify the differences between Wiesel's metaphysical and ontological concern as opposed to a more sociological orientation. Furthermore, some specific criticisms which Wiesel makes in his "Plea for the Dead" are weak and their weaknesses expose the limitations of Wiesel as a systematic thinker just as previous discussion has shown his power as a writer.

It seems clear that Wiesel's "Plea for the Dead" is written in response to Hannah Arendt's *Eichmann in Jerusalem*. The juxtaposition of Wiesel's tirade against judgment and Wiesel's insistence on an attitude of shared pain with the continual mention of Eichmann, *Judenarat*, and awards for good and bad conduct allows no other possible conclusion, for in every significant detail the position that Wiesel criticizes is the position which Hannah Arendt is said to hold by her major Jewish critics.[38] It is clear that for many, including Gershom Scholem, the manner in which Arendt said her piece was as offensive, if not more offensive, than what she said.

Wiesel's first criticism against many analytic studies of the Holocaust and presumably against Arendt involves the relationship of Nazi responsibility and Jewish behavior. Wiesel writes that:

Beyond the diversity of all theories, the self-assurance of

> which cannot but arouse anger, all unanimously con-
> clude that the victims by participating in the execu-
> tioner's game, in varying degrees shared responsibility.[39]

This charge, which is repeated by Alexander Donat in his criticism of Arendt[40] seems misplaced when directed at Professor Arendt.

She goes to great lengths to underscore the persistent differences between the conceptual universes of the Germans and that of the rest of the world. In one of the most poignant dialogues recounted in *Eichmann in Jerusalem,* Professor Arendt writes:

> Servatius declared the accused innocent of charges bear-
> ing on his responsibility for "the collection of skeletons,
> sterilizations, killings by gas, and *similar medical matters,*"
> whereupon Judge Halevi interrupted him: "Dr. Servatius,
> I assume you made a slip of the tongue when you said
> that killing by gas was a medical matter." To which
> Servatius replied: "It was indeed a medical matter, since
> it was prepared by physicians; it was *a matter of killing*
> and killing, too, is a medical matter."[41]

Servatius later repeated this remark. Arendt suggests that perhaps Servatius wanted to

> Make absolutely sure that the judges in Jerusalem would
> not forget how Germans—ordinary Germans, nor former
> members of the SS or even the Nazi party—even today
> can regard an act that in other countries is called
> murder.[42]

Professor Arendt in no way wishes to exonerate the Germans and in no way equates German responsibility with Jewish responsibility.

Wiesel criticizes numerous theoreticians for indicating what he calls a "shared responsibility"; however, the responsibility of the perpetrators is not in the same category as the response of the victims. Inadequate self-defense does not lessen the guilt of the murderer. One thinks of the feminist's insistence that whatever the behavior of the rape victim, it is the rapist who must be held responsible. When the feminists advocate preventative behavior on the part of the potential victim to minimize the possibility of rape, they in no way exonerate the rapist. Similarly, Arendt's study of the victim's behavior, as well as that of the perpetrators, is for the purpose of understanding and prevention rather than to minimize Nazi responsibility.

Wiesel's insistence upon the mystery of the Holocaust and upon the continuity between traditional anti-Semitism and the Holocaust runs the risk of mitigating against what is most basic to Arendt's and Hilberg's understanding of the Holocaust. What is most unique is their refusal to view the extermination of the Jews as a direct continuation of medieval and modern anti-Semitism. Arendt argues that to fully understand the concentration camps, the camps must not be seen exclusively in their Jewish context, i.e. as an unrestrained outbreak of anti-Semitism, but also as an extension onto the domestic front of the policies of imperialism which were the end result of the unrestrained expansionary drive of industrial capitalism. The Jews became the chosen victims not only because of the traditions of anti-Semitism but also because they were economically superfluous to Germany and possessed visible power without wealth.[43] One logical method of eliminating a superfluous population (and the reader must bear in mind that logical is not equivalent to moral or desirable) is by extermination. Arendt follows Raul Hilberg and argues that the Jewish institutions failed to perceive correctly their own situation and hence the responses that they had practiced for two millenium in dealing with anti-Semitism were hopelessly inappropriate to their unprecedented situation.[44] They did not understand the inherent lawlessness of the Nazi regime and the fact that the Nazis were operating without any of the traditional moral, social, political, and economic constraints which had restrained the scope; of previous anti-Semitic outbreaks.[45]

Arendt's treatment of Eichmann as a bureaucrat with the two basic skills of organization and negotiation is totally consistent with her understanding of the Holocaust. She seeks to analyze the man. Her understanding of Eichmann is often in direct conflict with the role ascribed to him by the prosecutor for the state of Israel[46] and with the role ascribed to him by Wiesel.[47] She describes him not as a demonic monster but as a bureaucratic functionary who would commit his full allegiance to any system that could reward his talents and arouse his enthusiasm.[48] This bureaucratic Eichmann is in a way far more dangerous than the demonic monster because of his prevalence in a modern technological society and because of his passionless amorality which can operate so methodically.

David Bakan has suggested that the two descriptions of Eichmann, the bureaucrat and the demon, are far closer to each other than one would ordinarily expect. He minimizes the area of disagreement:

> The externalization of neccessity is often buttressed by both an ultra-mythicism and an ultra-realism. Both were present, for example, in the great holocaust of naziism with the revival of German historical myths, on the one hand, and the complete banality—to borrow Hannah Arendt's term for it—and excessive realism of orderliness, obedience, bureaucracy, files, schedules, supplies, etc., of Eichmann, on the other. Although ultra-mythicism and ultra-realism appear to be poles apart, they are identical in that in both there is the externalization of necessity. There is only a superficial contrast between them.[49]

In both the demonic and the bureaucratic characterizations, Eichmann eludes the full measure of personal responsibility, in the one case because his extraordinary evil places him beyond the realm of ordinary humanity and in the other case because he is the victim and the creation of a depersonalized, technological system.

Another element of Wiesel's criticism of Holocaust theoreticians is his insistence on the mystery. This sense of mystery is in conflict with Arendt's struggle for comprehension. Arendt writes:

> Comprehension does not mean denying the outrageous, deducing the unprecedented from precedents, or explaining phenomena by such analogies and generalities that the impact of reality and the shock of experience are no longer felt ... Comprehension, in short, means the unpremeditated, attentive, facing up to and resisting of reality—whatever it may be.[50]

For Arendt the unpleasant reality that we must face is external: social, economic, psychological, political, historical, and moral. For Wiesel the reality that must be confronted, and the reality upon which we risk our souls in confrontation, is ontological. There is no reason why the one reality need preclude the other, though Wiesel seems to feel that the understanding of the psycho-social situation without asking the ontological question is limited and distorts reality. It is appropriate to suggest that the opposite is also the case and that Wiesel's insistence on the mystery threatens to distort parts of reality which must be confronted.

D

Wiesel's Defense of Mystery and the Roots of His Attraction to American Jewry: A Speculative Theory

The question must be asked as to why Wiesel's writings, with respect to the mystery of the Holocaust, find a responsive audience in American Jewry while the demystified writings of Arendt qua historian, of Rubenstein qua theologian, and of Bettelheim qua psychoanalyst meet with such hostility? Elsewhere, it has been suggested that the problem was related to Wiesel's reaffirmation of the viability of the Jewish symbolic system and to the other writers' detachment from that conceptual system. In this section I would like to offer the broad outlines of a psychoanalytic understanding of the mystery of the Holocaust. The leadership of American Jewry has responded quite hostilely to the three major attempts to demystify the history of the Holocaust and the one theological attempt which spoke in radically demystified terms. Only in the deep grounds well of support for the state of Israel has the Jewish community really confronted and responded to the Holocaust. The American Jewish community's refusal to face the Holocaust in a demystified way may have deep psycho-analytic roots.

From Wiesel's writings and from the writings of other authors, we learn of the patricidal and infanticidal impulses which were sometimes expressed in the behavior of the victims. It is not accident that the victims were burned, offered up, as it were, as sacrifices on an altar. The emphasis on the innocence of the victims seems to reflect the sacrificial requirement that the offering be without blemish. The innocence of the children particularly emphasizes the un-blemished quality of the offering. Several authors have also referred to the victims as messiahs, atoning sacrifices offered

up on an altar. Though these references are often unin-
tentional, their unconscious significance is important.

The contradictory attitudes toward the victims and the
survivors must also be considered. These attitudes reflect a
profound ambivalence and welcome a sense of mystery.
Eliezer Berkovits spoke of the 'holiness of the victims' and the
unique authority of the survivors. His writings are not alone in
their insistence upon an attitude of veneration and holiness with
respect to the victims and survivors. Yet, on the other hand,
Wiesel (and not only Wiesel) continually underscores the
compromised behavior of the inmates in the camps and that all
who have emerged are defiled. The unspeakable question
which is never asked of the survivor, "How did you survive?"
and the uncomfortableness which one feels in his presence may
relate as much to personal compromise as it does to holiness.

This sense of the holiness of the victims and the mystery
of the Holocaust may be rooted in what psychoanalysis has
termed the primal crime. Whether one understands the primal
crime in the Freudian sense of patricide or in the Bakanian
sense of infanticide is unimportant. The anger and the
competition that are present in the institution of the family as
well as the love and concern which are seen in that web of
relationships leaves us with an enormous sense of ambivalence.
Acting out either of these tendencies without restraint is
considered the most sinful of human acts. Any memory of
such sinful acts tends to be repressed, and resurfaces in the
extreme opposite of veneration and sacredness, for once the
hostility is expressed, the love and the concern which are the
other side of our ambivalent feelings are able to fully express
themselves. One need not argue that the victims and the
survivors were fratricidal or infanticidal. Rather, one may
speculate that our fears of our own actions under such
circumstances and our fright as to which series of emotions
would become the dominant one within us, leads us to
overestimate the behavior of the victims and to shroud the
event in mystery. We are trapped by our own ambivalence and
perhaps by the communal memory of some primal crime
(taken in a serious, though non-literal sense).

If this be the case, then Wiesel, an author whose
fundamental perspective on the Holocaust mirrors this ambivalence of sinfulness and holiness, mystery and the quest for

explanation, finds an audience of kindred souls in American Jews. Wiesel presents all sides of the questions raised by the Holocaust. He also stands at the brink with respect to God. He loves Him and hates Him, he fears Him and yet tries to live without Him. Common to his treatment of God, Israel, and the Holocaust is this standing on the brink. Wiesel is torn by ambivalence as he confronts the void.

1. In "The Guilt We Share" Wiesel writes:

    > Well known psychiatrists have attempted ot give some expla-
    > nations in their books dealing with the psychology of the
    > concentration camp ... But to attribute that acceptance (of Nazi
    > beastiality)—as they do—to the disintegration of the personal-
    > ity, or to the rising up of the "death wish," or to something in
    > Jewish tradition, can only be a partial explanation. The meta-
    > physical *why* is still lacking.
    >
    > (*Legends of Our Time,* pp. 209-10)

    Since Bettelheim mentions the death instinct in his writings on the Holocaust (Bruno Bettelheim, *The Informed Heart.* (New York: The Free Press, 1960, pp. 249-51), and since he is strongly criticized on this account (Alexander Donat, *Jewish Resistance.* [New York: Warsaw Ghetto Resistance Organi-zation, 1964]), it is safe to conclude that Wiesel had Bettelheim in mind when he wrote these words. My argument with respect ot Wiesel's attack on Arendt will be presented in Section Three of this chapter.

2. Wiesel's reference to "something in Jewish tradition" in the quote above may be a reference to Raul Hilberg's first chapter in *The Destruction of European Jewry* (Chicago: Quadrangle Books, 1961).

3. *The Informed Heart,* pp. 246-249.

4. *Ibid.,* pp. 247.

5. *Ibid.,,* pp. 218-20.

6. Alexander Donat, *Jewish Resistance,* p. 57. It is ironic that in Bruno Bettelheim's recent essay in the *New Yorker* entitled "On Surviving" he bitterly denounces the Wertmuller's movie *Seven Beauties* for its emphasis on survival at all costs. He is extremely frightened that our recent disappoint-ment in the free world may lead to a fascination with totalitarianism and that this fascination could easily lead to active acceptance. He is angry at Wertmuller's use of farce and comedy for it seems to neutralize evil and to make a sham of human dignity. So much for Bettelheim's commitment to survival at any price. Bruno Bettelheim, "Surviving" in the *New Yorker* (August 2, 1976) pp. 31-52.

7. Bettelheim's passionate concern with humanity and with the moral issues raised by the Holocaust are easily seen in the *New Yorker* review essay. He writes:

> Her film (Wertmuller's) deals with the most important problems of our time, of all times; survival; good and evil; and man's attitude toward a life in which good and evil co-exist, when religion no longer offers guidance for dealing with this duality. The late Hannah Arendt . . . stressed the utter banality of evil. I agree with her thesis. But what must concern us primarily is that evil is evil. . . . *Op. Cit.*, p. 33.

8. Elie Wiesel, "Talking and Writing and Keeping Silent," in Franklin H. Littell and Hubert Locke (eds.), *The German Church Struggle and the Holocaust*, (Detroit: Wayne State University Press, 1973), p. 270.

9. *Night*, p. 17.

10. *Ibid.*, p. 19.

11. *Ibid.*, pp. 12-17.

12. *Legends of Our Time*, pp. 43-51.

13. Treated in an earlier chapter. Ed.

14. *Night*, pp. 40-41.

15. *Ibid.*, p. 18.

16. *Exodus* XV: 1-19.

17. *Ibid.*, p. 21.

18. *Ibid.*, p. 41.

19. This is considered by many the major blow of Paul Hilheige's invaluable work.

20. *The War Against the Jews* (New York: Holt Rinehart, Winston, and The Jewish Publication Society, 1975) p. 343.

21. *Ibid.*, p. 345.

22. *Ibid.*, pp. 102-4.

23. *Ibid.*, pp. 116-24.

24. *Ibid.*, p. 124.

25. *Ibid.*, pp. 74-76.

26. *Ibid.*, p. 74.

27. *Legends of Our Time*, p. 233.

28. *Ibid.*, p. 228.

29. *Ibid.*, p. 228.

30. *Ibid.*, p. 229.

31. *Legends of Our Time*, p. 205.

32. *Ibid.*, p. 210.

33. *Ibid.*, p.212.

34. *Ibid.*, p. 223.

35. *Souls on Fire*, p. 111.

36. Elie Wiesel, "Talking and Writing and Keeping Silent," p. 274.

37 Elie Wiesel, "A Plea for the Survivors," in Shima Vol. 100, reprinted in *The Jewish Digest* (April 1976) p. 39.

38. See Ernst Simon, "A Textual Examination," and Alexander Donat, "An Empirical Examination," in "Revisionist History of the Jewish

Catastrophe: Two Examinations of Hannah Arendt," in *Judaism*, Vol. XII No. 4 (Fall 1963), pp. 388-435. Similarly, a strongly negative evaluation of Professor Arendt's work is to be found in Norman Podhoretz, "Hannah Arendt on Eichmann: A Study in the Perversity of Brilliance," in *Commentary*, Vol. XXXVI No. 9 (September 1963). The most positive review of Arendt's work is Bruno Bettelheim, "Eichmann: The System, The Victims," in *The New Republic* Vol. 148 No. 24 (June 15, 1963), pp. 23-33.

39. *Legends of Our Time*, p. 219.

40. See Note 38. This point on the complicity of leadership is made by Hannah Arendt as part of a much larger theory of totalitarian domination and should not be considered in isolation from the larger theory. Ironically, it was Arendt's work which set part of the agenda for future Holocaust research; an agenda which yielded the fruits of Isaiah Trunk's *Judenrat* and which will shortly yield Raul Hilberg's translation and commentary on *The Diary of Adam Cherniakow*, the leader of the Warsaw Judenrat.

41. Hannah Arendt, *Eichmann in Jerusalem* (New York: Viking Press, 1963), p. 69.

42. *Ibid.*, p. 69.

43. See Hannah Arendt, *The Origins of Totalitarianism*, (Cleveland: The World Publishing Company, 1951), most specifically Chapter One.

44. In *The Destruction if European Jewry*, Hilberg writes:

> Both perpetrators and victims drew upon their age-old experience in dealing with each other. The Germans did it with success. The Jews did it with disaster. (p. 17)

See also *Eichmann in Jerusalem*, pp. 117-118 ff.

45. For an updating of the dangers described by both Hilberg and Arendt see Richard L. Rubenstein, *The Cunning of History* (New York: Harper and Row, 1976). Here too, as in their theological work Rubenstein strives to describe the Holocaust in a radically demystified fashion while Wiesel is seeking to protect the mystery.

46. Gideon Hausner, *Justice in Jerusalem*, (New York: Harper and Row, 1965).

47. In the essay "The Guilt We Share," Wiesel describes Eichmann as a liar determined to save his own neck and thus he agrees with both the prosecution and the judges. However, he concedes that Eichmann may not have been a major actor in the German drama and thus he concurs on this fundamental point with Arendt.

There are any number of difficulties which stem from Wiesel's refusal to attack his adversaries by name and to enter into dialogue rather than standing aloof and remaining 'above' the dialogues. I find his course of action somewhat unwise.

48. *Eichmann in Jerusalem*, pp. 21-36.

49. David Bakan, *Disease, Pain, and Sacrifice* (Chicago: The University of Chicago Press, 1968), p. 117.

50. *The Origins of Totalitarianism*, p. viii.

ELIE WIESEL AND THE DRAMA OF INTERROGATION

by Ted L. Estess

> I pray to the God within me that He will give me the
> strength to ask Him the right questions.[1]

Elie Wiesel is typically indentified as a Holocaust writer. As such, he joins such figures as Josef Bor, Zdena Berger, Primo Levi, Eugene Heimler, and André Schwarz-Bart, all of whom have attempted in varying ways to find a voice with which to articulate the experience of the "final solution." Against a reality so grotesque and unsettling, we might well expect the imagination to go dumb. Indeed, with this group of writers, *what* and *how* they speak may not be so remarkable as *that* they speak at all.

While the critical response to Wiesel's artistry has appropriately emphasized his identity as a Holocaust writer, we need also to appreciate the manner in which his writing participates in broader currents of contemporary sensibility. It is important to interpret Wiesel as more than a representative of Job in the twentieth century and to see his literature as more than a convenient example of the death of God. An approach which places Wiesel in a wider context need not neglect the specifically Jewish and the narrowly religious elements of his literature, nor need it soften his witness to the uniqueness of the Holocaust. What it might do is to enrich our awareness of how Wiesel's creative verve transmutes his special life experience into art which is pertinent to the self-understanding of any person.

An initial step toward such an approach to Wiesel

involves emphasizing that his characteristic stance toward the human mysteries is one of interrogation. In its subject matter and, more importantly, in its fundamental vision, his art portrays that "the essence of man is to be a question, and the essence of the question is to be without answer" (*TBW* 186). While his questions certainly involve the Holocaust experience, the genesis of his interrogative vision resides in pre-Holocaust religious intensity.[2] Indeed, the opening scene of his first narrative initiates the process of questioning as Moché the teacher speaks to Eliezer: "Man raises himself toward God by the questions he asks Him.... That is the true dialogue. Man questions God and God answers. But we don't understand His answers. We can't understand them. Because they come from the depths of the soul, and they stay there until death" (*N* 16). The night of the Holocaust, in stripping away the answers of 3,000 years of Jewish religious and cultural history, was not the origination but the intensification of the very questions which sustained that history.

The questions which permeate Wiesel's literature are largely religious in character. They are religious in the ordinary, or what Tillich called the "narrow," sense of the word insofar as God, evil, and suffering are involved. With regard to this sense of the religious, it should be emphasized that through questioning Wiesel avoids a preemptory rejection of ancient patterns of religious meaning. Indeed, the stance of questioning is precisely that interpretative posture which maintains creative tension between the individual and the tradition. Moreover, as a specifically Jewish writer, his task is not to reject but to retrieve, not to invent but to repeat. His creative powers turn to renovate—with hermeneutical violence, to be sure—the tradition in which he stands.[3]

Wiesel's questioning, however, is religious in a broader sense as well, if by "religious" we intend "asking passionately the question of the meaning of our existence and being willing to receive answers...."[4] In his literature this willingness to question takes the distinctively modern shape of inquiry into the nature of the self. Following Nathan Scott's observation about contemporary sensibility, we might locate the expansive meaning of Wiesel's religious interrogation: "In a time of the eclipse of God, the most characteristic form of the religious question becomes the question of authenticity, of how we are to keep faith with and safeguard the 'single one' or the 'true self'—in a bullying world."[5]

Yet questions remain authentic only in the dialectic of question and answer, in the interaction of yes and no. While the presiding principle of creative integrity is that of the question, Wiesel's literature is also assertive. Other writers, such as Kafka and Beckett, with whom he shares affinities, are interrogative; yet their literatures linger more in the state of suspended interrogation than does his. Wiesel's work, parabolic and elliptical as it is, adds ethical intensity and human fullness through its attempt to provide an ideationally significant response to painful religious, social, and psychological dilemmas.

The questioning spirit in itself of course gives no special distinction to Wiesel. Man is questioner, as almost every significant philosophichal anthropology from Plato and Aristotle to Heidegger and Lonergan has emphasized. What finally distinguishes Wiesel is the shape his questioning takes and the significance that questioning has for meaningful dwelling in the world. The shape of his questioning is an ancient one—that of storytelling. And it is the stories that we ourselves must interrogate and be interrogated by in order to disclose the import and, possibly, the redemptive vision hidden in and evoked by Wiesel's questioning. In our interrogation, we will do well to remember with Wiesel that "these riddles are hard to solve, for the key is not found in our brains but in our hearts." (*BJ* 116).

INTERROGATION AND SELF-IDENTITY

"When he opened his eyes, Adam did not ask God: 'Who are you?' He asked 'Who am I?'" (*O* 11). The question of the first man is also the question of Wiesel: "Reduced to a mere number, the man in the concentration camp at the same time lost his identity and his individual destiny"; hence the survivor was compelled to enter onto a path of creation and discovery of self (*LT* 211).[6] Wiesel embarked on this path by writing in quick succession three novellas, which, taken together, constitute a triptych of self-definition. Eliezer in *Night*, Elisha in *Dawn*, and the nameless "I" of *The Accident* are characters without a future; they have only a past cruelly presided over by the smoke of the Holocaust and a present nostalgically punctuated by childhood memories of what was lost in the flames. The "I" has curled into a question mark.

After the manner of Job, Eliezer seeks to understand himself by questioning God. This questioning must be understood in light of Moche's teaching: "You will find the true answers, Eliezer, only within yourself" (*N* 16). External answers failing, Wiesel follows the path which characterizes almost the entirety of modern literature when he turns to "the within, all that inner space one never sees."[7] For the early Wiesel, the community and the family are in flames and the self is left "terribly alone in a world without God and without man" (*N* 74). The only place to go is within. This story of initiation into the drama of interrogation leaves the self not in the place where initiation rites should end—in a new community beyond the trials of the initiatory ordeal—but alone in the nadir of death. Yet, for all its power of muted outrage and endless suffering, *Night* is not a final answer to the question of the self; hence Wiesel's second book questions *Night*.[8]

Dawn questions precisely the notion that the answers will be found within by the solitary individual. Elisha again presents an image of the self as questioner: "So many questions obsessed me. Where is God to be found? In suffering or in rebellion? When is a man most truly a man? When he submits or when he refuses? Where does suffering lead him? To purification or to bestiality?" (*D* 24). As Eliezer's life of study was interrupted in Sighet by the operpowering force from the outside, so is Elisha surprised by Gad, who strides into his life like one out of the grand tradition of Jewish rebels and mysterious messengers. Gad refuses to allow Elisha to remain in his solitude, and in disturbing that solitude he suggests that the context for authentic questioning is that of the self not in isolation but in relationship.

Strangely enough, the relationship into which Elisha enters is that of executioner to victim. By way of Elisha's killing a British hostage as part of the struggle to create the state of Israel, the narrative suggests that all persons are related, even when they violate that relatedness with so profance an act as murder. In making his protagonist an executioner, Wiesel is not relativizing the unique guilt of the Nazis, nor is he merely suggesting that all persons are capable of murder. He is disclosing, rather, that all persons stand (or fall) together in finitude and moral ambiguity. As a later character remarks, "The man who tries to be an angel only succeeds in making faces" (*TBW* 188). Hence, the "dawn" to which the title refers is a dawning of the possibility for human community, not in moral perfection or self-righteousness, not in a division of the good from the evil, but in the acknowlegment that all persons share a common destiny: all are exiled from the garden of innocence.

The Accident marks the end of the first period of Wiesel's literary development and raises the issue of the invention of a new self to central thematic prominence. The protagonist again poses the question of self-identity: "You want to know who I am, truly? I don't know myself" (*A* 77). It seems from this admission that Wiesel's character is back at the point from which Eliezer begins in *Night*. What is happening, however, is a characteristic movement in Wiesel: he returns to the beginning with every book, as if seeking in the origin of things some secret to assist the process of creativity within a new situation. [9] His protagonists begin again and repeat the same process, either in the present time of the novel or in memory. With each repetition, the protagonist's stepping back to the beginning allows him, by the end of the narrative, to move further forward toward significant identity. This pattern embodies the recognition that the journey of the self is not one-dimensional but is a process in which one recoils repeatedly to the origins in order better to engage the fluid succession of present time.

In an important turn for Wiesel, the protagonist of *The Accident* unexpectedly decides to invent another self. If the "reality" of the self is insufficient or unbearable or non-existent, then one option is to fictuonalize another self by taking a mask.[10] As the protagonist says, "It's absurd: lies can give birth to true happiness. Happiness will, as long as it lasts, seem real" (*A* 126).

Self-invention as an answer to the problem of identity is, however, called into question by an artist named Gyula. Gyula's portrait of the protagonist functions to question the mask through which the protagonist has been seeing himself. Surely the mask of suffering and isolation behind which the protagonist has been hiding is authentically in touch with his life experience. But the interpretation of the self solely in negative terms is a dishonest masquerade which shields the person from the rich diversity of life. Viewing the portrait, the protagonist decides cynically to take another mask, this one of happiness. Sensing what has been decided, Gyula, in a violent and parabolic act of friendship, burns the portrait. With this, he emphasizes that the mask of solitary suffering must be rejected—it belongs more to the dead than to the living; it does not tell the whole story of the self. More importantly, Gyula's act suggests—and here Wiesel differs sharply from an artist such as Beckett—that an interpretation of the self as a series of inauthentic masks is an inadequate model of personhood. As Wiesel writes in another place, "A Jew has no right to wear disguises" (*OGA* 100).

While Wiesel rejects the inauthentic assumption of masks as an adequate model of the person, there is still a recognition that the self is unfinished. He writes that "reflected in all my characters and their mirror games, it is always the Jew in me trying to find himself" (*OGA* 213). The mirror for his protagonists is a friend. By looking into that mirror, the Jew—who on one level is every person for Wiesel—begins to question his habituated modes of self-interpretation and moves to imagine alternative ways of seeing himself. Ortega y Gasset sets the matter for Wiesel's characters: "It is too often forgotten that man is impossible without imagination, without the capacity to invent for himself a conception of life, to 'ideate' the character he is going to be. Whether he be original or a plagiarist, man is the novelist of himself...."[11] What Wiesel's protagonists have difficulty relizing is that one is not necessarily lying or pretending in acts of love and friendship. For, as later characters see, such acts are creative human possibilities which belong authentically to a person.

Wiesel's narrative strategy itself reflects the search for self which we have seen in the early stories. That strategy, reminiscent of the exploration of consciousness which occurs in Bergson, Proust, and Beckett, displays that the life of the self is not a straight-line march into the future but involves considerable dissociation and disunity. Evident in his early narratives and more prominent in the later ones, the rearrangement of the moments of clock time shows the self carrying into the future an ineradicable weight from the past. Through the familiar technique of montage in which the narrator associates, for reasons not always clear, one incident with another, the narrative pattern itself becomes a metaphor of the attempt of the self to find unity in the heterogeneity of experience.

The process of interrogation keeps the self open to new possibilities in the early novels of Wiesel; it, in the words of Amos Wilder, keeps "open the incursions of grace."[12] Just as evil and horror intrude with great surprise into the life of Wiesel's characters, so does grace unexpectedly enter in the form of love and friendship. As one character says, "The mystery of good is no less disturbing than the mystery of evil" (*BJ* 254). The interrogative stance, if it is to exercise fidelity to its own executive principle, must question the significance of those moments of goodness.

INTERROGATION AND AUTHENTIC INTERSUBJECTIVITY

Moving through the night of self-enclosed solitude and through a struggle with angelism, Wiesel carried his interrogation toward the day of dialogic intimacy in *The Town Beyond the Wall* and *The Gates of the Forest*. There are hints in this direction in the earlier novels, indicating that even in the darkest moments of his long night he has remained open to the full gamut of his life experience. But the voyage to recognizing the secrets in one's own experiences of authentic intersubjectivity is a lengthy one. As Yeats said, "It is so many years before one can believe enough in what one feels even to know what the feeling is."[13]

The process of interrogation is the central structural component of *The Town Beyond the Wall*. The entire narrative is related while Michael is being interrogated by Hungarian police about his illegal entry into the country. Ironically, this interrogation, is called "prayer," since the prisoner, like a praying Jew, must stand until he confesses or goes mad. Since the Holocaust, Wiesel's prayers have largely been questions, but the "prayers" in this book are no longer inquiries directed to God but are questions posed to Michael: Can he suffer the agony of this "prayer" to save a friend? It is Michael the interrogator who is being interrogated: his fidelity in friendship is on trial.

The journey of the self as portrayed in Michael recapitulates much of what we have observed in the earlier protagonists. Following the war, Michael retreats into isolation to "create a new skin ... a new life," firmly convinced that "love is for those who can forget, for those who seek to forget" (*TBW* 67, 87). Yet Michael's solitude is invaded by Pedro, who calls forth from Michael the capacity for friendship, a capacity which is exercised when Michael refuses to betray Pedro to the police during the interrogation. More importantly, Michael remains faithful to Pedro when he turns to "resume the creation of the world from the void" by retrieving a fellow prisoner from an almost catatonic silence. He repeats with another person what Pedro has done for him. The place to begin creating a town beyond the wall of death and despair is in the immediate situation, which, in Michael's case, is with the one fellow prisoner.

Michael, in a tendency increasingly important in the vision of Wiesel, translates the man/man relationship into an enactment of the God/man relationship. The Hasidic notion of God's hiding in the least likely stranger, ready to surprise the unsuspecting, informs the movement to attribute revolutionary intensity to friendship. Michael—the name means "Who is like God?"—discovers transcendent presence in those persons close at hand. Again, Pedro is the repository of wisdom: "He who thinks about God, forgetting man, runs the risk of mistaking his goal: God may be your next-door neighbor" (*TBW* 123).

The drama of interrogation leads to a re-cognition of the significance of relatedness in the lives of Wiesel's characters, while at the same time it discloses that relatedness is prior to and foundational for any interrogation whatsoever. Michael suggests as much when he remarked: "But to say, 'What is God? What is the world? What is my friend? is to say that I have someone to talk to, someone to ask a direction of'" (*TBW* 187). Even the possibility of asking a question is founded on the recognition that we are not, as Eliezer assumes in *Night*, finally "alone in the world." Furthermore, realizing authentic interrogating the meaning of those relationships in which and by virtue of which one already dwells in the world.

But the element of questioning carries a still further significance in *The Town Beyond the Wall*, since a simple

question—Why does Michael wish to return to his hometown?
—provides the chief element of narrative suspense. This question
is resolved when Michael confronts the spectator, a man who
stood passively at a window while the Jews were being deported
from the city. How can a human being remain an indifferent
spectator?—that is the question which compels Michael to return
to his home.

In one of the most dramatic moments in all Wiesel's
literature, Michael indicts the spectator with the sin—no, the
punishment—of indifference.[14] That indictment brings further into question the model of the self that we observed in *The
Accident,* the model in which a person plays an invented role,
in which there is a split between the self and its role, between
being and acting. To play at living, Michael suggests, is
insufficient; merely to pretend at happiness, friendship, and
love leads only to an indifference in which the real action and
death of men are viewed as morally neutral. In Michael's
perspective, the Holocaust is a final repudiation of an ethical
nihilism which he sees implicit within the metaphor of life as a
game: "If living in peace means evolving in nothingness, you
accept the nothingness. The Jews in the courtyard of the
synagogue? Nothing. The shrieks of women gone mad in
cattle cars? Nothing. The silence of thirsty children? Nothing.
All that's a game, you tell yourself. A movie! Fiction: seen and
forgotten. I tell you, you're a machine for the fabrication of
nothingness" (*TBW* 172).

Against the view that life is a game and the self is a player,
Michael affirms what Pedro calls "simplicity," in which there
are no disguises and no pretending. "'I believe in simplicity,'
Pedro said. 'When one loves, one must say: I love you. When
one wants to weep, one must say: I want to weep. When one
becomes aware that existence is too heavy a burden, one must
say: I want to die.... In driving Adam out of Paradise...God
merely deprived him of the power of simplicity'" (*TBW* 124-
25). For Michael a return to simplicity means things as
ordinary as working, loving, being a friend, and having a
family (*TBW* 173). In redeeming his own lifetime, Michael
moves to recover that "condition of complete simplicity," the
simplicity "costing not less than everything."[15]

But we misunderstand the complexity of Wiesel's interrogation of the self if we think that his world divides neatly

into such categories as victims, executioners, and spectators; that in the world there are persons who are simply playing at living while others embody the life of simplicity. As the various representatives of these life possibilities dialectically confront one another, Wiesel's literature suggests that the self is multidimensional. Michael seizes the insight: "Dwon deep, I thought, man is not only an executioner, not only a victim, not only a spectator: he is all three at once" (*TBW* 174). It is not, furthermore, a question of either being a person who invents himself or being a person who simply is what he is. It is a matter of dwelling in the dialectical tension of being both persons at the same time; it is a matter of being both authentic and inauthentic together. Not only is the self a quester, without identity and home and firm mooring; the self, speaking out of ancient wisdom, is also teacher and guide, possessing with Gyula and Pedro quiet confidence and deep simplicity.

The movement to simplicity, however, does not bring the stasis of the completed self, for there are other questions to explore. Also, the primary questions of God and evil and suffering remain unanswered because they are unanswerable. Michael's self-progression, however, does bring the equilibrium which accompanies the capacity to commit oneself in compassion to another. In caring one gains and expresses rootedness; in caring one comes home to the only place one can be—where one is—and there, even in a prison cell, one can act to alleviate suffering.[16] Michael's prayer, "God of my childhood, show me the way that leads to myself," finds a response: the way "leads to another human being" (*TBW* 135, 127). In moving toward another, the self finds a place in which the secrets of reality and the questions of man are conjoined in revelatory dialogue. There a person must risk "to ask the great questions and ask them again, to look up at another, a friend, and to look up again: if two questions stand face to face, that's at least something. It's at least a victory" (*TBW* 187). As Gyula says, "Maybe God is dead, but man is alive. The proof: he is capable of friendship" (*A* 123).

The "town" to which Michael returns is in all respects unlike the town from which he was torn by the Holocaust. Yet, to our surprise, it is very much like that town, for it is a place—no, a way—in which persons with integrity of words and actions dialogically share their lives. The lines of Eliot again trace the voyage of Wiesel's characters:

> We shall not cease from exploration
> And the end of all our exploring
> Will be to arrive where we started
> And know the place for the first time.[17]

INTERROGATION AND ACTION

Wiesel's early protagonists are incapable of initiating independently chosen actions. They are characterized more by what happens to them than by what they are able to make happen. Returning from the Holocaust denuded of self and stripped of a community in which to act, these cripples have little interest in doing anything whatsoever.

This inability to interact significantly with the external world reinforces the impression that the primary concern of Wiesel's literature is with character, not with plot or action. Indeed, he at times accentuates the interest in character by telling the reader the outcome of action at the beginning of the narrative. His plotting in the longer stories is extraordinarily loose, providing only an external frame for the exploration of the interiority of his characters. Unlike what we find in a tightly structured, sequential narrative, the actions of his characters in the external world tend to follow *after* not *from* one another.

Despite the retreat of his characters from action and despite a narrative strategy which de-emphasizes interconnection of events in time, the drama of interrogation in Wiesel is a preparation for action. This occurs in several stages: first, the protagonist secludes himself for a period of introspection; then there occurs an intrusion by a compelling individual who attempts to engage the protagonist with the living; narrative interest increases in the contrast between the protagonist's inaction and his friend's willingness to love and act; finally, the protagonist, after enduring the loss of the friend and after further suffering, evolves to the moment of choice and action. In *The Town Beyond the Wall, The Gates of the Forest,* and *A Beggar in Jerusalem,* this pattern occurs in each of its major components. Gregor, toward the end of *The Gates of the Forest,* exemplifies the culmination of this process when he decides to return to his wife and attempt to rebuild the marriage.

Forcefully, he asserts: "I am what I choose to be: I am in my choice, in my will to choose. There is no divorce between self and its image, between being and acting. I am the act, the image, one and indivisible" (*GF* 219).

Wiesel's protagonists move toward action because they wish to gain a story for their own lives. They realize that without action there is no story to life; without action, there is only atmosphere. David suggests as much when he remarks in *A Beggar in Jerusalem*, "I'm also looking for a story" (*BJ* 157). His plan to fight and die in the Arab-Israeli war is his effort to find some definitive action, even if only to die, which will give shape to an amorphous, storyless existence. The plan involves an agreement with an Israeli soldier named Katriel that if one of them should die in the war, the survivor will tell the other one's story. But it is Katriel who is "missing in action"; hence David faces the dilemma of whether he, in addition to telling Katriel's story, should live out that story through marrying Katriel's widow. David comes to possess a story for his own existence, as do all of Wiesel's later protagonists.

In sharp contrast to the protagonists' inability to act is the capacity of their close companions to commit themselves. The secret of Katriel's power over David and of the power of Gyula, Gad, and Pedro is that, though they have suffered in the Holocaust and have teetered at the brink of madness, they are still able to engage the living through a self-initiated agency. Katriel is "missing in action"; and it is toward a destiny of being willing to lose oneself in action that Wiesel's protagonists move. Only in that path will they, in addition to being the tellers of the stories of the dead, be able to achieve that little taste of immortality that is given to mankind: that immortality which is gained by having a story of one's own which can be told by another after one is gone.

The resolve to act, while it might appear in this brief synopsis as a dramatic appendage to the development of the characters, is not a shallow voluntarism or a Sartrean turn to Wiesel's sensibility. It is rather the culmination—and by that I do not mean "termination"—of an ongoing process of self-interrogation, self-creation, and self-discovery. We are somewhat surprised when Michael and Gregor and David come decisively to the moment of action; but they apparently realize, in the words of Graham Greene, that "sooner or later

... one has to take sides—if one is to remain human."[18]

The Hasidic rebbe, who ascends to such a powerful influence in the final pages of *The Gates of the Forest*, brings Gregor to see the unavoidability of choosing. To Gregor's question of how belief in God is possible after the Holocaust, the rebbe replies, "How can you *not* believe in God after what has happened?" (*GF* 192). But, as the rebbe in great wisdom sees, belief or nonbelief is not a final answer. He painfully admits that God "has become the ally of evil, of death, of murder, but the problem is still not solved. I ask you a question and dare you answer: 'What is there left for us to do?'" (*GF* 197). With a despair beyond the antinomy of hope and despair and a faith beyond the opposition of belief and unbelief, the rebbe continues to probe the question of doing. There are no adequate answers, theological or philosophical or psycho-analytical; yet the individual remains to face life and to do what one can to alleviate suffering, to respond to the need of persons to be loved, to act in behalf of friendship. David sets the dilemma: "Do you understand now that love, no matter how personal or universal, is not a solution? And that outside of love there is no solution?" (*BJ* 172). Having only proximate answers to unanswerable questions, Wiesel's protagonists take courage and act.

The movement to the possibility of action indicates something about the drama of interrogation itself. It suggests that the questioning of Wiesel is not a sophistry which engages argumentation for its own sake, nor is it a cynical detachment which relativizes away all differences among human responses, nor is it a thinking severed from the concrete situation of life with others. His interrogation is a process in which the person recovers a reserve of self-integrity, of wholeness, of health. The self comes to what Ortega y Gasset calls *ensimismarse*, "within-oneselfness," which is taking a stand within the self so as to empower the person to act freely in the relationships in which he stands.[19] Interrogation, while it involves exploration of what is within, does not finally abstract Wiesel's protagonists from the exigencies of the historical situation in which they dwell but instantiates them in that situation more fully. The end of the process is not self-enclosed thinking or solitary contemplation: it is action in behalf of that which is disclosed in the process of interrogation.

As Gregor comes to see in *The Gates of the Forest,* "Nothing is easier than to live in a cloistered universe where I am alone with God, alone against God.... The man that chooses solitude and its riches is on the side of those who are against man ..." (*GF* 219). What confronts us—indeed, what interrogates us—in Wiesel is an ongoing process of enacting those insights which are disclosed through questioning while at the same time questioning those insights which inform action

In seeing the importance for Wiesel of enacting insight, we do well to remember that the lives of most of his protagonists carry the imprint of two distinct dispensations, one from the mother and the other from the father. It is the mother who carries the son to the Hasidic rebbe for a blessing; it is she who condones, even encourages, an interest in the esoteric wisdom of the cabbalists and the paradoxes of the Hasidim. In dialectical tension with the mother, the father is the active advocate for the concrete needs of persons in the community. The father reminds the son that "God, perhaps, has need of saints; as for men, they can do without them" (*LT* 17). These two dimensions do battle in Wiesel, and surely both are integral to the full image of the self that he portrays. In his literature, the turn toward mystical solitude is checked by an awareness of the desperate needs of persons in history; similarly, the loss of the self in frenetic activism is inhibited by an attentive listening to dark mysteries.[20]

Action comes to occupy a large place in Wiesel's sensibility because he experienced so deeply in the Holocaust the consequences of the failure to act. It was an indifference to life on the part of executioners, spectators, and even the victims themselves which, in Wiesel's view, allowed the destruction of the 6 million. Indifference is the enemy of action; apathy is choosing death in life. And storytelling is Wiesel's action against indifference and for friendship/"We tell the tale of the Holocaust," he says, "to save the world from indifference."[21]

INTERROGATION AND STORYTELLING

Every story, to some extent, is about storytelling. This is true of all Wiesel's tales; yet storytelling fully emerges as the central action in his latest novel, *The Oath.* This action is performed by an old man named Azriel, who is the sole survivor of a pogrom against the Jews of a small European village earlier in this century. Azriel—since that awful irruption of hate and suspicion destroyed the entire village, Gentile and Jew alike—has kept the "oath" of silence, the pledge of every Jew not to narrate the story of the pogram if he by chance should survive. If speaking of man's atrocities and God's failures were insufficient to accomplish deliverance from such pogroms, then perhaps silence would stir the conscience of mankind and disturb even the indifference of God in a way that speaking did not. Azriel has survived for fifty years, carrying in silence the terrible burden of memory. One night in an attempt to dissuade a young man from committing sucide, he tells the story of death in order to serve life, thinking that in hearing the story the young man will be placed in such a relationship with the dead that he will not forsake the living. Perhaps the young man will choose life, if for no other reason than to interrogate the meaning of Azriel's story.

In placing storytelling at the center of *The Oath,* Wiesel focuses the dynamic which has sustained his writing from the beginning. With the Holocaust, he entered into a night of silence. It seemed that any description of the dignity, faith, and complicity of the victims, that any tale about the hate and indifference of the executioners and spectators—that any act of speaking whatever would betray the victims, immortalize the executioners, and corrupt the living. On what basis could one break the silence and attempt to speak the unspeakable? The protagonist of *The Accident* answers, "I am a storyteller. My legends can only be told at dusk. Whoever listens questions his life" (*A* 77). Or, as David remarks, "Men's tales put me in jeopardy" (*BJ* 159).

Storytelling, at least in Wiesel's view, is an act which initiates the listener into the drama of interrogation. And the moments of that drama, as we have already seen, include inquiring into self, attending to significant relationships, envisaging and effecting chosen actions. In short, the drama of interrogation is a process by which one can come to have a story of one's own. That is precisely what Azriel sees when he dissuades the young man from suicide in *The Oath.* Suicide, Azriel suggests, is a foreclosure on the possibility of having one's own story, for suicide is an answer whose finality cannot be revoked.[22] One gains a story through interrogating experience, and experience belongs only to the living. "Some writings," Wiesel comments, "could sometimes, in moments of grace, attain the quality of deeds" (LT viii). Storytelling attains the "quality" of action in Wiesel when it catalyzes a process of questioning that effects change in the life of the hearer and the reader.

If the reader in his own confrontation with the tale is initiated into the drama of interrogation, the action of storytelling must be, as I have proposed throughout this essay, an interrogatory venture for the teller himself. Wiesel comments, "I write in order to understand as much as to be understood" (*OGA* 213). There is, however, in Wiesel a tension between coming to understand through storytelling and coming to understand through rational inquiry. A significant moment for several of his protagonists, and perhaps for Wiesel himself, is their turning to and quickly from philosophy. Also important are the comments scattered throughout his literature which place strictures on the efficacy of a rigidly logical address to the questions which possess the characters.[23] Occurring here is another dimension of the battle between the way of the mother and that of the father: the way of the mother is that of storytelling after the manner of the great Hasidic masters; that of the father is of philosophy. The longer narratives combine both, for in the frame of a story there is considerable talk which has the appearance of philosophizing. But ultimately, narrative succeeds philosophical discourse as the mode of interrogation in Wiesel. Questioning is not the *subject matter* of his narratives; rather, the narratives are his way of questioning any subject matter. Narrative, Henry James observed, "bristles with questions."[24] It does so, Wiesel might say, precisely because narrative is questioning.

This discussion indicates that, for Wiesel, the end of telling a story is not to make an object of beauty which will be the focus of passive contemplation, though his stories are at times beautiful in their aesthetic shape; nor is storytelling playing with words to pass the time, after the manner of someone like Samuel Beckett. Rather, storytelling is Wiesel's mode of inquiring into the nature of things. In this action, he is doing something analogous to what the philosopher attempts to do: to interrogate all experience and attempt to disclose the way in which things cohere in significant patterns of meaning. This is why, I think, we see the gradual expansion of the canvas and of the subject matter in Wiesel's career as a writer. From the brief story which dealt with the Holocaust experience, he has turned to increasingly longer narratives which probe deeper and deeper into Jewish history. Hence, he recently composed *Souls on Fire,* a book on the Hasidic masters of the eighteenth and nineteenth centuries, and is presently writing on the patriarchs. His interrogative adventure enlarges as he seeks to incorporate the stories of all men into his own story; it expands as one question leads to another, as he finds in storytelling "answers to all questions and questions for all answers" (*A* 119).

It is precisely this understanding of the nature and function of storytelling and of the literary text that several students of the art of interpretation have with persuasive arguments been attempting for a number of years to lead us to see.[25] Storytelling, indeed all speaking whatever, is, we are told, a coming-into-understanding of that which discloses itself to an attentive inquirer. Moreover, the relationship which, according to these thinkers, characterizes the address of the reader to the story is one of mutual interrogation. The reader brings to the text a history of habituated modes of response and a certain value orientation which, if the confrontation with the literary text is to do what it ought, are placed in question by the horizon of understanding speaking through the text. A challenge comes to the interpreter from the text, a challenge to allow his own perspectives to be interrogated and his horizon of understanding to be altered and expanded. Accordingly, the hermeneutical event involves not merely dissection or explication of the text itself, but a dialogue by which the text and reader act on each other in such a way that neither the reader not the text will any longer be the same.

The narrator of *The Accident* appears to have this type of dialogic intensity in view when he remarks: "To listen to a story under such circumstances is to play a part in it, to take sides, to say yes or no, to move one way or the other. From then on there is a before and an after. And even to forget becomes a cowardly acceptance" (*A* 95). And, again, after relating the story of a child who served the perverse pleasure of German officers, the narrator comments, "Whoever listens to Sarah and doesn't change, whoever enters Sarah's world and doesn't invent new gods and new religions, deserves death and destruction" (*A* 96). Engaging and being engaged by the story at this deep level is not altogether a consciously intellectual or verbal matter. It involves listening to the silence which resonates through the story. Clara (clarity) has this in view when she speaks to Gregor: "you stop at words.... You must learn to see through them, to hear that which is unspoken" (*GF* 176). It is this painfully creative process, with all the risk and courage and sensitive openness which it demands, that situates itself into the life of the hearer of Wiesel's tales. "Do you know that it is given to each of us to enrich a legend simply by listening to it?" (*BJ* 131).

It might appear with this understanding of the act of storytelling, along with the previous discussion of friendship and action, that in the vision if Wiesel the ethical subsumes the aesthetic. It might even appear that there is a submerged moralism in Wiesel, that the interrogative drama opens itself up finally to the soliloquy of the imperative. To be sure, his interrogation, so as not to be an act of bad faith, a dramatic pose, or a mere game, includes an attempt to answer the questions. His interrogation involves an effort to distinguish options and to pursue with appropriate clarity and passion the matters at hand. Patiently, with honest and disturbing self-revelation, Wiesel has negotiated the treacherous movement between forgetfulness and madness. In this movement he has dared, imperatively at times, to affirm, refusing to retreat to the solitude of mere negation.

Moreover, we must acknowledge that Wiesel's greatest strength is with the anecodote, briefly related without elaboration or commentary. Thus it is perhaps unfortunate that a recurring convention in his longer narratives, beginning with the final pages of *The Town Beyond the Wall,* is to bring the teacher into the story and to provide him a platform from which to attempt an answer to the questions posed in the narrative.[26] In the structure of the story, the speeches sometimes unhappily intrude as appendages to the narrative movement. While the drama of interrogation provides the movement and energy to the stories of Wiesel, the moment of answering the questions often mars aesthetic power and narrative effectiveness. "Art," Samuel Beckett has commented, "is pure interrogation, rhetorical questioning, less the rhetoric."[27]

Wiesel's art occasionally edges toward the rhetorical; in doing so, the rhetoric threatens to break precisely the interrogative engagement which the stories themselves might effect. Moral outrage tempts Wiesel at times to do too much for the reader, to tell all, instead of narrating and allowing the interrogative process to wend its way in the silence.

These demurrers aside, the final weight of Wiesel's storytelling is aesthetic, not narrowly moral; it is interrogative, not obstinately declarative or imperative. His storytelling gains its ethical intensity in part because it does precisely that which the aesthetic intends: it awakens the sense of surprise. Pedro accents this motif in *The Town Beyond the Wall:* "Blessed is he capable of surprising and being surprised. If I had a prayer to address to God, it would be, 'O God, surprise me. Bless me or damn me: but let thy benediction or thy punishment be a surprise'" (*TBW* 133). Indifference is that inhibitor of action against which all of Wiesel's literature inveighs, and the antidote to indifference is the capacity of being surprised by lying *and* by truthfulness, by evil *and* by good, by dying *and* by living. We are surprised to find love where we might have foreseen hate, to happen upon hope when we might have anticipated despair, to come upon evil when we might have predicted good, to find destiny when we might have expected mere chance.

Through awakening the sense of surprise, which in many respects is the same as eliciting an interrogative vision, Wiesel's literature achieves its moments of greatest power. Art, whenever it is in the service of surprise, while fulfilling a noble aesthetic function, is at the same time initiating that interrogative drama which is essential to ethical judgments and which best expresses the religious tenor of our time.

1. Elie Wiesel, *Night*, trans. Stella Rodway (New York: Hill & Wang, 1960), p. 16. Hereafter pagination for quotations from Wiesel's literature is given in parentheses in the text. The following abbreviations and editions are used: *A=The Accident*, trans. Anne Borchardt (New York: Avon Books, 1962); *BJ=A Beggar in Jerusalem*, trans. Lily Edelman and the author (New

York: Avon Books, 1970): *D=Dawn* trans. Frances Frenaye (New York: Avon Books, 1970): *GF=The Gates of the Forest,* trans. Frances Frenaye (New York: Avon Books, 1967); *JS=The Jews of Silence,* trans. Neal Kozodoy (New York: Signet Books, 1967); *LT=Legends of Our Time* (New York: Avon Books, 1970); *N=Night: O=The Oath,* trans. Marion Wiesel (New York: Avon Books, 1970); *OGA=One Generation After,* trans. Lily Edelman and the author (New York: Avon Books, 1972); *SF=Souls on Fire,* trans. Marion Wiesel (New York: Vintage Books, 1973); *TBW=The Town Beyond the Wall,* trans. Stephen Becker (New York: Avon Books, 1970).

2. For extensive exploration of man as questioner, see Bernard Lonergan, S.J., *Insight: A Study of Human Understanding* (New York: Philosophical Library, 1956). Also see Michael Novak, *The Experience of Nothingness* (New York: Harper & Row, 1971), pp. 44-51.

3. Wiesel remarks, "To transmit is more important than to innovate Every question a disciple will ask his Master, and that until the end of time, Moses already knew. Yet, we must ask the questions and make them ours by repeating them" (*SF* 257). For a discussion of Wiesel as a "reconstructionist of faith," see Byron L. Sherwin, "Elie Wiesel and Jewish Theology," *Judaism* 18 (1969): 39-52.

4. Pa;ul Tillich, "The Lost Dimension in Religion," in *Ways of Being Religious,* ed. Frederick J. Streng et al. (Englewood Cliffs, N.J.: Prentice-Hall, Inc.), p. 356.

5. *Three American Moralists: Mailer, Bellow, Trilling* (Notre Dame, Ind.: University of Notre Dame Press, 1973). p. 221.

6. In the life story of at least one of Wiesel's protagonists, the question of self-identity is explicitly a pre-Holocaust issue. Kalman, the teacher of Michael in *The Town Beyond the Wall,* instructs his student to question his soul. And Michael records that for weeks he was obsessed with such questions as, Who am I? and What am I? (*TBW* 49). The location of this question prior to the Holocaust is an instance of Wiesel's seeking to discern threads of continuity, fragile as they may appear, between his pre- and post-Holocaust history (see *LT* 215-37).

7. Samuel Beckett, *Three Novels: "Molloy," "Malone Dies," "The Unnamable"* (New York: Grove Press, 1958), P. 10. For discussion of the turn within as an element of modern sensibility, see Erich Heller, *The Artist's Journey into the Interior and Other Essays* (New York: Vintage Books, 1968).

8. The movement from one novel to the next in Wiesel displays the question/answer dialectic in that each succeeding narrative attempts more fully to answer the question of the previous, while at the same time it questions the answer given by the earlier narrative. See "Against Despair," First Annual Louis H. Pincus Memorial Lecture, United Jewish Appeal, 1974 National Conference, New York, December 8, 1973. There, Wiesel comments: "Somewhere ... there lives a man who asks a question to which there is no answer: a generation later, in another place, there lives a man who asks another question to which there is no answer either—and he doesn't know, he cannot know, that *his* question is actually an answer to the first." To this story, Wiesel adds. "To us, however, questions remain questions."

9. *The Oath,* Wiesel's most recent long narrative, is an exception, for its

protagonist is the first who is not a survivor of the Holocaust .But, in accord with the pattern I point out here, the protagonist does imaginatively return to his own holocaust, a pogrom which occurred earlier in this century.

10. In his turn to fictionalizing the self, Wiesel's protagonist joins the parade of characters who people the literature of such figures as Gide, Pirandello, and Beckett. For a discussion of the function of masks in the literature of these figures, see Eurico Garzilli, *Circles without Center: Paths to the Discovery and Creation of Self in Modern Literature* (Cambridge, Mass.: Harvard University Press, 1972).

11. Quoted by Frank Kermode, *The Sense of an Ending: Studies in the Theory of Fiction* (New York: Oxford University Press, 1966), pp. 140-41.

12. The Uses of a Theological Criticism," in *Literature and Religion,* ed, Giles Gunn (New York: Harper & Row, 1971), p. 45.

13. Quoted in N. Jeffares, *W.B.Yeats: Man and Poet* (New York: Barnes & Noble, 1966), p. 38.

14. Wiesel himself suggests that indifference is not only a sin but a punishment in "Storytelling and the Ancient Dialogue," lecture delivered at Temple University, November 15, 1969.

15. T.S. Eliot, "Four Quartets: Little Gidding," in *The Complete Poems and Plays* (New York: Harcourt Brace & Co., 1952), p. 145.

16. For a sensitive discussion of caring, see Milton Mayeroff, *On Caring* (New York: Harper & Row, 1971).

17. Eliot, p. 145.

18. Graham Greene, *The Quiet American* (New York: Viking Press, 1956), p. 230.

19. Jose Ortega y Gasset, "The Self and the Other," trans. Willard Trask, in *The Dehumanization of Art, and Other Writing on Art and Culture* (Garden City, N.Y.: Doubleday & Co., 1956), p. 167. This essay has several parallels with Wiesel in its discussion of the self, thought, and action. Ortega writes: "Unlike all the other beings in the universe, man is never surely *man; on* the contrary, *being man* signifies precisely being always on the point of not being man, being a living problem, an absolute and hazardous adventure, or, as I am wont to say: being, in essence, drama!" And, again: "Man's destiny, then, is primary *action.* We do not live to think, but on the contrary, we think in order that we may succeed in surviving" (pp. 173, 174).

20. Michael evidences this polarity when he speaks: "Mother wants me to be a rabbi. Father would rather have me study for a doctorate in philosophy.... My mother lives body and soul for Hasidism: she devotes her actions and thoughts to God. My father adores reason: he devotes all his time to skepticism about the eternal verities. To make peace between them I promised to study religion *and* philosophy" (*TBW* 30).

21. Interview on the "Today Show," NBC television, May 20, 1974.

22. The similarity between Wiesel and Camus, as it is in many ways, is apparent in this judgment on suicide (see Camus, *The Myth of Sisyphus,* trans. Justin O'Brien [New York: Vintage Books, 1955]).

23. For a discussion of the limits of a logical address to certain questions, see *LT,* pp. 215-37. Of attempts to explain the Holocaust, Wiesel writes: "To find one answer or another, nothing is easier: language can mend anything.

What the answers have in common is that they bear no relation to the questions.... All the words in all the mouths of the philosophers and psychologists are not worth the silent tears of that child and his mother, who live their own death twice" (*LT* 222-23).

24. Henry James. *The Art of the Novel* (New York: Charles Scribner's Sons, 1939), p. 3.

25. I have in mind the work in hermeneutical theory of such figures as the philosophers Martin Heidegger and Paul Ricoeur and the theologians Ernst Fuchs and Heinrich Ott. For a helpful discussion of these matters, see Nathan A. Scott, Jr., "Criticusm and the Religious Horizon," in *Humanities, Religion, and the Arts Tomorrow*, ed. Howard Hunter (New York: Holt, Rinehart & Winston, 1972), pp. 39-60. I am indebted to Scott's essay for the phrase "drama of interrogation" (p. 49). For further consideration of interpretation theory, see Stanley R. Hopper and David L. Miller, eds., *Interpretation: The Poetry of Meaning* (New York: Harbinger, 1967).

26. Wiesel is as much the teacher as he is the artist; as much the guide as the quester. This recognition suggests that the pairs which dominate his literature are two parts of the author himself. Interestingly, Wiesel has recently taken a teaching post at the City college of New York. This reinforces what we already know from his art: that to be a teachaer of great power is perhaps a higher calling than to be a "pure" artist. Or, more accurately stated, the highest calling for Wiesel is to be an artist who, through his storytelling, is at the same time a compelling teacher.

27. "Denis Devlin," *Transition* 27 (April-May 1938): 289.

ELIE WIESEL'S SONG: LOST AND FOUND AGAIN

by Robert McAfee Brown

The mystery of the coming of Messiah, the belief that history moves toward a culmination and fulfillment, is one thing Jews and Christians share in common, even though they stand on opposite sides of a great divide in their interpretation of that hope.

Over forty years ago, Martin Buber, in an essay on "The Two Foci of the Jewish Soul," described the ultimate division between Judaism and Christianity messianically, but also suggested that our point of deepest division was the very area in which we have the most in common. What we have in common, he said, is "a book and an expectation." To the Christian the book is a forecourt, to the Jew it is the sanctuary. But, he went on, "In this place we can dwell together, and together listen to the voice that speaks here." The Christian's expectation, he said, "is directed toward a second coming, ours to a coming which has not been anticipated by a first." But, he continued, "we can wait for the advent of the One together, and there are moments when we may prepare the way before him together."

Buber could state realistically that "Pre-messianically our destinies are divided. Now to the Christian the Jew is the incomprehensibly obdurate man, who declines to see what has happened; and to the Jew the Christian is the incomprehensibly daring man, who affirms in an unredeemed world that its redemption has been accomplished." Even in this division, Buber concluded, we can engage in a common watch, holding fast to our own separate faiths, but caring "more for God himself than for our images of God." (Buber,

Israel and the World, Schocken Books, New York, 1948, pp. 39-40)

It is in this spirit that Christians must approach, with profound gratitude, the throbbing, despairing and yet strangely hopeful song that Eli Wiesel has recovered from his Hasidic childhood and sung again for us in *Ani Maamin* (Random House, $7.50). It is an old song, a song about the Messiah and his failure to appear, a probing that is by turns insistent, pleading, tearful, strident, despairing and yet finally full of hope, both veiled and visible, that can, in spite of all the horror and heartache, enable us to face the future.

The Messianic coming, as Buber intimates, poses different problems for Christians and Jews, and part of the Jewish contribution to Christian Messianism is a reminder that a claim that the Messiah has come is as much a problem as it is a solution. Our problem, of course, is that if the Messianic hope has been fulfilled in Jesus of Nazareth, if redemption has come, evil nevertheless persists demonically in the "redeemed" world. What kind of Messiah is it that we announce as "good news," when the world seems so unchanged by his advent? Indeed, are we not worse off if the world we must announce as the result of Messiah's work within it is a world in which evil persists and suffering continues unchecked? Better no Messiah, it might be claimed, than such a one.

If those are not real "problems" to Christians, then Christians need more than ever to hear the voice of Jews, who, as Buber reminds us, "experience, perhaps more intensely than any other part, the world's lack of redemption." For if Christians have a problem that forces them to ask, "Why, if the Messiah has come, is the world so evil?," Jews also have a problem that forces them to ask, "Why, with the world so evil, has the Messiah not come?" Further questions unfold: What will it take to bring him? If God's children stand in such crushing need of deliverance, why is the deliverance withheld? Can one, in such a world, have any hope for the future? Can one hope that even yet, at this late time, fulfillment and redemption may still come? Most poignant of all, may it not be the case that even if Messiah comes, *he will come too late?*

Wiesel, out of the horror of his own experience at Auschwitz and that of his entire generation, has wrestled with the Messianic problem in an autobiographical chronicle, half a dozen novels, and three books of essays. With infinite variety, the Messianic theme is raised, the question is asked, reponses are sought. The strands of hope seem slender and often virtually invisible, but there always remains a willingness to persist in asking the questions. For if man often seems to be "hope turned to dust," he is also, amazingly, "dust turned to hope." On occasion, most notably perhaps at the conclusion of *The Gates of the Forest,* a hope is expressed that the Messiah is not one man, but can and must be present in all men, whose very presence in the world, singing, praying, crying, and obdurately questioning, is somehow a sign that forsakenness is not the only world.

Ani Maamin is Wiesel's latest and most poignant pressing of the Messianic question. It is the libretto of a contata, set to music by Darius Milhaud, and appears in the text in both French and English. The writing is in blank verse, spare and taut, and its very economy of line, apparent in both languages, contributes to the enormous anguish built up as the questions addressed to God assume an almost unbearable poignancy. *Ani maamin beviat ha-Mashiah* is one of Maimonides' thirteen articles of faith: "I believe in the coming of the Messiah." Wiesel sang the song as a young Hasidic Jew in Transylvania, and believed it. He heard it sung in the death camps and wondered how it could continue to be sung. How could one "believe in the coming of the Messiah" during and after the holocaust? So the song was "lost." Could it possibly be "found" again? The book is Wiesel's exploration of that possibility. No telling can capture it at second-hand, but even a telling at second-hand can force one toward an encounter with the tale at first-hand.

The cantata retells the old story of Abraham, Isaac, and Jacob wandering the earth, only this time they are doing it during the era of the holocaust. They return to the heavenly precincts to plead the cause of the Jews before God in this, the time of greatest tribulation. Each recounts a crucial event from his own past, Abraham as the first to affirm God as the Redeemer of men, Isaac as the one who faced his own sacrifice uncomplainingly, and Jacob as the one who dreamed of a ladder to earth from heaven. Each insists that God has abandoned the future promised to them and their children, a future that has been turned to ashes. Jacob asks:

You promised me to watch over Israel

Where are You? What of your promise?
You promised me blessings for promise?
You promised me blessings for Israel
Is this your blessing?

The patriarchs weep. The angels weep. But God does not weep. God remains silent.

Again they implore him:

Faithful God, behold the torment
That bears your seal,
As does the faith
Of your victims.

The slaughter, the devastation, continues, even as they speak. And with each Jewish death, another fragment of the Temple goes up in flames. Hope is being murdered as never before. But from the celestial tribunal, only silence.

The pleaders intensify their urgency. Abraham did not know that the road from Ur to Canaan would end in Treblinka. Isaac did not know that the vision from Mount Moriah would include Majdanek. Jacob on his way to Bethel did not know

That every road
At dusk
Would lead to Auschwitz.

Each gives an example of the utter destruction the holocaust has brought: a bunker in Warsaw where a Jewish hand had to silence forever the cry of a Jewish child, a death march in a forest where a father cannot console a son, a despairing suicide in a concentration camp. The Chorus supports the patriarchs and cries out to Heaven: "Your children implore you: Hear and answer." But Heaven remains silent.

There follows a plea not only for those who have been slaughtered but also for those who have survived and feel guilty for surviving. There is an anguished question about the divine capriciousness that grants indulgence to executioners while chastisements are inflicted on children.

Finally the silence of heaven is broken, not by God, but by an angel who comes to plead his cause. We hear the familiar arguments offered in the book of Job: Who are men to question the divine power or plan? God has his reasons. Man is not to challenge but to accept. There will be salvation in the end.

But Abraham interrupts with the crucial question:

You showed me messianic times
But what kind of messiah
Is a messiah
Who demands
Six million dead
Before he reveals himself?

The angel can only respond:

God consoles.
That is enough.

At that, the pleading turns to anger. It is *not* enough! It can never be enough. Abraham, Isaac, and Jacob respond that they and their people will never be consoled. It is impossible to be "consoled" for Belsen, or "rewarded" for Birkenau, or "forgetful" of Majdanek.

And so they decide to leave heaven. All they can do in the face of such response is to return to earth and tell their people that there is no hope: "For now it is clear: God knows—and remains silent. God knows—so it must be his will." The executioners win, for God is silent. They step back to leave, and God is still silent.

Each of the patriarchs, as he withdraws from the heavenly throne, recounts a tale in which, in the face of insurmountable odds and a silent heaven, a Jew nevertheless affirms. In one instance, a child expresses belief in the one who is carrying her, futilely, away from the Nazi machine guns. In another, a Jew in a doomed village suddenly "sings/ Of his ancient and lost faith," proclaiming that he still believes in the coming of the Messiah, even though he is late, even though God be unwilling. In a third, a Jew in a death camp on the first night of Passover, unable to celebrate the meal nevertheless can say,

Still, I recite the Haggadah
As though I believe in it.
And I await the prophet Elijah,
As I did long ago,

ending with the affirmation:

I shall wait for you.
And even if you disappoint me
I shall go on waiting.

"Auschwitz," he declares, "has killed Jews/But not their expectation."

After each of these recitals of an indomitable willingness to go on waiting, to refuse to succumb fully to despair, the Narrator informs us that God is being moved. The first time "a tear clouds his eyes," then "a tear streams down God's somber countenance," and finally, "God, surprised by his people, weeps for the third time—and this time without restraint, and with—yes—love." No one sees this weeping. It is veiled from the sight of Abraham, Isaac, and Jacob. But his children's faith has moved him, deeply. Moved him, indeed, in the most literal sense of the word, for as Abraham, Isaac and Jacob go away, the Narrator informs us that although they do not know it, "They are no longer alone: God accompanies them, weeping, smiling, whispering." So finally God *does* speak, and "The word of God continues to be heard. So does the silence of his dead children."

The presence of God is a veiled presence. No one knows of it. But there is another hope as well, suggested in each of the examples that finally moves God to a weeping and smiling engagement with his people. This is the hope that Abraham, Isaac, and Jacob have in their children, in the ongoing life of the Jewish community. Before the machine guns, the child bespoke faith; in the village, a Jew continued to believe; in the death camp an inmate affirmed that, even there, he would wait for the Messiah to come. These acts of presence are not veiled. And it is out of such affirmation, of a presence and a hope both veiled and unveiled, that the story of God's people continues to be written.

Wiesel does not only write a song *about* the hope for a future that lies in Israel's children. He places himself within the circle of that hope by dedicating the book to his own child:

> For Shlomo-Elisha
> Son of Eliezer,
> Son of Shlomo,
> Son of Eliezer.

These are the first words one reads after the title page. They cannot really be read until after one has read the final page. Then they become a smile through tears.

Buber told us that "we can wait for the advent of the One

together, and there are moments when we may prepare the way before him together." Wiesel in *Ani Maamin* makes his contribution to that preparing of the way. He has given us a creation of fearful beauty. He has found a lost song. He has sung it for us. If we are to "prepare the way ... *together*," our own present task is, in the fullness of gratitude, to listen.

... Which would be, of course, a dramatic place to conclude. Who could blame Wiesel, or any Jew—or any person sensitive to the sufferings of others, for that matter—for concluding there? A plea had been made (*Do* something ... send the Messiah) and the plea had been ignored.

But the song does not conclude. It goes on. Something new enters in. The chorus, which has been supportive of the patriarchs' outcry, ceases to echo the outcry, and instead invokes blessing upon them. Blessing! God seems not to provide a blessing, so Israel will provide it. If God remains silent, Jews who have revered his name will not.

ELIE WIESEL: THE JOB OF AUSCHWITZ

by Maurice Friedman

In contemporary literature the meeting of literature and religion stands under the sign of that pervasive existential mistrust that Martin Buber has described as the "eclipse of God." This literature must not be misunderstood as merely atheist, pessimistic, or absurd, as is so often thought. Part of our existential and religious hope lies in our confrontation with that contemporary literature which in its depth asks us *the* religious questions of our time. In our day the only way to the positive, perhaps, is not through the negative certainly, but through the tension of the absurd, the contradictions of modern existence, through the absence of a modern image of meaningful personal and social existence and the attempts to create such an image in response. Our image of hope, therefore, is not the antithesis but the completion of our image of despair. It is the image of a new courage, a new religiousness which can only be reached by contending for meaning within the Dialogue with the Absurd. It is a two-fold revelation of the hidden human image — out of its original hiddenness and out of the denigration and eclipse of the human image in our day.

"How is life with God still possible in a time in which there is an Auschwitz?" writes Martin Buber.

> The estrangement has become too cruel, the hiddenness too deep. One can still "believe" in the God who allowed those things to happen, but can one still speak to Him? Can one still hear His word? ... Dare we recommend to the survivors of Auschwitz, the Job of the gas chambers: "Give thanks unto the Lord, for He is good; for His mercy endureth forever"? ... Do we stand overcome before the hidden face of God like the tragic hero of the Greeks before faceless fate? No, rather even now we contend, we

too, with God.... We do not put up with earthly being;
we struggle for its redemption, and struggling we appeal
to the help of our Lord, who is again and still a hiding one.[1]

Auschwitz is here only a symbol for all of the extermination camps in which, as Buber said when he accepted the
Peace Prize of the German Book Trade, "Millions of my people
and fellow believers were exterminated in a systematic
procedure the organized cruelty of which had no precedent in
human history." Even when one speaks, as I often do, of
Auschwitz and Hiroshima together, we have to realize that we
cannot really compare 6 million deaths with 70,000 or 80,000
or even, as in the bombing of Dresden, 120,000. The figure
staggers the imagination. People the world over have been
moved by *The Diary of Anne Frank* because it enabled them to
experience her part of the holocaust from within. But who can
experience from within the death of 6 million or even a portion
of that many?

This failure of the imagination was also experienced by the
Jews of Europe themselves before they were deported. No one
could really imagine, even in those rare cases where individuals
came back and insisted that the deported were not being taken to
work camps, as they had been told, but to extermination
centers — no one could imagine something which so destroyed
the very cement of social confidence beyond ordinary enmities,
beyond anti-Semitism as it had been known, beyond anything
conceivable, since society itself implies a certain minimal
communication. No one could understand what had never had a
precedent in history—that they were going to be turned into
cakes of soap, such as I myself have seen on Mount Zion in
Jerusalem, with the letters "R.J.F."—"Pure Jewish Fat"—on
them. No one could understand because it had not happened,
because actuality does not grow out of potentiality but the other
way around, because only when it did happen did it become a
very real possibility that can be repeated again and again in
human history, despite the solemn pledge of all the nations at the
United Nations that never again will a genocide be allowed to
take place. The Modern Job begins with the scientific
extermination of six million Jews and a million Gypsies, *and*
with those who have had to continue living in the face of these
unimaginable horrors.

The most impassioned complaint, the most stubborn and

faithful Dialogue with the Absurd, the most moving embodiment of "the Job of the gas chambers" is found in the work of Elie Wiesel, as in the man himself for those of us who know him. His slim volumes form one unified outcry, one sustained protest, one sobbing and singing prayer.

In the first, *Night,* Wiesel tells the story of how he was deported with his family from his Hungarian-Jewish village when he was a child of twelve, how his mother and sister were metamorphosed into the smoke above the crematories, how he and his father suffered through Auschwitz, Buchenwald, and forced winter marches until finally, just before liberation, his father died. For Wiesel the "death of God" came all at once, without preparation—not as a stage in the history of culture but as a terrifying event that turned the pious Hasidic Jew into a Modern Job whose complaint against "the great injustice in the world" can never be silenced.

> Never shall I forget those flames which consumed my Faith forever. Never shall I forget that nocturnal silence which deprived me, for all eternity, of the desire to live. Never shall I forget those moments which murdered my God and my soul and turned my dreams to dust. Never shall I forget these things, even if I am condemned to live as long as God Himself. Never.[2]

On a later day when he watched the hanging of a child with the sad face of an angel, he heard someone behind him groan, "Where is God? Where is He? Where can He be now?" and a voice within him answered: "Where? Here He is—He has been hanged here, on these gallows." When after the liberation of Buchenwald he looked at himself in a mirror, a corpse gazed back at him. "The look in his eyes, as they stared into mine, has never left me."

Wiesel's novels are continuous with the autobiography. In *Dawn* he places this same boy, now called Elisha, in the position of a Jewish terrorist, killing English soldiers in an effort to secure the independence of the Jewish state in Palestine. Elisha had wanted to study philosophy at the Sorbonne in order to rediscover the image of man that had been destroyed for him by the extermination camps: "Where is God to be found? In suffering or in rebellion? When is a man most truly a man? When he submits or when he refuses? Where does suffering lead him?

To purification or to bestiality?" Instead Elisha gives his future to the "Movement," the first group in his knowledge which changes the destiny of the Jew from that of victim to executioner. It is he himself who must execute the English hostage, Captain John Dawson, whom the Movement has sentenced to die as a reprisal for the hanging by the British of one of their number. He comes to realize, in taking upon himself an act so absolute as killing, that he is making his father, his mother, his teacher, his friends into murderers. He cannot rid himself of the impression that he has donned the field-gray uniform of the Nazi S.S. officer.

Elisha rediscoveres the presence of God when he spends the last hour with the hostage before shooting him. His victim-to-be is sorry for Elisha and troubled by him — an eighteen-year-old turned terrorist — while Elisha tries in vain to hate him as if the coming of the Messiah were dependent upon the Jews finally learning "to hate those who have humiliated and from time to time exterminated them." But when he kills John Dawson, he feels that he has killed himself, that he himself has become the night.[3]

In *The Accident* this same child of *Night*, somewhat older and now an Israeli correspondent at the United Nations, is almost killed by a taxi, and in the course of a long and painful recovery confronts the fact that he had seen the taxi, that he wanted to die, that he did not fight to stay alive even in the hospital but left the burden entirely on the doctor. Even "love" gives him no incentive for living in the present. He is one of the "spiritual cripples" whom the world does not dare to look in the eye, amputees who have lost not their legs or their eyes but their will and their taste for life. The sufferer is the pariah, the Modern Exile who must live apart from men because he tells them something about their common humanity that they cannot bear.

> Suffering pulls us farther away from other human beings.
> It builds a wall made of cries and contempt to separate us.
> men cast aside the one who has known pure suffering,
> if they cannot make a god out of him; the one who tells
> them: I suffered not because I was God, nor because I was
> a saint trying to imitate Him, but only because I am a
> Men cast aside the one who has known pure suffering,
> if they cannot make a god out of him; the one who tells

ambitions; such a man frightens men, because he makes them feel ashamed.... He poisons the air. He makes it unfit for breathing. He takes away from joy its spontaneity and its justification. He kills hope and the will to live.[4]

The accident occurs the day after he has entered into an agreement with his mistress Kathleen that he knows is meaningless—an agreement to let her make him happy and forget the past.

In the last chapter of *The Accident*, Wiesel introduces the Hungarian painter Gyula who is at once foil and image of man and who provides the final judgment on the hero.

Gyula was a living rock. A giant in every sense of the word. Tall, robust, gray and rebellious hair, mocking and burning eyes; he pushed aside everything around him: altars, ideas, mountains. Everything trembled, vibrated, at his touch, at the sight of him.... We encouraged each other to stick it out, not to make compromises, not to come to terms with life, not to accept easy victories.[5]

Gyula visits the hospital room repeatedly to do his portrait. He tries to tell Gyula his secret—that the accident was no accident, that on the deepest level he wanted to die—but Gyula will not listen. Yet when Gyula shows him the completed painting, he knows that he has guessed. The eyes are those of "a man who had seen God commit the most unforgivable crime: to kill without reason." Gyula confronts his friend's will to death with the silent offer of friendship—a proof that if God is dead, man is alive. Man's duty is to make suffering cease, not to increase it, Gyula tells him. This means a rejection of the lucidity that exchanges the light of hope for the clear darkness of the absurd.

"Lucidity is fate's victory, not man's. It is an act of freedom that carries within itself the negation of freedom. Man must keep moving, searching, weighing, holding out his hand, offering himself, inventing himself." ... "The dead, because they are no longer free, are no longer able to suffer. Only the living can. Kathleen is alive. I am alive. You must think of us. Not of them."[6]

Gyula poses the choice of life or death, but to Eliezer only lies can make happiness possible while the truth is on the side of death. Sensing his decision for death by the intensity with which he looks at the painting, Gyula puts a match to the canvas and burns it up. "No!" Eliezer exclaims in despair. "Don't do that! Gyula, don't do it!" For a long time after Gyula has closed the door behind him, he weeps. Gyula's angry act of friendship brings tears to the eyes of the man who cannot weep and brings him one step forward toward the Modern Job.

Next to Camus' *The Plague*, the clearest presentation in literature of the progression through the Modern Promethean to the Modern Job is Wiesel's novel *The Town Beyond the Wall*. The plot of the book is the return of Michael after the war to his native Hungarian city. Entering by means of the black market, the only organization that can get through the "Iron Curtain," he is arrested by the police and forced to say "prayers," i.e., to stand eight hours at a stretch before a wall without moving, eating, or drinking. The police hope to extract from him a confession as to who helped him get into the country—a confession that would condemn his friend Pedro to death or imprisonment—but they have reckoned without his tenacious loyalty to his friend and his capacity to endure by going inward to the sources of memory.

After the war and the extermination camps, Michael went to Paris and lived in utter solitude in order to seek his God, to track him down. Even in his determination not to give in so easily as Job, even in his insistence that he will be a match for God and will defy his inhuman Justice, he still remains within his dialogue with his God. "He took my childhood; I have a right to ask Him what He did with it." Michael combines the Modern Promethean and the Modern Job, and he shows the link between them: In our time man *has* to go through the first to reach the second, but he may not remain in the first. At the death of the "little prince"—a Jewish boy pampered by the Nazis in the concentration camps only to die under a truck in Paris— Michael's suffering leads him to the verge of madness.

> An immense wrath, savage and destructive, welled up suddenly in Michael. His eyes flashed. The little prince's death—this death—was too unjust, too absurd. He wanted to pit himself against the angel as Jacob had: fell him with a blow, trample him. One gesture, just one, but a gesture in proportion to his misery.[7]

But Michael recognizes that greater than the mad revolt of the Modern Promethean is the tension of the Modern Job who refuses to go mad. "The man who chooses death is following an impulse of liberation from the self; so is the man who chooses madness.... To keep our balance then is the most difficult and absurd struggle in human existence." Madness is an easy, comfortable escape, a once-for-all act of free will that destroys freedom. Michael understands that madness represents a moral choice as well as a psychological compulsion. Michael's friend Pedro, "a living rock" like Gyula, warns him against the mad revolt which tempts him.

> "You frighten me," Pedro said. "You want to eliminate suffering by pushing it to the extreme: to madness. To say 'I suffer, therefore I am' is to become the enemy of man. What you must say is 'I suffer, therefore you are.' Camus wrote somewhere that to protest against a universe of unhappiness you had to create happiness. That's an arrow pointing the way: it leads to another human being. And not via absurdity."[8]

These, of all Pedro's words, are the ones that later come to Michael's aid.

In the prison cell — Michael's last "prayer" — Michael comes closest of all to madness, to "a door opening onto a forest, onto the liberty in which anything is permitted, anything is possible." Michael is obsessed by King Lear "who preferred suffering at the hands of men to flight into a trackless desert," who faced treason and cowardice directly and said, "I am here and nowhere else!" Yet he berates him for not going mad as a way of spitting in their faces, protesting against pain and injustice, rejecting their life and their sanity. Like Ivan Karamazov, Michael wants "to turn his ticket in" — not to reject God but his world. Madness is, indeed, the way of the Modern Promethean — Melville's Captain Ahab and Dostoevsky's Kirilov and Ivan. To resist it without glossing over *or* submitting to the suffering that gives rise to it is the way of the Modern Job. The Pedro whom Michael now imagines coming to speak with him in his cell points this latter way and shows it for the sober, courageous revolt that it is:

> "The only valuable protest, or attitude, is one rooted in the uncertain soil of humanity. Remaining human — in spite of all temptations and humiliations — is the only way

to hold your own against the Other, whatever it may
be.... To see liberty only in madness is wrong: liberation,
yes; liberty, no."[9]

Michael finds the alternative to going mad in making
himself responsible for his prison cellmate, a young boy who is
completely silent and, until he responds to Michael's heartbreaking efforts, completely out of touch. In bringing Eliezer
back into dialogue Michael brings himself back to humanity.
Pedro has taught Michael and Michael teaches Eliezer the
necessity of clinging to humanity. "It's in humanity itself that
we find both our question and the strength to keep it within
limits." To flee to a nirvana through a considered indifference
or a sick apathy "is to oppose humanity in the most absurd,
useless, and comfortable manner possible." Like Doctor Rieux
in *The Plague,* Michael recognizes that "It's harder to remain
human than to try to leap beyond humanity." The real heights
and the real depths of humanity are found "at your own level, in
simple and honest conversation, in glances heavy with existence." Man asks the question within himself ever more deeply,
he feels ever more intimately the existence of an unknowable
answer, and Michael brings both of these into the dialogue with
Eliezer, into his Dialogue with the Absurd.

The Modern Job does not contend with an entirely alien
Other, hostile and indifferent, such as Captain Ahab's White
Whale or Caligula's absurd. Even the absurd reality over
against us has a meaning — a meaning which can only be
revealed in our trusting and contending. The dialogue, or duel,
between man and his God does not end in nothingness: "As the
liberation of the one was bound to the liberation of the other,"
says the legend at the end of the novel, "they renewed the
ancient dialogue whose echoes come to us in the night, charged
with hatred, with remorse, and most of all, with infinite
yearning."

Malach, the Hebrew word that is usually translated
"angel," actually means "messenger." *The Gates of the Forest* is
the story of the lasting effect of two "messengers" on the life of
Gregor, a young Jewish refugee. Gavriel, the nameless
messenger to whom he gives his own Hebrew name, and the
much more tangible Leib the Lion, accompany him — in person
or in memory — through the spring when he hides from the

Nazis in a cave in the forest, through summer when he plays the role of a feebleminded mute in the village where Maria, the former family servant, passes him off as her nephew, through autumn when he joins the partisans fighting under the leadership of his childhood friend, Leib the Lion, and through winter when he seeks a way forward in postwar New York where he has gone with his wife Clara, once the girl friend of Leib.

Gavriel tells Gregor that the Messiah has already come, that he is among men, that nonetheless the horror has taken place, and that all that is left is to learn to laugh in the face of the horror—a terrible, mad laugh that defies the absurd. It is the laugh of a man poised midway between the Modern Promethean and the Modern Job and holding the tension of both. The message which this messenger brings Gregor is that of the "final solution," the unsuspected extermination of the Jews. His father will not come back. No one will come back. His family has left without hope of return.

When the Hungarian soldiers come with dogs, Gavriel gives himself up to prevent their discovering Gregor. Before going, he tells Gregor of how he discovered the Messiah in a simple beadle who at night wept for the destruction of the Temple, for the exile of Israel and that of the Shekinah. When the Nazis came, Gavriel went to Moshe the Silent and demanded that he do his duty and disobey God for the sake of saving from annihilation the people of the witness, the martyr people, the people of the covenant. But the "Messiah" laid down his arms without resisting and let himself be taken prisoner and executed. "I tell you, Gregor," says Gavriel, "that hope is no longer possible nor permitted: ... the Messiah has come and the world has remained what it was: an immense butchery." When Gregor goes to live with Maria in her village and impersonates a deaf-mute, he is forced to play Judas at the school play and is almost killed in the frenzy of the crowd. "Miraculously" casting off his dumbness and speaking with the voice of a prophet, he forces the people, including the priest, to beg Judas' pardon—for it is *he*, not Jesus, who is the crucified one. Yet Gregor resists his desire for vengeance. When he announces that he is not the son of Maria's sister Illeana but a Jew, a smile not of victory but of pity illuminates his face.

Escaping to the forest, he makes contact with a band of

Jewish partisans and rediscovers his childhood friend Leib the Lion. When they were boys, Leib had taught him to fight the gang of children that descended on them on their way to school with cries of "dirty Jews!" and "Christ-killers!" on their lips. The mythic proportions that Leib took on then in Gregor's eyes are now realized in fact in his role as leader of the Jewish partisans, a latter-day Bar Kochba. Gregor informs Leib of what has been known for a long time already in Washington, London, and Stockholm but which no one had taken the trouble to radio to the Jews of Transylvania — that the deported Jews were not being taken to factories or labor camps but to extermination centers. The shocked and almost unbelieving Leib orders an attempt to liberate Gavriel from prison to ascertain the truth of Gregor's report and is captured himself in the process. It falls on Gregor to inform the other partisans that their leader is taken and to discover through their dismay and grief the image of man that he represented for them:

> Every one of his words and gestures enriched their hope by giving to it simplicity and humility: we shall prevail, for inasmuch as it has any meaning, victory is within the domain of the man and of that which elevates rather than denies him.[10]

Gregor makes the Promethean laughter of Gavriel and the Jobian courage of Leib his own, and they sustain him and give him strength until that distant day in postwar New York when he is confronted by a Hasidic rabbi who recognizes both his suffering and his pride. When Gregor admits that what he wants is that the rebbe cease to pray and that he howl instead, the rebbe, with a movement of revolt, says to him, slowly, accentuating every word and stopping after every phrase: "Who has told you that force comes from a cry and not from a prayer, from anger and not from compassion? . . . The man who sings is the brother of him who goes to his death fighting." The dancing, the singing, the joy of the Hasid is *in spite of* the fact that all reason for dancing, singing, and joy has been taken from him.

> "He's guilty; do you think I don't know it? That I have no eyes to see, no ears to hear? That my heart doesn't revolt? That I have no desire to beat my head against the wall and shout like a madman, to give rein to my sorrow and disappointment? Yes, he is guilty. He has become an ally

of evil, of death, of murder, but the problem is still not solved."[11]

The revolt of the Modern Promethean is unmasked by the rebbe as only a romantic gesture. It still leaves the question of what to do, of how to live, of the direction from which salvation and hope must come.

Unable to bear any longer the way his wife Clara betrays him by remaining faithful to her first lover, the dead Leib, Gregor has resolved to leave her. Now, after joining a *minyan* in reciting the *kaddish*—the prayer for the dead—he knows that he will return to Clara to take up again the battle of winning her back to the present, to life. It does not matter whether or not the Messiah comes, Gregor realizes, or the fact that he is too late. If we will be sincere, humble, and strong, the Messiah will come—every day, a thousand times a day—for he is not a single man but all men. When Clara learns to sing again and Gregor to weep, it will be he that sings and weeps in them.

Gregor's last *kaddish* is for Leib the Lion, his old comrade in battle, who, while alive, incarnated in himself what is immortal in man. This prayer for the dead is also a prayer for life—a prayer that the dead Leib will allow Gregor and Clara to live, but also that, despite their loyalty to the past, Eliezer, the "I" of *The Accident,* Michael, Gregor, and Elie Wiesel himself will be able to live for the living and not for the dead. It is a prayer for all of us—for we are all the inheritors of Auschwitz and Hiroshima—that we work our way through to the trust and contending of the Job of Auschwitz who meets the living present, including the absurd, with the courage that these "messengers on high" have bequeathed.

The original title of Wiesel's book *Chants des Morts* ("Songs of the Dead") might well be the title of all his books. But so also might be the English title, *Legends of Our Time.* Elie Wiesel, as anyone knows who has ever heard him speak, belongs to the oldest profession in the world, that of the storyteller—the man who preserves the awesome life of the tribe in the form of myths and legends—dramatic events— rather than of connected historical accounts. The art of story-telling was an oral one for countless millennia before it became a written one as well. Wiesel retains this oral quality not only in his speaking but also in his writing. In a series of poignant and powerful writings, he has woven together words and silence into tales of unexampled beauty and terror. In each successive work he has wrested an image of humanity from his Dialogue with the Absurd—his contending with the Nazi holocaust and the monstrous shadow which it cast on his life. The Job of Auschwitz "will always take the side of man confronted with the Absolute." God's presence, or his absence, at Treblinka or Maidanek "poses a problem which will forever remain insoluble." Nor does it matter that "loss of faith for some equaled discovery of God for others." Both stood within the Modern Job's Dialogue with the Absurd: "Both answered the same need to take a stand, the same impulse to rebel. In both cases it was an accusation."

"My generation has been robbed of everything, even of our cemeteries," says Wiesel in *Legends of Our Time*.[12] Where there are no cemeteries, the dead refuse to stay dead, and the living must give proper burial through creating a structure within which mourning can take place. The whole of Wiesel's writing is just such a work of mourning, of witnessing to the living dead: "The act of writing is for me often nothing more than the secret or conscious desire to carve words on a tombstone: to the memory of a town forever vanished, to the memory of a childhood in exile, to the memory of all those I loved and who, before I could tell them I loved them, went away." These include his playmates, his teachers, Moshe the Madman, the beadle, and his family—all from his town of Sighet. But they also include men whom he knew in the extermination camps, such as the man who went laughing to his death after he had fasted on Yom Kippur as a Job of Auschwitz must fast: "Not out of obedience, but out of defiance."

"Man defines himself by what disturbs him and not by what reassures him." Elie Wiesel lets himself be disturbed, and he disturbs us by insisting, in the face of *all* who turn away from it, on "the guilt we share." Witnessing the trial of Eichmann, Wiesel conducts a worldwide trial: of the indigenous populations of Hungary and Poland whose eagerness to become *Judenrein* alone made it possible for "the cattle trains with their suffocating human cargo" to "roll swiftly into the night"; of "the whole outside world, which looked on in a kind of paralysis and passively allowed" the murder of six million Jews, a number that could never have been reached had Roosevelt,

Churchill, and the pope let loose an avalanche of angry protestations; of the American Jewish community which did not use its political and financial powers to move heaven and earth to save five to ten thousand Jews from murder each day; of Chaim Weizmann who put off for two weeks the messenger of the holocaust who had told him that "every passing day meant the lives of at least ten thousand Jews" ("How did Brand not go stark raving mad?" Wiesel asks.); of Gideon Hausner, Ben-Gurion, and the Israelis who tried Eichmann without crying out "in a voice loud enough to be heard by three generations: We never attempted the impossible — we never even exhausted the possible." From this trial, Wiesel concludes that "with the advent of the Nazi regime in Germany, humanity became witness to what Martin Buber would call an eclipse of God." It was above all, in fact, in the name of the "Job of Auschwitz," that Buber called this an age of the "eclipse of God."

It is Auschwitz that will engender Hiroshima and perhaps that extinction of the human race by nuclear warfare that "will be the punishment for Auschwitz, where, in the ashes, the hope of man was extinguished." At the time of the holocaust, those outside did not speak out. "One need only glimpse through the newspapers of the period to become disgusted with the human adventure on this earth." Nor were the inmates of the camps ignorant of this. Their seemingly weak "acceptance" of their death became, in consequence, "an act of lucidity, a protest" not only against their torturers, but also against the rest of humanity that had abandoned, excluded, and rejected them. "It is as though every country — and not only Germany — had decided to see the Jew as a kind of subhuman species" whose disappearance did not weigh on the conscience since the concept of brotherhood did not apply to him.

The most masterful expression of Wiesel's fight for the hidden image of man is his haunting and compelling novel of the Six Day War, *A Beggar in Jerusalem*. In *A Beggar in Jerusalem* the holocaust and the threat of extermination that seemed to hover over the people of the state of Israel on the eve of the Six Day War fuse into one reality. "They were alone," writes Wiesel, "as earlier in Europe in the time of *Night*." Perhaps it was the overwhelming feeling that Wiesel himself was the first to articulate — that we could not allow this extermination to happen twice in one lifetime — that gives this book a different time sense from all his other novels. In all of them there are flashbacks and the easy—and enormously painful—intermingling of what has been and what is. But only in *A Beggar* are all the ages present simultaneously. One of the circle of "beggars" who sit before the Wall during the long and story-laden nights after the Six Day War tells of when he came up to the man Jesus as he hung on the cross and said to him, "They will kill millions of your people in your name," at which Jesus wept so bitterly that the man who stood beneath him wept too. In *A Beggar*, as in *One Generation After*, there appears the bitter irony that alive, Jesus, the Jew, is the enemy of mankind; whereas once he is safely dead he becomes their God. "We have been crucified six million times," Wiesel seems to say, "and no amount of worship of the crucified ones will stay the hand of the next slayer who comes looking for a victim."

The plot of *A Beggar*, insofar as there is one, is the story of two men, David and Katriel, the one present throughout, the other both present and absent. We come to feel that David and Katriel are one person even before David is recognized by Katriel's wife Malka, whom he has never met before yet who is his wife. Nor is it clear to David which one of them, himself or Katriel, is "the beggar of Jerusalem"—the man who will come and tell you your own story in such a way that you will recognize in it your life and death.

Commenting on those Jews who wished, before the Six Day War, to define themselves simply as men and only accidentally as Jews, Wiesel neatly reverses the formula and suggests that in our day "one cannot be a man without assuming the condition of the Jew." "The Jew is the most exposed person in the world today," wrote Martin Buber in 1933. The inhumanity which has been unleashed upon the Jew since then so threatens the humanity of all men that only in sharing that exposure can any man today become man. Today we must all suffer with the "Modern Exile" or lose our birthright as men. When David recognizes himself as the permanently exiled stranger in a story of Katriel's, he speaks for every hero of Wiesel's novels and for Wiesel too:

> Disguised as a stranger, I might have been living beside women who were mistaking me for someone else. The real me remained below, in the kingdom of the night, prisoner of the dead. . . . I was nothing more than an echo

of voices long since extinguished.... I thought I was living my own life. I was only inventing it.[13]

This state of exile is also the state of God today, *A Beggar in Jerusalem* suggests. The Messiah does not dwell above in glory, but below in the suffering and exposure of men. God too has need of a witness: "In the beginning was the Word; the Word is the history of man; and man is the history of God." The Shekinah, the indwelling Glory of God, remains in Jerusalem yet follows all Jews everywhere into exile. The Shekinah dwells in the contradiction, and the greatest and most tormenting contradiction of all is to kill for the sake of God men who are created in the image of God: "He who kills kills God. Each murder is a suicide of which the Eternal is eternally the victim." This contradiction is similar to the question that haunts Elie Wiesel throughout each of his novels: How is it possible to live for the living without betraying the dead?

The answer to this question lies in bringing forth from its concealment the hidden human image. If man is created in the image of God, then the only way that that image can be transmitted is through transmitting the image of man. It is for this that a whole people set out to march for a third time, and with the living marched the dead: "Israel conquered because its army, its people included six million additional names." Only Elie Wiesel in our generation has been capable of uniting the holocaust and the emergence and survival of the state of Israel without denying the mystery or reality of either or turning one into historical cause and the other into historical effect. In this sense, all of Elie's other books were preparations for *A Beggar in Jerusalem;* for only here do the living fight *with* the dead and not against them, only here is it possible for David to stay with Malka despite their loyalty to Katriel. By its dedication, "For Marion," and by the unification of past and present in the figures of Katriel, Malka, and David, *A Beggar in Jerusalem* convinced me that Elie too was now ready to live in the present, without turning his back on the reality of the past.

In what he himself says will be his final book on the holocaust, *One Generation After,*[14] Wiesel repeatedly asserts that in the holocaust man betrayed his image and that whether or not the murder of a million children makes any historical sense, it denies and condemns man. The Job of Auschwitz hears above all the command to witness to what has happened, recalling and telling every detail, writing down his testimony moments before dying in agony, surviving in order to be able to tell—to howl against the wall of death that crushed a whole people. It is only this—and the hope that someone might listen to this recounting—that enables the Job of Auschwitz to continue at all. Nothing so concisely sums up Elie Wiesel's mission as a person and a writer as his own sentence, "I do not demand of the raconteur that he play the role of master but that he fulfill his duty as messenger and as witness." What it means to "hold fast to one's integrity" in this calling of messenger and witness Wiesel has shown us in every one of his novels and stories and in *Night* and *The Jews of Silence*.

Wiesel's identification with the state of Israel does not entail a hatred for Israel's enemies. The victorious Jew "is no longer a victim, but he will never become a torturer" or seek to break the will of the vanquished. The state of Israel in no way cancels out the extermination of six million Jews. It may nonetheless be permitted to the Job of Auschwitz—the survivor who trusts *and* contends and holds fast to the integrity of *man* in so doing—to see in Israel "a victory over the absurd and the inhuman." "I belong to a generation," writes Elie Wiesel, "that has not known many such victories." This victory is not incompatible with the continued exile of the Shekinah, the mark of an unredeemed world, as the last chapter of *A Beggar in Jerusalem* makes clear. David looks at Malka, *his* wife and not Katriel's, touches her and loves loving her; yet something in him shrivels and rebels, and he is compelled to walk so as to punish his body for keeping time imprisoned and punish his spirit for having resisted. If the madmen that dwell in David's soul (the madmen who have reappeared constantly in Elie Wiesel's novels) come close to being appeased in Jerusalem, the one city where time welcomes the weary exile instead of expelling him, the key to peace is still in Katriel, and it is perhaps David who is dead and Katriel the survivor. David is the beggar of Jerusalem who knows how to wait but who will also have to decide, to retrace his steps, to find the forgotten road back that no one walks with impunity.

A victor, he? Victory does not prevent suffering from having existed, nor death from having taken its toll. How can one work for the living without by that very act betraying those who are absent? . . . Of course, the mystery of good is no less disturbing than the mystery of evil. But one does not cancel out the other. Man alone is capable of uniting them by remembering.[15]

Even Wiesel's concern with "the Jews of silence"—the Jews of the Soviet Union the discrimination against whom Wiesel has done more than any other person in the world to make known—stands under the sign of the Modern Job. *Simhat-Torah,* the day of the rejoicing in the giving of the Torah, "will henceforth be associated with the Jews of silence," Wiesel testifies after going to Moscow for a second time to see the thousands of young Jews, deprived of their heritage, publicly affirming and celebrating their existence as Jews. "For those who participate in their dancing, each moment becomes privileged: a victory over silence." From these Soviet Jews Wiesel learned that those who make of their Judaism a song are of equal value with those who make of it a prayer. "The staunchest Hasid could learn from the most assimilated Jewish student in Moscow how to rejoice and how to transform his song into an act of belief and defiance." Out of a situation of constraint these young Jews made an act of choice, out of what should break and humiliate them they drew their force of resistance.

In *One Generation After,* Wiesel tells a young German of the New Left that he confuses the lack of discipline with independence, feeling the need to challenge the regime—whatever it may be—and reject authority—whatever its source. He is, in short the Modern Promethean. Wiesel wants him to be angry at being born "into the midst of a fanaticized and stubborn people that repudiated its Führer only after his military defeats and not for his crimes." If he does not despise his guilty fathers, he will become inhuman himself and unworthy of redemption. Wiesel demands that he face up to the reality of the past or become guilty of the holocaust himself. "I shall not hate you," Wiesel declares in an echo of Camus' "Letter to a Nazi Friend" that he quotes from at the head of his essay, but "I shall denounce, unmask, and fight you with all my power."

In "To a Young Jew of Today" God himself is brought

to trial as he was by Job and two and a half millennia later by the Hasidic rebbe Levi Yitzak of Berditshev. "If God is an answer, it must be the wrong answer." There is no answer: "the agony of the believer equals the bewilderment of the non-believer." All there is, is a question which man must live and formulate and in so doing challenge God. This challenge is permissible, indeed required. "He who says no to God is not necessarily a renegade. . . . One can say anything as long as it is for man, not against him, as long as one remains inside the covenant." Here contending means faithfulness; to betray the present means to destroy the past, whereas to fulfill oneself means choosing to be a link "between the primary silence of creation and the silence that weighed on Treblinka."

The task of the Job of Auschwitz is contending for meaning within the Dialogue with the Absurd. If he rakes over the ashes of the holocaust, it is because "to be a Jew today . . . means to testify," to bear witness with fervent, if saddened, joy to the Israel that is and to bear witness with "restrained, harnessed anger, free of sterile bitterness" to the world of the six million Jews that is no longer. "For the contemporary Jewish writer, there can be no theme more human, no project more universal."

"Was it not a mistake to testify, and by that very act, affirm their faith in man and word?" asks Wiesel, and replies for himself and the Job of Auschwitz, "I know of at least one who often feels like answering yes." This note of doubt and bitterness also belongs to the Job of Auschwitz as it did to the original Job. He would be a dishonest rebel if he did not sometimes say with Wiesel: "Nothing had been learned; Auschwitz has not even served as warning. For more detailed information, consult your daily newspaper." The storyteller is left with a sense of guilt and impotence. Writing itself is called in question; for by its uniqueness the holocaust defies literature. The storyteller who sees himself essentially as a witness realizes in anguish that he cannot "approach this universe of darkness without turning into a pedlar of night and agony." The messenger unable to deliver his message knows that "no image is sufficiently demented, no cry sufficiently blasphemous to illustrate the plight of a single victim, resigned or rebellious." And yet the story had to be told for the sake of our children. "We needed to face the dead again and again, in order ... to seek among them, beyond all contradiction and absurdity, a symbol, a beginning of promise."

It is precisely this tension between the powerful urge to keep silent and the equally powerful call to witness that forms the heart of Wiesel's novel *The Oath*. Set in two time periods before and after the holocaust, *The Oath* only gradually reveals itself as the most terrifying of Wiesel's works in its suggestion of the possibility of the permanent eclipse of the hidden human image. It is, by the same token, a powerful comment on the holocaust itself—not just as a sickness of the Nazis or of modern man but of humanity. In the first instance, this is European, Christian humanity, but in the end it is the human as such that is tainted by senseless hatred and ultimate stupidity.

The Oath is structured around a dialogue between an old man with a terrible secret protected by a solemn communal vow and a young man contemplating suicide who just thereby tempts him to break his vow. On a deeper level still, it is the hidden image of Moshe the Madman, a recurrent figure through each of Wiesel's works, and the story of Kolvillàg, a "small town, somewhere between the Dnieper and the Carpathians." The story of Kolvillàg is an awesome embodiment of Rabbi Nachman of Bratzlav's parable of a town that contains all the towns of the world. In this town is a street that contains all the streets of the world, and in this street a house that contains all the houses of the world, and in this house a room that contains all the rooms of the world, and in this room a man who contains all the people in the world, and this man laughs—with the laughter of madness!

The Oath begins and ends with visions of apocalyptic terror and of the dread beast of the Apocalypse. The beast at work was "alternately savage and attentive, radiant and hideous, ... reducing to shreds whoever saw it at close range," turning the town into "a desecrated, pillaged cemetery," crushing all its inhabitants into a twisted and tortured monster with a hundred eyes and a thousand mouths all of which were spitting terror. Witness to this ultimate destruction, the narrator has not been silent by choice. Rather silence has been his master, drawing "its strength and secret from a savagely demented universe doomed by its wretched and deadly past."

If, despite this, the old man reveals all to the youth, it is because of a residue of responsibility which forms the final stage of every encounter even in the era of the eclipse of the human. "Whoever says 'I' creates the 'you.' Such is the trap of every conscience. The 'I' signifies both solitude and rejection of solitude." The narrator admonishes the youth not to oppose evil to evil, committing one more injustice by killing himself. "'I am not telling you not to despair of man, but not to offer death one more victim, one more victory.'" Every death is absurd, useless, ugly. Whether life has a meaning or not, what counts is not to make a gift of it to death. "It is not by legitimizing suffering—and what is death if not the paroxysm of suffering—that one can disarm it." To defeat evil one must help one's fellowman; to triumph over death one must begin by saving one's brother.

The name of the old man is Azriel, but he is also called by some Katriel. Like Wiesel's own teacher, whom he portrays in "The Wandering Jew" in *Legends of Our Time,* Azriel is a mysterious figure, someone equally at ease quoting from the Talmud or Mao Tse-tung, master of seven ancient tongues and a dozen living ones, "haughty with the powerful, humble with the deprived," and above all a *Na-venadnik,* one whose destiny is never to put down roots in any one place. Azriel's chronicler father and his mad teacher Moshe, by making him the repository of their tragic truths, doomed him to be a survivor, a messenger, and a perpetual exile—revealing and attaching himself to no one, watching over the inhabitants of the secret world inside him. In his daydreams it is not he but his village that is roaming the roads in search of help and redemption: He is but a link, the hyphen between countless communities.

There is nothing paradoxical in this; for Azriel's message is the message of silence—of events too monstrous to be told, too bewildering to be imagined. It is the silence of the holocaust, the burden of which the youth of today have inherited without its mystery. The Exterminating Angel has turned all men into victims, not least those who attempt to use its services. The culmination of fanaticism and stupidity affects equally victims and executioners. "Whoever kills, kills himself; whoever preaches murder will be murdered. One may not accept any meaning imposed on death by the living. Just as every murder is a suicide, every suicide, is a murder." To kill the other, like the sin of Cain, is to murder the brother in oneself. To kill oneself is to murder oneself in one's brother.

A central motif in *The Oath*, as in *The Gates of the Forest*, is messianism—the inverted messianism of a cursed century. Man clamors for the Messiah, but he is fascinated by death. The Christian Messiah expires on the cross, leaving others to bear his shame. But the Jewish Messiah survives all generations, perhaps ashamed to reveal himself or ashamed for a world in which men claim to be brothers and are nothing but wild, solitary beasts. "In these days exile is becoming ever harsher. To have hope in God is to have hope against God." "What is the Messiah," said Moshe to Azriel, "if not man transcending his solitude in order to make his fellow-man less solitary?" "Every truth that shuts you in, that does not lead to others, is inhuman." In defying Moshe's vow of silence, Azriel is allowing Moshe, the hidden image of the human, to speak through him to the young man. Conversely, in forcing Azriel to reinvent a meaning to his quest, the young man is unwittingly helping Azriel even as Azriel is helping him. "May God save you not from suffering but from indifference to suffering," Moshe had said to Azriel, and it is out of gratitude to the young man for saving him from this indifference that Azriel breaks his oath.

Moshe is a great Kabbalist with miraculous powers who channels his fervor into prayer, study—and madness. Moshe takes as his only disciple Azriel, the son of Ahmuel—the chronicler responsible in his generation for the Book of Kolvillàg. Both—Shmuel and Moshe—are trying to attain the same messianic goal, the one through memory of the past, the other through imagination of the future. The Messiah, Moshe tells Azriel, will not come to save men from death but from boredom, mediocrity, the commonplaces of routine. Yet when Moshe is married to a homely girl by a maneuver of the community, he brings his understanding of the messianic into his tender and confirming relationship with his wife Leah:

> He knew that nothing justifies the pain man causes another. Any messiah in whose name men are tortured can only be a false messiah. It is by diminishing evil, present and real evil, experienced evil, that one builds the city of the sun. It is by helping the person who looks at

> you with tears in his eyes, needing help, needing you or
> at least your presence, that you may attain perfection.[16]

When the Jews of Kolvillàg are threatened with a pogrom triggered by the disappearance of a Christian hoodlum who torments birds and children alike, Moshe takes it upon himself to save the community by meeting the prefect's demand for a Jewish name on which the pin the supposed murder. Beaten into unconsciousness by the sadistic sergeant to whom he "confesses," Moshe takes on the role of a Modern Job. "Nothing justifies suffering," he thinks, but "nobody is required to explain it, only to fight it." One cannot confer a meaning on death.

> "To turn death into a philosophy is not Jewish. To turn
> it into a theology is anti-Jewish. Whoever praises death
> ends up either serving or totally ignoring it.... We ...
> consider death the primary defect and injustice inherent
> in creation. To die for God is to die against God. For us,
> man's ultimate confrontation is only with God."[17]

"What is essential," Moshe tells the boy Azriel, "is to live to the limit. Let your words be shouts or silence but ... nothing in between. Let your desire be absolute and your wait as well.... Whoever walks in the night, moves against night."

Moshe's desire to be a martyr for the sake of Israel is not granted, for once stirred up, the senseless hatred will not stop until everything is destroyed. Through the intervention of the friendly prefect, Moshe is allowed to summon the whole of the Jewish community to an extraordinary session where he sweeps everyone up into his own rebellion against the traditional Jewish task of pleasing God by becoming the illustrations of their own tales of martyrdom. Jewish memory, it was held, robbed the executioner of his final victory by preventing his attempts to erase the evidence of his cruelty, haunting his conscience, and warning humanity present and future of his crimes. Murdered, plundered, humiliated, oppressed, expelled from society and history, forbidden the right to laugh or sing or even cry, the surviving Jews turned their ordeal into "a legend destined for men of good will." "The more they hate us, the more we shout our love of man." But now, says Moshe the Madman, the time has come to put an end to this Jewish role of being mankind's memory and heart.

"Now we shall adopt a new way: silence." By refusing to testify anymore, we can break the link between suffering and the history of suffering, thereby forestalling future abominations. With all the mystic power till now held in check, Moshe leads the whole community to take an oath that whoever may survive the massacre and humiliation which await the Jews of Kolvillàg will go to their graves without speaking of it, and he seals this oath by placing the entire people of Israel under the sign of the *Herem*—the dread word of excommunication and damnation!

What rules in Kolvillàg just before the attack is fear, fear "ready to rob you of vision and life and of your very desire to go on living." Heralding disaster, fear becomes disaster." Fear operates in the besieged community of Kolvillàg exactly as the plague in Camus' Oran:

> Fear is absorbed and communicated like poison or leprosy. Once contaminated by fear, you too become a carrier. And you transmit it the way primary experience is transmitted: involuntarily, unwittingly, almost clandestinely; from eye to eye, from mouth to mouth.[18]

A father describes a pogrom to his daughter as worse than hell; for in hell there is no blind cruelty, no gratuitous savagery, no desecration, no trampled innocence. A pogrom is "insanity unleashed, demons at liberty, the basest instincts, the most vile laughter." Even the Hasidic rebbe says, "We were wrong ... to try, wrong to hope.... A Jew must not expect anything from Christians, man must not expect anything from man."

At this point in his narrative, Azriel shares from the Book of Kolvillàg some of the records of earlier pogroms from the twelfth century onward. One of these is the story of Zemakh, a vignette which unforgettably portrays the hidden human image revealed in response to the very eclipse of the human. Zemakh the beadle, who cleaned, tended the hearth, carried messages and packages, Zemakh the man who never in his life said no, defies unto death Lupu, the monster squire. When Lupu demands that Zemakh tell him that he is a man endowed with many talents and indescribable virtues, Zemakh responds, "Whoever feels compassion for a man without pity will in the end be ruthless with a man of compassion.... I shall not lie to please you." "To glorify the executioner is the basest of slaveries," says Zemakh the rebel. "To make him into a god the worst of perversions." Zemakh was "one of those Just Men whose hidden qualities are revealed only at the hour when body and soul no longer obey the same call."

When the attack comes it is "primitive and absolute hate," an apocalyptic vision of "horsemen and beasts" which announces "the explosion and end of the world." This terrifying inhuman night does not stop at destroying the Jews but spreads to all, the killers and the killed. "It is a night of punishment, of supreme ultimate stupidity," Moshe says to the prefect who tries in vain to save him. "They kill themselves by killing, they dig their own graves by murdering us, they annihilate the world by destroying our homes." What follows is a babel of mutual murder that spares no one. "The killers were killing each other, senselessly, with swords, hatchets, and clubs. Brothers and sisters striking one another, friends and accomplices strangling one another." Here the two voices of Elie Wiesel—the memory of Shmuel and the silence of Moshe—are united in an unbearable vision of a "Second Coming": "Suddenly I understood with every fiber of my being why I was shuddering at this vision of horror: I had just glimpsed the future." The narrative, which dooms the youth to survival while allowing Azriel to return to Kolvillàg to die in his stead, Azriel concludes in the name of his mad friend Moshe, the "last prophet and first messiah of a mankind that is no more."

Elie Wiesel did not become great, like Lincoln, through his unique response at the time of the historical event. During his years in the extermination camps, he was only a boy. Nor does he suggest in *Night* that he was more admirable than any of the other citizens of the "kingdom of night." He became great, rather, in a lifetime of living with the most terrible event in human history. In his living and writing, in his lectures and tales, he has responded ever more deeply and faithfully to the holocaust and has become, through this responding, the conscience of mankind.

The most sublime and impassioned protest of this Job of Auschwitz, the most remarkable fusion of religion and literature in his works, is neither novel, play, nor essay but the cantata *Ani Maamin*, which in November 1973 was performed at Carnegie Hall to music composed for it by the great French composer Darius Milhaud in honor of the hundredth anniversary of the Hebrew Union College-Jewish Institute of Religion. It is the haunting and powerful plaint of Abraham, Isaac, and Jacob, the traditional intercessors for Israel, who, in the face of the holocaust, turn to God and then away from God to Israel to share the fate of the exterminated millions and the tormented survivors. Maimonides' statement of perfect faith that, though the Messiah tarry, he will come, is not here the affirmation of those pious Jews who went to their deaths in the gas chambers singing these words as a hymn. It is Wiesel's and our affirmation *despite* God and *despite* man, an affirmation that is as much contending as trust.[19] It is the Dialogue with the Absurd embodied and voiced by the man who, more than any other living human being, has become in his own person the "Job of Auschwitz." This Job of Auschwitz is not the person who was exterminated, but, as Buber stated when he coined the phrase, that *survivor* of the holocaust who does not put up with faceless fate but struggles for redemption *with* and *against* our "cruel and kind Lord" whose revelation in our times is only a deepening of his hiddenness.

Elie Wiesel's story-telling witness points to the only redemption that we can hope for. We cannot bring the human image shining and beautiful out of the holocaust, out of Hiroshima and Nagasaki, out of Vietnam, out of Biafra and Bangladesh. The only thing we can do is to face the eclipse of the human image sufficiently honestly and courageously, that in affirming the human, insofar as we can, we do not lose sight of what has all but obscured it—that monstrous inhumanity which we can never affirm. If we try to affirm the human less honestly that that, we shall not be affirming it at all—and the human image will only be more fully and terribly eclipsed. "The era of the moon opens at the very moment that, reluctantly, the age of Auschwitz comes to a close," writes Wiesel, and the concentration-camp man seals off his memory and steps down from the witness stand. Elie Wiesel—the messenger, the witness, the Job of Auschwitz—may carry on his Dialogue with the Absurd from now on in quite other legends and tales or someday even in silence. But in that silence—for generations to come—there will reverberate the awesome and somber fervor of his Books of Job, each one of which sears flaming light into the darkest recesses of our souls.

1. Martin Buber, *On Judaism*, ed. by Nahum Glatzer (New York: Schocken Books, 1967), pp. 224 f.

2. Elie Wiesel, *Night*, Foreword by François Mauriac, trans. from the French by Stella Rodway (New York: Avon Books [paperback], 1969), pp. 43 f. I have inserted into this chapter the section on Elie Wiesel in my *To Deny Our Nothingness: Contemporary Images of Man* (New York: Delacorte Press, 1967; Delta Books [paperback], 1968), Chap. 18, "The Dialogue with the Absurd," pp. 348-353.

3. Elie Wiesel, *Dawn*, trans. by Frances Frenaye (New York: Avon Books [paperback], 1970).

4. Elie Wiesel, *The Accident*, trans. by Annie Borchardt (New York: Avon Books [paperback], 1970), pp. 105 f.

5. *Ibid.*, pp. 110 f.

6. *Ibid.*, pp. 120

7. Elie Wiesel, *The Town Beyond the Wall*, trans. by Stephen Becker (New York: Avon Books [paperback], pp. 95 f.

8. *Ibid.*, p. 127.

9. *Ibid.*, p. 183.

10. Elie Wiesel, *The Gates of the Forest*, trans. by Frances Frenaye (New York: Avon Books [paperback], 1969), p. 161.

11. *Ibid.*, p. 196.

12. Elie Wiesel, *Legends of Our Time* (New York: Avon Books [paperback], 1970).

13. Elie Wiesel, *A Beggar in Jerusalem*, trans. by Lily Edelman and Elie Wiesel (New York: Random House, 1970), pp. 132 f. I have slightly altered the translation for the sake of faithfulness to the French original.

14. Elie Wiesel, *One Generation After*, trans. by Lily Edelman and Elie Wiesel (New York: Random House, 1970).

15. Wiesel *A Beggar in Jerusalem*, p. 210.

16. Elie Wiesel, *The Oath*, trans. from the French by Marion Wiesel (New York: Random House, 1973), p. 138.

17. *Ibid.*, p. 189.

18. *Ibid.*, p. 251.

19. Elie Wiesel, *Ani Maamin: A Song Lost and Found Again*, music for the Cantata composed by Darius Milhaud, trans. from the French by Marion Wiesel (New York: Random House, 1973).

THE JOURNEY HOMEWARD:

The Theme of the Town in the Works of Elie Wiesel

by Ellen Fine

> "only my village exists, it is its
> image I see reflected in the world."
> *A Beggar in Jerusalem*

Elie Wiesel's first three books, *Night, Dawn* and *The Accident,* describe the voyage away from his origins, the long descent into night which dispossessed him of his identity, his tradition, his town. In the works that follow, the author embarks on the painful journey homeward in search of his pre-Holocaust past. He is like a pilgrim setting forth upon a quest for a sacred place, a kingdom lost somewhere between the Dnieper River and the shadow of the Carpathian mountains— his native town of Sighet. He is the witness looking for the object of his testimony, located in a small Transylvanian village.

After the journey to the end of night, the pilgrimage to the town marks yet another phase in the Wieselean itinerary. On one hand, it is filled with anguish, confirming the traveler's worst fears that the town no longer exists and that he is condemned to perpetual exile. The theme of the "dead" town dominates most of the texts, both fiction and non-fiction, which deal with the return. On the other hand, Wiesel struggles to revive the dead voices of the town he once knew, as he becomes aware of his role as messenger of the destroyed Jewish community, representative of so many other Eastern European "shtetls" devastated by the Nazi invaders. By going back to his past and rediscovering his sources, Wiesel is able to establish his own voice/vocation as witness, incarnating the story and history of his particular community and that of the Jewish people. He, consequently, becomes the meeting ground of past and present, responsible for re-creating and transmitting the tale of his town to future generations.

The Dead Town

Unlike other writers preoccupied with returning to their origins, Wiesel's exploration of the past is structured by historical reality. The loss of his childhood and the disappearance of his town did not come about within the normal course of events. As an adolescent of fifteen, he was eye-witness to the abrupt collapse and dispersion of the Jewish community of Sighet, presently located in Rumania but which was a part of Hungary during World War II.[1] Hungarian Jews were relatively safe until March 1944 when the installation of the pro-German government brought Eichmann himself to Hungary in order to carry out one of the most concentrated and systematic deportations in Europe. In the spring of 1944 with the end of the war in sight, the Nazis deported and eventually wiped out 450,000 Jews in Greater Hungary, including Sighet's 15,000 Jews. After the war, the Jewish population of Sighet amounted to approximately fifty families.

Wiesel, along with his friends and family, was thus plunged from the stability of the small-town life into the grotesque, dehumanized world of systematized torture and mass murder. After the liberation, he refused to be repatriated to Sighet and, as a result, was sent to Normandy, France along with 400 other orphans. At the border the passengers were asked if they wanted to become French citizens and Wiesel, unable to understand French, failed to respond. Consequently, he remained stateless until 1963 when he received his United States citizenship.

During the ten years following the war, Wiesel became a journalist. Based in France, he travelled all over the world—to such places as Africa, India, Israel. As he roamed from one country to another, he obsessed more and more about his home town. In "The Last Return," a narrative description of his actual return to Sighet in 1964, he reveals that he was unsure as to whether he travelled "in order to get away from Sighet, or to find it again. The town haunted me, I saw it everywhere, always the same as it had been. It invaded my dreams, it came between me and the world, between me and myself. By trying to free myself from it, I was becoming its prisoner."² The town is both imprisoned in his memory and imprisons him. "Since the end of the nightmare I search the past, whose prisoner I shall no doubt forever remain," he states in "A Plea for the Dead." (*Legends of Our Time,* 231)

The compulsion to wander masks a longing to journey homeward as Wiesel discloses in an account of his former teachers. "I began to wander across the world, knowing all the while that to run away was useless: all roads lead home. It remains the only fixed point in this seething world." (*Legends of Our Time,* 26) The themes of exile and flight are linked, then, to the theme of the return. Just as the liberated prisoner craves to visit the prison in order to know that he is free and the madman is propelled toward his madness, the stateless stranger is compelled to go home.

The further the wanderer flees from his point of departure, the more it haunts him; the town becomes "une idée fixe," driving him to the point of fantasizing that the entire universe is an extension and a projection of his birthplace. "The whole universe is but an extension of that little town, somewhere in Transylvania, called Marmarosszighet," Wiesel says in "My Teachers." (*Legends of Our Time,* 26) "Perhaps the whole universe is nothing 'but a phantasmagorical projection of Sighet; perhaps the whole universe is turning into Sighet," he remarks in "The Last Return." (*Legends,* 147) And in the parable recounted by Katriel in *A Beggar in Jerusalem,* the traveler in search of the big city returns unknowingly to his native town, realizing that "only my village exists, it is its image I see reflected in the world."³ Azriel, the narrator of *The Oath,* is also haunted by his native town of Kolvillàg destroyed by a pogrom: "I am still in my native town, I have left it only in my dreams, I have done nothing but change dreams."⁴

The town of Sighet embodies not only the author's past, dominated by Hassidic traditions, but becomes a paradigm for all the Jewish towns of Central and European Europe that were devastated by the Nazi regime. Sighet also serves as a model for all of the towns, villages, and cities described by

Wiesel in his works. Transposed into fiction, the little town of Sighet becomes "the Town," transcending the real and taking on legendary and universal significance as Szerencsevàros, ironically named "the city of luck" in *The Town Beyond the Wall*, the triumphant, reconquered city of Jerusalem in *A Beggar in Jerusalem*, and the annilihated community of Kolvillag (translated as "all the world" in Hungarian) in *The Oath*. The "Town," in effect, assumes a character of its own which structures the texts as noted by the importance given to the name of the town in each of these novels. (In French, *The Oath* is entitled *Le Serment de Kolvillàg.*) *The Gates of the Forest* is the exception where the village depicted is devoid of Jews and retains its anonymity, playing a secondary role to that of the forest. The development of the theme of the town which leads to the expansion of the town's boundaries beyond the immediate and the particular, parallels, in a sense, the role of the returning wanderer whom we can call the "pilgrim-protagonist"; he evolves from a spectator to a witness, becoming aware of his mission as collective survivor who must articulate the testimony of all those who were a part of his former world, thereby giving a voice to a town which has been silenced by the forces of night and death. Ultimately, he reconstructs a new town out of the ruins.

If we superpose Wiesel's various narratives, essays and novels, we can observe certain recurrent motifs which characterize the return trip of the pilgrim-protagonist. The prevailing mood of the journey homeward appears to be one of uncertainty, questioning and fear. The pilgrim-protagonist has embarked upon a quest which is unclear; he is the messenger looking for a message, the storyteller in search of a story, the speaker who has not found his voice, the witness not yet aware of his mission. As Frederick Garber observes, his is "a homecoming made by one who sees what he has come back to look at through a long tunnel filled with the thick smell of heavy smoke."[5] However, despite the equivocal nature of the voyage, three underlying motives predominate: (1) curiosity to see what the town has become or the "retrospective glance" as represented by the figure of Lot's wife (2) the desire to relive one's childhood or the search for time lost and (3) the need to re-establish contact with one's roots, to overcome the anonymity of self-imposed exile.

The retrospective glance is illustrated in *The Town Beyond the Wall*, the first novel written after the *Trilogy* and the first to directly deal with the theme of the return. Michael, the protagonist-survivor who has lived in Paris after the war, finds himself back in his home town of Szerencsevàros, having clandestinely entered with the help of Pedro, the head of an international smuggling ring in Tangier. Michael aimlessly wanders through the streets of the town now controlled by Hungarian secret police. In an attempt to comprehend the reasons for his visit, he thinks, above all, of Lot's wife whose curiosity drove her to disobey the law by looking back at the destroyed city of Sodom and therefore, to be punished by God:

> What have I come here to do? To what call had I responded? Of course, there was simple curiosity: to look back. Lot's wife was more human than her husband. She too had wanted to carry with her the image of a city that would live—that would die—without her. Doubtless there was something of that in my need to retrace my steps.[6]

The frozen pose of Lot's wife looking backward towards her town recurs throughout Wiesel's works. Instead of traditionally condemning the "don't look back" impulse embodied by the Biblical figure, the author depicts Lot's wife as sympathetic and humanly curious in her zeal to carry with her and thus, to perpetuate the image of her town. "Lot's wife, by glancing backward appears to us more human than her husband; her gesture poses the problem not of justice but of continuity," Wiesel states in the French version of his essay, "Appointment with Hate," describing his trip to Germany after the war which emphasizes the need of the victim as well as the criminal to return to the scene of the crime.[7]

While the retrospective glance is a fundamental aspect of Wiesel's own thinking and writing, he points out the danger of retracing one's itinerary solely on the basis of intellectual curiosity, noting, for example, in the essay, "A Plea for the Dead":

> And Lot's apprehensive wife, was right to want to look back and not be afraid to carry the burning of doomed hope. 'Know where you come from,' the sages of Israel

said. But everything depends on the inner attitude of whoever looks back to the beginning: if he does so purely out of intellectual curiosity, his vision will make of him a statue in some salon. Unfortunately, we do not lack statues these days: and what is worse, they speak, as if from the top of a mountain.

(*Legends*, 220)

The author here rejects the grandiose and narcissistic form of bearing witness to the past, perhaps expressing his own fear of transforming the retrospective glance into a sterile vision. He may also be responding to those contemporary critics who denounce testimony to the past as empty words proclaimed by false peophets.

Wiesel has himself been compared to Lot's wife in a positive way.[8] Indeed, as he makes his final departure from Sighet in 1964, he turns his head for a prolonged last look at the town—source of fear and fascination, of innocence and atrocity: "Sighet had long sunk below the horizon and I still kept my head turned toward it, as though it were possible for me to carry it away in my gaze." (*Legends*, 164) He is glancing back to a world which is no longer his and at the same time, he serves as the link between the past and the present, between the dead and the living.

The retrospective glance joins the themes of continuity and rupture; it is both a recognition of the ties to the past and an acknowledgement that those ties have been cut off. In a circular motion, it brings the past into the present and blinds the beginning to the end. "A man's last vision of what was his beginning is like no other, for like that beginning, it becomes part of him, irrevocable and unalterable," Wiesel observes in *One Generation After*.[9] But while the look to the past is an attempt to make a circle of history, it is also a way of lending a new dimension to the present and in a sense, moving forward. Going backward in time is for Wiesel the expression of an aspiration towards continuity and connectedness that is important both in the psychology of survivors and in Jewish thought:

I stress the word 'return', so basic in our tradition. 'Treshuva' to me signifies return, not repentance. Whoever returns to the source does not remove himself from the present. On the contrary; he lends it a new dimension. For he then realizes that in Jewish thought, everything is connected.[10]

If the retrospective glance connects the end to the beginning, the return to one's origins is also for Wiesel as for other authors such as Nerval and Proust, the search for the lost idyllic world of childhood, the second motive for the journey homeward, "To become a child again" is a key expression in the Wieselean vocabulary. Wiesel seeks to recreate the town of his past as seen through a child's eyes. By resurrecting the child in himself, he aspires to bring "back to life some of the characters that peopled his universe, the universe of his childhood," as he notes in *Souls on Fire*.[11] By becoming a child again, the author places himself in the position of the receiver of legends and tales told by his Hassidic masters. For example, when David, the narrator of *A Beggar in Jerusalem,* listens to Dan, one of the other beggars who tells tales about the lost Jewish kingdom, he observes: "As I listened, I became a child again." (47) "Dan would describe his kingdom which the child within me, envious and fascinated, had tried to fathom long ago." (53) Listening to the old master speak in "The Wandering Jew," the author-narrator also feels likd a child again: "I listened, straining painfully, as I had listened long ago, as a child, amazed, to the stories the Hasidim used to tell with such fervor ..." (*Legends,* 127) As he himself speaks, he becomes aware of his own fear and ignorance in front of the old master: "I was going to lose the use of my tongue, become a child again, speechless, innocent." (*Legends,* 131) And in the narrative, "The Itinerary of an End" which appears in the French version of *One Generation After,* the author tells of his meeting with the old Rabbi who had known his grandfather: "In his presence, I became once again the child that I had been long ago, accustomed to listening and to waiting."[12]

If the theme of childhood is associated with the themes of innocence, waiting, listening, and silence, it also is linked to the notion of seeing the world through the perspective of a child's eyes as a form of paradise, a golden age.[13] In the memory of the survivor, the town becomes a kind of Eden, "Szerencsevaŕos, that blasted Paradise where all had once seemed so simple." (*The Town Beyond the Wall,* 85) The returning wanderer is like a child looking for a reunion with the mother, the source, the beginnings, "this town which gave me everything" (*Legends*, 148), "my own city where I first saw my mother." (*Town*, 149) The pilgrimage to the town, in effect, reactivates in the stranger profound feelings of belonging to someone, something that has an existence outside of himself, a past, a tradition: "The joy of not being alone, of belonging, of being bound to someone, to someone who had lived before me and was living outside me," (*Town*, 149), Michael recollects as he thinks about seeing the image of himself and his mother reflected in the mirror for the first time. At the same time, however, he realizes that this attachment no longer exists. The town which gave him everything took it all away; Paradise has been followed by the Fall. "And here I am alone. Mother is no more." (*Town*, 149) The child, expelled from paradise has died, just as his mother and the town as he knew it have disappeared. The theme of the dead child thus dominates the mood of the journey homeward as it did the voyage into the night. The dead child represents the dead town, the dead past and above all, the dead self.

The pilgrim-protagonist is ambivalent toward the dead child in himself. On one hand, he acknowledges the strangeness that separates his present self from his former self as Michael tells Milika, a survivor from his home town whom he meets in Paris after the war: "He [the little boy] didn't survive. He's dead. I deny him. Never saw him, never knew him. A stranger. An unidentified corpse. I have nothing in common with him." (*Town*, 87) On the other hand, he realizes that the dead child, still a part of himself, evokes a past which continues to haunt his present life and cries out to be revived. Michael discloses to Milika: "I know he's dead but I also know that he won't leave me. He follows my trail; he walks in my footsteps ... When I run, he runs along behind me." (*Town*, 87) It is ultimately through the dead child in himself that the exiled traveler can be guided back to his town, recover his past and his identity, and make restitution to those who have died as David in *A Beggar in Jerusalem* affirms: "there was a child waiting for me in my past and I was afraid to follow him; I knew one of us was dead. I also knew that he alone could lead me to our teachers ..." (30)

The conflicted attitude with regard to the dead/resuscitated child is related to the theme of the town. The pilgrim-protagonist is afraid of seeing the town again and afraid of not seeing it. He fears a vision of ruins but also dreads the sight of a reconstructed town that bears no resemblance to the town he once knew.

> What would be waiting for me when I arrived? The dead past or the past revived? Total desolation or a city rebuilt again and a life once more become normal? For me, in either case, there would be despair. One cannot dig up a grave with impunity.
>
> (*Legends*, 146)

The dispossessed voyager wants to be reunited with the dead child in himself and reclaim that child's lost kingdom but at the same time, painfully perceives that the town like the child no longer exists. He experiences what Proust calls "the contradiction brought about by searching in reality for images from the memory."[14]

The confrontation of past and present, of memory and reality creates continuous tension in the Wieselean protagonist, often leading him to the brink of insanity. Like Shakespeare's King Lear, a character who haunts Michael, the exiled survivor struggles against madness because he too has been dispossessed of his kingdom: he no longer is sure what is real and what is imagined. The town simultaneously exists and does not exist for him. "Your town still exists, your town no longer exists. It survives only in the delirium of the mad," David tells the young madman in *A Beggar in Jerusalem* who questions his own perceptions of reality and believes that his town has been rid of all Jews. (38)[15] In *The Oath*, Azriel tells the young man: "Kolvillàg does not exist any more. I am Kolvillàg and I am going mad." (14) The author, like his protagonists, also comes to doubt not only that the town exists in its present state but that it ever existed. For example, in the retrospective narrative, "Journey's Beginning," he observes: "That town. I see it still, I see it everywhere. I see it with such clarity that I often mock and admonish myself: continue and you'll go mad; the town no longer exists, it never did." (*One Generation After*, 21) "The Last Return" concludes with the paradoxical statement, "For it had never existed—this town that had once been mine." (*Legends*, 164) Wiesel thus questions the validity of his own memory and his own identity as he slowly discovers that the eden of his childhood is "not the lost paradise but the paradise which never existed."[16] This contradictory recognition of the town's existence and non-existence recalls, in effect, certain aspects of the French "Nouveau Roman" and novels by Samuel Beckett. Nevertheless, while the result may be similar, for Wiesel it is not a question of experimenting with literary techniques which contest and interrogate the nature of reality, but rather of expressing the anguish caused by the inconsistencies inherent in the Holocaust experience itself.

Despite the risk of madness, the pilgrim-protagonist seeks to combat the sense of alienation brought about by his nomadic existence and returns to the site of this dead town in an attempt to rediscover his roots which is the third motive for the journey homeward. We have seen that the survivor has chosen the life of a wanderer after the war and the figure of the Wandering Jew is familiar throughout Wiesel's work, represented by the traveler, the vagabond, nomad, refugee—all those who fall into a class of statelessness, travelling about without attachments and living in anonymity. In *Legends of Our Time* an entire narratave is devoted to "The Wandering Jew," one of the author's former masters who was a type of "vagabond-clown" of unknown origins, spoke about thirty languages and inspired fear and admiration because of his supernatural abilities. The Wandering Jew is also depicted by such characters as Moishe-the-Madman and Elie, the prophet, who constantly appear throughout the texts. The image of the Wandering Jew is evoked, as well, in *The Town Beyond the Wall* on the day of deportation when old men and children, rabbis and invalids parade through town, their sacks on their backs as they unknowingly head toward their extermination. (160)

The Wieselean protagonists are all wanderers, living in what Lothar Kahn calls "the tradition of exile and flight" that distinguishes the characters of Wiesel's novels.[17] "I am the clandestine traveler who has come home without even knowing why," Michael says in *The Town Beyond the Wall*. (153) In *The Gates of the Forest,* Gregor characterizes Gavriel as "one of those dreamers, who wander on mountainsides or roads the world over, who have chosen exile in order to detach themselves from time and to exorcise it."[18] And David in *A Beggar in Jerusalem* realizes after listening to Katriel's parable about the misled traveler: "Suddenly I understood that Katriel's traveler might have been myself." (159) During a tortured night of hallucinations, he imagines: "I am the haggard traveler, wandering aimlessly, looking at men but taking nothing from them." (173) In *The Oath* as well, Azriel is condemned to be a "Na-venadnik" or eternal wanderer "in perpetual exile, a stranger among strangers." (52)[19]

The figure of the Diasporic Jew embodies the image of modern man as stranger, representing what Cioran in his essay, "A People of Solitaries," calls "the alienated existence *par excellence* or, to utilize an expression by which the theologians describe God, the *wholly other*."[20] The state of estrangement is epitomized by the pilgrim-protagonist whose eventual homecoming makes him more than ever aware of his homelessness. He feels he is an intruder in the town that was once his; he is like Moses unable to enter the inaccessible and forbidden Promised Land:

> I felt myself a stranger, if not an intruder, in this sinister town which was stripped of all vigor, of any life of its own. I searched for the people out of my past, I searched for my past and I did not find them.
>
> (*Legends*, 159-60)

The condition of undesirable stranger, of being rejected from one's own past, from time itself is echoed in *The Town Beyond the Wall:*

> This is my city, I was born here. Here, I became a part of time, here I was launched upon the river, here is my source, here burrow my roots: and yet here I am an unwanted stranger; just as my own memories deny me.
>
> (*Town*, 91)

We see here two important motifs related to the theme of the town: (1) the bewitched or forbidden town and (2) expulsion from time. In the first case, the expatriate returns to find the town of his childhood lifeless, menacing and sinister because it has been cursed by outsiders who have condemned the life of its Jewish inhabitants. The bewitched town, imbued with evil and destruction, is the counter-part of the town as paradise. The Holocaust has left the cursed town scorched, arid, dried up and devoid of all life in the mind of the undesirable stranger. "My pilgrimages kept leading me back to a source run dry. The life of the town, by continuing, had thrust me out," says the madman in *A Beggar in Jerusalem*. (38)

This leads us to the second motif—the expulsion from time. Once a part of a harmonious community, the returning survivor is met with the indifference and obliviousness of the townspeople. Along with the other victims, he has not only been uprooted from the town but driven out of time itself. As he roams the streets desperately hoping to be recognized, he realizes that he lives in a time different from that of the passers-by who do not see him. For them, he is a thing longtime dead and forgotten; his return is of no consequence to them. Just as in the concentration camp he was reduced to a number, a nonentity, so, too, in post-Holocaust times, he has become a discarded object whose past and present existence remains unacknowledged. The apathetic inhabitants of the town have not only erased the deported victims from their memory, but in addition, they have no place in their consciousness for the survivors. "In their eyes, I was not even an invisible person, nor a fleeting shadow, but a thing without weight, without a past,"[21] Wiesel tells us in "The Last Return." As he walks down the streets of his home town, he is aware that he is a non-person in the minds and eyes of the townspeople: "If I had spoken to them, they would have continued on their way ... As if I did not exist. Or rather, as if I had never existed." (*Legends,* 157) Michael, too, in *The Town Beyond the Wall* experiences the feeling of being a corpse among the living: "The people come and go, not stopping before him. They do not see him. Perhaps they are pretending. For them he is already dead. For them he has never existed." (91)

In addition to being ignored by the passers-by, the pilgrim-protagonist's estrangement is intensified by his discovery that the sites and people of his former world have been replaced. On one hand, the town has remained intact except for the disappearance of its Jewish population but on the other hand, the pilgrimage to the once-familiar landscape reveals significant changes. For example, Michael runs toward the public square where the old synagogue used to stand and to his dismay, is struck not only with the absence of all traces of the pillar of the Jewish community but with the presence of a modern three-story edifice that stands in its place. The sanctuary had been razed to the ground by the Germans who by destroying the "Temple" were following in the footsteps of the Romans centuries ago in Jerusalem. Here, then, is a literal example of a pilgrimage to a holy place which no longer exists and which has been supplanted.

While the theme of substitution can be applied to the physical structure of the town itself that has undergone demolition and reconstruction, the idea of being replaced by others is even more painful than finding an empty or torn-down building. When the young madman in *A Beggar in Jerusalem* perceives strangers living in his former house, he believes that the vision is a result of his madness: "You may not believe this, but I seemed to discover strangers even in my own home, at my parents' table." (38) Michael in *The Town Beyond the Wall* makes his way back to 17 Kamár Street where his house and father's store still stand, unchanged from the outside. When he enters the store and sees a man of about fifty appear before him, he momentarily entertains the illusion that it is his father. Dream and reality, past and present merge as Michael is torn between the desire to resuscitate his father and the recognition that his father is dead:

> Was this my father? Was that my father's voice? No, a strange face, a strange voice. And yet I wasn't convinced, not absolutely sure and convinced. My father might have changed; I might have changed; my eyes and ears might have changed.
>
> (152)

The theme of substitution is related here to the theme of the strange voice, the one which has replaced the familiar one. Michael is ambivalent toward this substitution. In one respect, he cannot accept that another man walk in his father's steps and that in another respect, he has a strong need to confirm his father's death. He reveals this confusion to Pedro, the leader of the smuggling ring who becomes his confident: "My father is dead, Pedro. I saw him die. I was with him right to the end. Or almost. As far as the threshold. But just the same: if it was only a dream? If he had just pretended to die? To leave? If he were dead only in my dream?" (152)

Although Michael eventually acknowledges that the storekeeper is not his father, he has a sudden longing to reclaim his stolen territory, to announce his identity, to shout to the merchant, "I am Michael. This is my store, this is my house. You're living off my store and in my house." (154) However, this desire to cry out only occurs in the protagonist's fantasy, being stifled in reality, as the survivor remains an unknown, silent stranger. Michael is unable to resurrect his father just as he is incapable of recapturing the town of his childhood. Bringing the past into the present makes him more and more aware of his own impotence.

This impotence is especially evident in "The Last Return" when the author-narrator dramatically describes his nocturnal visit to his old house that is now inhabited by strangers. He feels like a thief, encircling the domicile, gazing at its closed shutters, preparing himself for penetration into the inner sanctum. But his role as outsider is perpetuated as he is only able to reach the courtyard. A dog ("friends of the enemy, all demons, all anti-Semitic ... the true victor in this war," *Legends,* 156) suddenly barks and chases him away, thus preventing him from completing his exploration of the past. His desire for repossession is frustrated; he has not dared to awaken the person now sleeping in his bed. Instead, he flees through the dark streets, the intruder, the fugitive, the eternal wanderer plunged into prolonged "déracinement" and expelled once again from the place of his origins. Just as he had, minutes before, run towards the house, almost flown like some Chagall-like angel ("I no longer run, I fly, I am the angel who soars above the roof-tops"[22]). He subsequently runs away in a painful state of rage and shame: "driven out a second time ... I took to flight, as I had long ago." (*Legends,* 156)

Having unsuccessfully attempted to embrace the past, the pilgrim-protagonist once again is forced to take to flight, a recurring theme in Wiesel's works. As in *The Accident,* where the narrator's confrontation with Sarah resulted in the need to escape and repudiate the prostitute who embodied his inhuman past, the pilgrim turns his back on the forbidden town, the shrine that for him has been transformed into an oppressive graveyard. He retreats into a second exile because he realizes that it is impossible to re-establish a sense of connection with the town. Like the precious Bar-Mitzvah watch unearthed by the narrator in the tale, "The Watch," (*One Generation After*) and then buried once again in its tomb-like box, the memory of the past cannot be excavated and left exposed. The rusty and worm-ridden watch is a relic of time lost and putting it back in its native soil is in some way indicative of the survivor's desire to leave a trace behind, a reflection of his presence which might some day be dug up by an unsuspecting child who would learn that there had been Jewish inhabitants in the town. Nonetheless, the survivor knows he must bury the past, bury the town itself and that he is doomed to silent impotence, an onlooker mutely crying out in the middle of the night in a vain attempt to arouse the sleeping town. "I shouted but no sound came out. The town went on sleeping with no fear of the silence." (*Legends,* 153)

The voice of the survivor, like the voice of the town, has been suffocated by the forces of night, "night continued and extinguished all voices." [23] The enveloping nocturnal silence is essentially the silence of isolation, exile and death. Like the once flourishing Jewish community that is now mute, the pilgrim-protagonist is incapable of making himself be heard. He is grappling with the process of becoming a witness for he knows that it is he who must give a voice to the stilled town whose life is imprisoned within his memory; he is the link between the theme of the town and that of the night:

> Here I am alone in the town, alone in the night. I am their link. I say aloud to myself: 'My town, my night'... the town, the night, and I, who am their meeting ground.[24]

However, his choked voice makes him conscious of the futility and ineffectiveness of his attempt to communicate. He is thus forced into the role of a silent spectator instead of a defiant spokesman whose voice could make an impact on the world around him. The return of the pilgrim-protagonist to his town is a form of second death for it confirms his worst suspicions: the Holocaust, while leaving the outer structure of the town unimpaired has, in effect, turned it into ashes—the town has died, and with it the memory of the victims as well as of the survivors.

Nevertheless, while the Wieselean protagonist basically remains a stranger imprisoned by silence in a dead town that ignores him, he eventually refuses his anonymity and speaks out. By letting his voice be heard, he is transformed from a transparent non-entity to a messenger who represents and, in some way, resurrects his deported and devastated community.

The tension created between the assertion of the voice and the retreat into silence is at the core of the journey homeward. The dead town becomes the resurrected town, for if death is exile and silence, the regaining of lost speech is an attempt to bring to life that which has died; the witness reclaims possession of origins through the power of the voice. By closely examining Michael's verbal confrontation in *The Town Beyond the Wall*, we can observe the process of liberation from exile through the spoken word.

The Resurrected Town

Like Elisha in *Dawn* and the nameless narrator in *The Accident*, Michael in *The Town Beyond the Wall* is a concentration camp survivor who after the war lives in Paris, frequenting the world of the vagabonds and spending hours roaming through the streets in a state of estrangement. He dwells as Joseph Friedman says in "the malaise of alienation."[25] After becoming a journalist for a Paris weekly, he is assigned to cover a story in Tangier and meets Pedro, the head of a smuggling ring. Despite Michael's apparent refusal to be repatriated to his home town in Hungary, he confides to Pedro that his most profound wish is to return to Szerencsevaròs. Pedro is able to get Michael clandestinely into Hungary, now controlled by secret secret police and part of the Iron Curtain.

Uncertain of what has compelled him to return, Michael aimlessly wanders through the streets of his town, finally visiting the square where the old synagogue once stood. As he encircles the modern building that has replaced the synagogue, a sudden image surges from the depths of his unconscious. In Proustian fashion, his involuntary memory forces the recall of a face impassively looking out of a window above the public square where the Jews were being rounded up. The violent souvenir of this onlooker who watched the entire procedure without emotion enlightens Michael as to the real purpose for his return home—he has come back to confront, accuse, humiliate and perhaps to understand the Other, the impassive witness, representative of all those neutrals indifferent to the fate of the Jewish people under the Nazi regime and depicted in the text by the grotesquely puffed-up face in the window:

the others—the Other—those who watched us depart
for the unknown; those who observed us without
emotion, while we became objects—living sticks of
wood—and carefully numbered victims. (*Town,* 159)

The spectator comes to personify the average man, the
townspeople and the world itself, all those who refused to take
sides and who participated in what Lothar Kahn calls "the
witness psychology, the policy of non-involvement in the
injustices done to others, the pursuit of self and safety."[26]
Moreover, Kahn suggests that the silent witness is the
Witness-God, "the silent unconcerned God who also watched
and allowed things to happen."[27] One might say, in a broad
sense, that the spectator symbolizes all of humanity and
especially us, *the reader,* suggested by the fact that when
Michael finally confronts the bystander in his apartment, he is
in the middle of reading a book.

"We have all become the faceless ones in the windows,"
says Norman Friedman who describes the indifferent witness
as "the Bureaucratic Cipher," the docile, obedient, con-
forming twentieth-century citizen who lives in a techno-
logically dehumanized society.[28] The "faceless" face in the
window appears to represent fear, malice, and incompre-
hensibility. According to Naomi Bliven in a *New Yorker*
review of the book, the lack of detail used to portray the
spectator makes him seem like "a figure in an allegory" rather
than a fully developed character; she points out the possiblility
that Wiesel left the bystander almost blank to allow each one of
us to fill in."[29]

The figure in the window does, indeed, take on an
allegorical aspect, recalling the conclusion of Kafka's *The
Trial.* When K is about to be killed in the quarry, the window
of a nearby house is suddenly flung open and a human figure
leans forward, stretching out both arms. K wonders: "Who
was it? A friend? A good man? Someone who sympathized?
Someone who wanted to help? Was it one person only? Or was
it mankind? Was help at hand?"[30] Despite the futility of the
gesture, the form in the window in Kafka's novel conveys a
feeling of hope, the extended arms offering possible assistance
or at least some sign of communication to the helpless victim.
By contrast, in Wiesel's book, the figure in the window is

reduced to a blank face with an empty stare. Both of these onlookers resemble each other, however, by their lack of involvement, passivity and silence with regard to the persecuted, and by their similar postures—looking down from above—which suggest a state of superiority and detachment as well as that of a spectator viewing a theatrical performance.[31]

The confrontation between Michael and the bystander that did not occur the day of the deportation, finally does take place twenty years later. The protagonist quietly walks into the apartment of the man and makes it clear that he has come to humiliate this impassive individual who did nothing as the Jews were being sent to their death. Michael exchanges some hostile words with him, flings a glass of wine in his face but the latter continues to calmly, coldly, and silently glare at the unwelcomed visitor without flinching. His attitude reflects a total absence of emotion and a refusal of any feeling of guilt or shame. Michael does not succeed in humiliating this indifferent witness.

Nonetheless, the encounter has revealed to Michael that the neutral bystander is the third point of the mysterious triangle that links executioners, victims, and spectators and that one man can be all three at the same time. By interrogating the spectator, Michael risks becoming one himself: "For the game can be played indefinitely: who observes the spectator becomes one. In his turn, he will question me." (*Town*, 163) In effect, Michael's attitude of contempt toward the onlooker and his accusations of cowardice and passivity are counter-acted by the spectator's own charges that the victims docilely let themselves be led to the slaughter-house without resisting: "You were afraid, you preferred the illusion to the bite of conscience and the game to a show of courage," he tells Michael. (163) On the whole, the confrontation suggests an identification between the survivor and the spectator which the author perpetrates if not on a manifest level than on an unconscious one.

If we make a brief comparison of Michael and the spectator, we can observe certain common characteristics, albeit from different points of view. First of all, both exist in a state of anonymity. Walking through the streets twenty years after his banishment, Michael feels like a non-person, a forgotten object, a dead man in the eyes of the townspeople.

He, in turn, perceives the spectator as a debased object, something less than human:

> The spectator has nothing of the human in him: he is a stone in the street, the cadaver of an animal, a pile of dead wood. He is there, he survives us, he is immobile. The spectator reduces himself to the level of an object. He is no longer he, you, or I: he is 'it.' (171)

Michael's view of the spectator reflects the most negative and inhuman aspect as his own sense of self. The expressions used to describe the man as subhuman, stone, piece of dead wood, dead animal, recall the language of the concentrationary universe where, according to Nazi ideology, the victim was considered to be outside of the human race. We see here a link between the victim, survivor, and spectator who come to represent the dehumanized, faceless, nameless modern citizens caught up in the evils of society.

A second characteristic associated with Michael and the spectator is that of voicelessness or silence. Both are soundless onlookers—Michael, as he roams the streets of his town without being seen and without speaking out and the spectator, as the observer behind the window who is omnipresent but invisible and silent. When Michael returns to his father's store, he is unable to verbalize a protest by proclaiming his identity and reclaiming his family's appropriated belongings. The spectator likewise abstains from making a protest or from any dissension as he sits by the window. However, whereas Michael's voice is choked, the spectator's is absent; Michael has been coerced into silence, his voice rendered impotent by the forces of night and violence, while the spectator has chosen the silence of evasiveness and non-involvement which is ultimately the silence of betrayal as Wiesel comments in the essay, "A Plea for the Dead": "The cruelty of the enemy would have been incapable of breaking the prisoner; it was the silence of those he believed to be his friends—cruelty more cowardly, more subtle—which broke his heart." (*Legends*, 229)

Even if the deadened voices of the survivor and the spectator stem from different points on the triangle and have different meanings, the result is the same: their muteness implies impotence, resignation to and acceptance of the situation or the society such as it is. Nevertheless, there is a movement from the absence of the word to its presence, from speechlessness to expression, from non-involvement to action on both the part of the pilgrim-protagonist and the impassive witness. Michael and the spectator follow a parallel course: by speaking out, the former to humiliate and the latter to protect himself, they each undergo a form of transformation.

Michael's transformation from the silent stranger to the messenger of the dead occurs during the course of his confrontation with the spectator. His verbal assault on this man who has come to personify the indifferent world is a cry of defiance that releases him from his silent exile, his isolation and state of anonymity. By returning to the onlooker's apartment, to the so-called scene of the crime, the survivor has gathered up "the courage to vomit the collective poison, to spit the bitter taste of the world into the faces of all those who want to turn away from it."[32] "The witness of the night becomes a fighter," Emmanuel Haymann, a French critic, says of Wiesel[33] and this applies here to the protagonist of *The Town Beyond the Wall.* Michael's indictment of the unconcerned bystander is an attempt to express his own personal revenge and thereby, assert his own identity and purpose. His final outburst is "une prise de conscience" of his role as *messenger of the dead,* a position characteristic of Wiesel's protagonists and assumed here in a challenging, revengeful, almost contemptuous manner: "The dead Jews, the women gone mad, the mute children—I'm their messenger. And I tell you they haven't forgotten you. Someday they'll come marching, trampling you, spitting in your face. And at their shouts of contempt you'll pray God to deafen you." (172-3)

Once delivered, Michael's message brings a sense of relief, a resolution of the tension built up throughout the years and an acknowledgement of his rupture with past. As Thomas Idinopulos points out: "Honoring the memory of the dead, he has begun to earn the right to live. And for the first time in his stories, Wiesel has his character speak as a healed man."[34] Michael has exorcised himself through words: "I had come, I had seen, I had delivered the message: the wheel had come full circle. The act was consummated. Now I shall go. I shall return to the life they call normal. The past will have been exorcised. I'll live, I'll work, I'll love ... No more double life, lived on two levels. Now I am whole." (173) Michael's verbal discharge resembles that made by the narrator of *the Accident* to Kathleen, his girlfriend; words bring relief but at the same time incur contamination. However, Kathleen is a pure and innocent recipient of the message in *The Accident* while the spectator in *The Town Beyond the Wall* is the intended object of contempt and humiliation. The verbalization of things which have remained unsaid for a long time is an appeal for a modification in attitude an acceptance of responsibility on the part of this "symbol of anonymity, the average man." (*Town,* 164) Michael's demand for a change is comparable to the narrator's statement in *The Accident:* "Whoever listens to Sarah and doesn't change, whoever enters Sarah's world and doesn't invent new gods and new religions, deserves death and destruction."[35]

Michael's own shift from silence to speaking out, from passivity to action, eventually produces an alteration in the position of the spectator who responds to the former's accusations by instantly denouncing him to the Hungarian police. When Michael is picked up at the street corner by the police car, his eyes meet those of the spectator's in the car mirror. Although their final encounter is a silent one, the eyes of the man so long emotionless reflect "defiance, an anticipation of victory, saying, 'Now you'll have to hate me!'" (174) Michael's words have given a voice to the spectator, albeit a negative one. In contrast to the silence of betrayal, he now deceives the survivor by the word. In effect, the stand taken by the "neutral" in the post-war police state is similar to this position twenty years before. During the war he took refuge in the silence of anonymity while in the present, he also renounces his freedom by collaborating with the police. Nonetheless, Wiesel indicated that becoming envolved in any way is better than indifference, a motif stressed in the last section of *The Town Beyond the Wall* and directly linked to the theme of the witness. By taking action and showing some expression of emotion, the spectator has in some way left the realm of the inhuman:

> To be indifferent—for whatever reason—is to deny not only the validity of existence, but also its beauty. Betray, and you are a man; torture your neighbor, you're still a

man. Evil is human, weakness is human; indifference is
not. (188)

If Michael's encounter results in the "contamination" of
the spectator who leaves the security of his window seat to
jump out onto the stage, it also brings about the protagonist's
own condemnation. Ironically, the survivor who has returned
to his home town to accuse, once again becomes the accused.
Michael is charged by the Hungarian police with being a spy,
having entered the country without identity papers and he is
forced to spend three days standing in a prison cell called the
"Temple" where he is interrogated. This method of torture,
reminiscent of Nazi techniques, is called "the prayer" because
the prisoner stands facing a wall, unable to move. Under these
conditions, Michael comes close to insanity but remains silent
in order to give his friend, Pedro, time to leave the country
without danger.

The former victim seeking to inflict punishment upon
mankind by finally speaking out and accusing is again
punished himself and re-enacts his victimization by returning
to prison. Irving Halperin in *Messengers from the Dead* feels
that Michael becomes a victim out of a sense of survivor-guilt:

> Thus it may be adduced that Michael's need to return to
> his hometown stemmed not only from an impulse to
> confront the spectator but also to satisfy an involuntary
> inclination to self-victimization. It is as though he must
> *sacrificially* become a prisoner again in order to placate
> a sense of guilt for having survived the Holocaust.[36]

While it is true that the survivor is often motivated by his
guilt, the theme of prison in *The Town Beyond the Wall* has more
profound and positive implications than the satisfaction of "an
involuntary inclination to self victimization." The prison as a
place of torture and degradation represents the oppressive
regime of modern political tyranny illustrated in the novel by
the Hungarian police state. But it can also by considered a
paradigm for the concentration camp experience, as Halperin
himself observes:

> The wall is not only a wall in a jail but symbolically the
> dead-end anguish of European Jewry during the Hitler
> years. It may also represent the sum total of the satanic
> means—the gas chambers, burning ditches, gas wagons,

deadly serums, machine-gun mass executions—used to destroy the bodies of Jews.[37]

The walls of the prison like the walls of the ghetto isolate man from the rest of humanity; they are the walls of sequestration and lamentation. However, paradoxically while they confine, they also liberate. Cut off from the outer world, the prisoner is free to explore the inner dimensions of time and space. The prison in *The Town Beyond the Wall,* ironically nicknamed the "Temple," serves as a place of refuge, a haven for contemplation and recollection which enables the protagonist to escape from the captivity of his present state by evoking images of the past. The theme of the prison is used by the author as a fictional device for the retrospective glance or the reordering and reconstitution of memories which permit his character to mentally reconstruct the town of his childhood. In prison, time is suspended, thus giving a dimension of freedom to the narrative itself which consists of flashbacks to the protagonist's childhood in Hungary (First Prayer), his adolescence in Paris (Second Prayer), and adult life as a journalist in Tangier (Third Prayer). After the three prayers that correspond to the three days of forced silence in front of the "Temple" wall, Michael loses consciousness and awakens in a cell with three other prisoners characterized as the Religious One, the Impatient One and the Silent One. "The Last Prayer" occurs in this cell and is mainly a narrative focusing on a detailed flashback of the journey homeward and the encounter with the spectator. At the same time, the past narrative joins the present moment revealing Michael's interactions with the other prisoners who are eventually transferred elsewhere. The only one who remains is the Silent One, the mad youth who comes to represent an important stage in the protagonist's own development.

Rather than reject the mindless, speechless young boy who like Sarah in *The Accident* reflects the inhuman part of himself, Michael attempts to restore the dead self to life, the mad self to sanity. Because of his concentrated efforts, the sensibility of the demented deaf-mute is gradually awakened, Michael gives a voice to the Silent One, a name (Eliezer) to the nameless. By saving the life of one human being, he feels that he is saving the life of all humanity, a recurring Wieselean theme. "He was suddenly responsible for a life that was an inseparable part of the life of mankind. He would fight. He would resume the creation of the world from the void." (183) By reaching out to another person and helping him "return" to the world of the living, Michael is re-establishing a new mode of being based on dialogue, friendship, and solidarity. The theme of return then is linked to the theme of re-creation. The pilgrim-protagonist here is clearly aspiring to restore a dynamic connection to the outside world. *The Town Beyond the Wall* is, in effect, a pivotal work because the protagonist for the first time is affirming his own sense of self and his responsibility toward the Other, toward others. By doing so, he is re-creating his own universe and rebuilding his own self.

The silence of the cell has given a voice to the inner self. Michael's retreat into the concentrated and intimate silence of the prison cell endows him with certain creative powers and prepares him for a spiritual rebirth. The cell becomes a kind of womb, calling to mind participation in initiation rites that involve a return or "regressus ad uterum" which, according to Mircea Eliade in *Myth and Reality*, corresponds to the state of "prenatal darkness" or the "Night before Creation,"[38]

One might say that the rites of initiation in the sanctity of the Temple are represented by the "prayer" imposed upon the prisoner and which prepares him for his exit. The prayer is both a means of torture and a metaphor for the creative act, taking on a religious, sacred aspect. It is an act of atonement through which the survivor-protagonist can rid himself of his guilt by resurrecting his lost, dead objects. Within the prison walls, Michael becomes aware of his heightened perception, his ability to hear and subsequently to bring to life the voices, sounds, and echoes of another world. He realizes that he has the power to evoke images which resuscitate and immortalize the characters who peopled the world of his childhood:

> Upright, facing the wall, he finds himself able to hear a thousand voices at a time, each distinct, to see a thousand paths, to weigh a thousand destinies ... His sensibilities sharpen, his being opens: as to the Rabbi of Nicholsburg, all the sounds and echoes of land and sea come to him. He senses even the ultra-sounds that certain creatures and certain destinies, give off.
>
> (104)

The pilgrim-protagonist recognizes in the Temple, place of terror and house of worship, that he cannot recover any meaning in the town such as it exists in its present oppressive state but he is able to create meaning by reconstructing the fragments of his souvenirs. If the actual pilgrimage to the town is a confirmation that it is "dead," the inner journey homeward enables the survivor to resurrect the town of his childhood. He becomes the link between the reality of the dead town and the legend of the resuscitated one. The quest for the town shifts from the outer to the inner world, from disintegration to creation, from dispersion to unity. In prison, the act of memory saves the protagonist from succumbing to madness and permits him to master his situation. The real town is now a cemetery, immobile and empty, silent and abandoned, but it is also a source of myths, tales, images, names and faces, as Michael tells Pedro: "I don't like graveyards. And the city of luck is just that: a great cemetery. And lying in it are faces and legends, holidays and hopes ..." (16-17)

Michael seeks to transform this graveyard into a living monument by resurrecting the town in himself. He has mythicized, fantasized, and internalized the town so that ultimately, he *is* the town, the lost paradise, the Promised Land, his dead friends and family, his mother, father, and little sister who are brought to life as he perceives and remembers them. Writing for Wiesel is "an invisible tombstone, erected to the memory of the dead unburied" (*Legends*, 25) and the book, therefore, becomes the author's means of constructing a memorial designed to commemorate the town. The exiled wanderer finally reaches his point of departure by discovering within his own memory the collective memory of the community and of the Jewish people as a whole. Just as the town comes to represent all the towns of Eastern Europe, the self of the pilgrim-protagonist is expanded to the collective Self. For Wiesel, to be Jewish is to be "Sum, synthesis, vessel. Someone who feels every blow that ever struck his ancestors."[39] "To be a Jew is to work for the survival of a people—your own—whose legacy is its collective memory in its entirety ... Time is a link, your 'I' a sum total." (*One Generation After*, 217) In order to be a Jew, one "must claim kinship with all the generations who have achieved these triumphs, these sorrows, these overpowering experiences."[40]

If in *The Town Beyond the Wall,* the pilgrim-protagonist is not yet consciously aware of his role as transmitter of tales, the reconstitution of his own personal history and the town's history that he relives as he recounts and imagines it, is an essential part of the process of becoming a witness. We see an evolution in Michael from the alienated spectator to the witness who realizes that he is not only on a quest for his own past but for the collective past of his people. By returning to his sources and reviving the voices of the "dead" community, he comes closer to establishing his own voice/vocation as messenger of that community. The discovery of the inner town helps him to restore a sense of continuity and solidarity to his life and to his tradition. The true journey homeward occurs when the author through his characters re-creates a new town built upon the ruins of the old one, a town which becomes the meeting ground of the dead and the living, the past and present.

The return to the town ultimately frees the imprisoned voice of the pilgrim-protagonist who assumes the role of the collective witness, a theme that permeates such works as *The Gates of the Forest, A Beggar in Jerusalem,* and *The Oath.* Wiesel's characters slowly come to grips with their past, linking their personal history to Jewish history and finally to the history of mankind. They become consumed with the desire to bear witness, to transmit the story and history of their town to future generations. They realize that the town cannot die because the witness is still alive and by speaking out, he will continue to immortalize the town in a work of art. As Pedro tells Michael in *The Town Beyond the Wall:* "Man may not have the last word, but he has the last cry. That moment marks the birth of art." (103)

1.   First a part of the Austrian Empire, Sighet was given up to Hungary, then handed over to Rumania and subsequently, taken back by Hungary at the beginning of W.W.II. During the war, Germany incorporated the town into the Third Reich. The Soviet Union took over at the end of the war, finally rendering Sighet to Rumania. Wiesel refers to the town's history in

The Town Beyond the Wall N.Y.: Avon Books, 1964), p. 16 and in *One Generation After* (N.Y.: Avon, 1970), p. 22.

2.   Elie Wiesel, *Legends of Our Time* (New York: Avon Books, 1968), p. 146. All further references to this work are given in the text parenthetically.

3.   Elie Wiesel, *A Beggar in Jerusalem,* trans. Lily Edelman and Elie Wiesel (New York: Avon Books, 1970), p. 149.

4.   Elie Wiesel, *The Oath,* trans. Marion Wiesel (New York: Avon Books, 1973), p. 59.

5.   Frederick Garber, "The Art of Elie Wiesel," *Judaism,* 22, No. 3, Summer 1973, p. 305.

6.   Elie Wiesel, *the Town Beyond the Wall,* trans. Stephen Becker (New York: Avon Books, 1964), pp. 154-55.

7.   Elie Wiesel, "Rendez-vous avec la haine," *Entre Deux Soleils* (Paris: Editions du Seuil, 1970), p. 96 (my translation). This quotation has been omitted in the English version of the text, *One Generation After.*

8.   *Bulletin du Cercle Juif,* No. 72, November 1962.

9.   Elie Wiesel, *One Generation After,* trans. Lily Edelman and Elie Wiesel (New York: Avon Books, 1970), p. 20.

10.   Elie Wiesel, *From Holocaust to Rebirth* (New York: Council of Jewish Federations and Welfare Funds, 1970), p. 3.

11.   Elie Wiesel, *Souls on Fire,* trans. Marion Wiesel, (New York: Vintage Books, 1972), p. 255.

12.   "Itineraire d'une fin," *Entre Deux Soleils,* p. 9 (my translation).

13.   Robert Jay Lifton in *Death-in-Life* (New York: Vintage Books, 1969) speaks of the image of a "golden age," of idyllic childhoods often presented by concentration camp survivors discussing their early lives. This phenomenon serves to idealize the dead and allows the survivor to "reactivate within himself old and profound feelings of love, nurturance and harmony, in order to be able to apply these feelings to his new formulation of life beyond the death immersion." (p. 534).

14.   Marcel Proust, *A la recherche du temps perdu* (Paris: Bibliotheque de la Pleiade, 1954), p. 427 (my translation).

15.   Elie Wiesel, *Le Mendiant de Jerusalem* (Paris: Seuil, 1968), p. 32 (my translation).

16.   "Elie Wiesel, l'Orant," *Techniques Nouvelles,* March 1972 (my translation).

17.   Lothar Kahn, *Mirrors of the Jewish Mind* (New York: Thomas Yoseloff, 1968), p. 179.

18.   Elie Wiesel, *The Gates of the Forest,* trans. Frances Frenaye (New York: Avon, 1966), p. 22.

19.   While Wiesel uses the expression "the Wandering Jew" throughout his works, in an interview with Lily Edelman, "A Conversation with Elie Wiesel," (*National Jewish Monthly,* November 1973) p. 12, he distinguishes between the Wandering Jew and the Na-venadnick, claiming that the Wandering Jew is "a Christian concept, growing out of a medieval legend about a Jewish cobbler who taunted Jesus on the way to the crucifixion and was cursed to wander thereafter until Jesus' return." In the Jewish tradition, "the Jew as wanderer is usually symbolized by the *Lamed Vavnik,* "The

Just Man ... before the Just man could be revealed he had to become a Na-venadnik, wandering about and hiding his own identity so as to attract and help others anonymously."

20.   E.M. Cioran, *The Temptation to Exist*, trans. Richard Howard (Chicago: Quadrangle Books, 1968), p. 80.

21.   Elie Wiesel, *Le Chant des Morts* (Paris: Seuil, 1966), p. 162 (my translation).

22.   Ibid., p. 157 (my translation).

23.   Ibid., p. 159 (my translation).

24.   Ibid., p. 152 (my translation).

25.   Joseph Friedman, "The Shame of Survival," *Saturday Review*, 25 July 1964, p. 26.

26.   Lothar Kahn, *Chicago Jewish Forum*, XXIII, Fall 1964, p. 53.

27.   Lothar Kahn, *Mirrors of the Jewish Mind*, p. 182.

28.   Norman Friedman, "God Versus Man in the Twentieth Century," *Reconstructionist*, XXII, No. 12, 28 October 1966, pp. 26-27.

29.   Naomi Bliven, Review of *The Town Beyond the Wall*, *New Yorker*, 9 January 1965, pp. 115-116.

30.   Franz Kafka, *The Trial* (New York: Modern Library, 1937), p. 286.

31.   The leitmotive of the play runs through Michael's encounter with the spectator; Michael likens the deportation scene to a Greek tragedy in which the characters are condemned before the curtain rises. The Jews play the role of these characters, following the instructors of an invisible director who sends them to their tragic destiny. The spectator admits that walking around the half-empty city after the deportation was "like being onstage an hour after the end of the show." (*Town*, 168)

32.   *L'Herne*, No. 3, pp. 215-216.

33.   Emmanuel Haymann, "Elie Wiesel: témoin de la nuit," *La Tribune Juive*, No. 192, 3-9 March 1972, p. 10 (my translation).

34.   Thomas A. Idinopulos, "The Holocaust in the Stories of Elie Wiesel," *Soundings*, No. 2, Summer 1972, p. 206.

35.   Elie Wiesel, *The Accident*, trans. Anne Borchardt (New York: Avon, 1962), p. 96.

36.   Irving Halperin, *Messengers from the Dead* (Philadelphia: Westminster Press, 1970), p. 90.

37.   Ibid., pp. 87-88.

38.   Mircea Eliade, *Myth and Reality* (New York: Harper and Row, 1963), pp. 80-81: "the *regressus ad uterum* is accomplished in order that the beneficiary shall be born into a new mode of being or be regenerated."

39.   Elie Wiesel, *Messengers of God*, trans. Marion Wiesel (New York: Pocket Book, Simon & Schuster, 1976), p. 10.

40.   Elie Wiesel, *A Small Measure of Victory: An Interview* by Gene Kippel and Henry Kaufmann (Tuscon: The University of Arizona, 1974), p. 17.

NOTHING WAS THE SAME AGAIN:

A Meditation on the Holocaust, Elie Wiesel's *Messengers of God*, and American Experience

by John K. Roth

> "Seek good and not evil so that you may live, and that Yahweh, God of Sabaoth, may really be with you as you claim he is. Hate evil, love good, maintain justice at the city gate, and it may be that Yahweh, God of Sabaoth, will take pity on the remnant of Joseph." — Amos 5:14-15 (The Jerusalem Bible)

A. All Events Are Linked

The words of this essay took form in October, 1976, about a month before the American electorate made a choice between President Gerald Ford and his challenger, Jimmy Carter. To be precise, they were written on Yom Kippur, the day of atonement and forgiveness. By my typewriter, I recall, there was a copy of the *New York Times Book Review* from the day before. Under its "Best Seller List" I noted the ten entries on the non-fiction side of the ledger.

Items one and two were: *Passages* by Gail Sheehy, a work that deals with "adult life crises"; and Wayne Dyer's *Your Erroneous Zones*, described as "breezy self-help pep talk."[1] Additional books dealt with post-Watergate analysis: *The Final Days* by Bob Woodward and Carl Bernstein, the Washington reporters who helped to expose the scandal originally; and *The Right and the Power* by Leon Jaworski, the former Watergate special prosecutor. Vidal and Beverly Sasson had scored with (perhaps the most problematic Bicentennial title of all) *A Year of Beauty and Health,* a study of "how to eat, exercise, reduce, etc." Include the fact that Alex Comfort's *The Joy of Sex* continued to be a leading paperback and at least a portion of the picture of how American publishers and readers celebrated the nation's two hundredth birthday-year begins to focus. History—(distant as well as recent), do-it-yourself psychology, pursuit of the "good life" (i.e., pleasure)—these ever-new-and-always-old concerns accounted for a lot of American ink in 1976.

Other dimensions need to be mentioned however. One is touched by the fact that two of the books on that *Times Book Review* list—interestingly enough, the most recent and the longest-standing entries—dealt with Jewish life: Arthur Koestler's *The Thirteenth Tribe,* a study of the ancient Khazars in Eastern Europe; and Irving Howe's *World of Our Fathers,* a highly praised account of the Eastern European Jews who immigrated to New York City in large numbers at the turn of the century. Not only do such works indicate that ethnicity— along with issues about male-female roles and relations— remained fundamental for American life in 1976. They also provide a link for noting that the subjects of death and dying were additional literary focal points during our Bicentennial year. Indeed considerable concern crystalized around the Holocaust, the destruction of European Jews under Hitler.[2]

Although we are hardly dealing with "Great Awakening" proportions, an increasing number of Americans have discovered, or re-discovered, the Holocaust. Heretofore, if Americans were aware of the Holocaust at all, many tended to regard it as somebody else's problem, as the worry of a neurotically obsessed minority. Undefined as it may be, our recent recognition of the event is different and significant; its timing may be important as well. To launch a third century of American life in the midst of what can now be seen as a Holocaust Universe—that dream-and-reality cries out for soul-searching and judgment, courage and rebellion, healing and atonement, of the first magnitude. Particularly at a time when evangelical Christianity revives in American life—not least in the enthusiasm of a Carter or even in the more placid spirituality of a Ford—the issue of whether God "may really be with you as you claim" is posed by Holocaust flames. The Holocaust is a potential time-bomb in American religious experience. Its long-delayed explosion could be starting now, and one factor in that process could be Elie Wiesel's gift to us in 1976.

I refer to *Messengers of God: Biblical Portraits and Legends,* a series of story-meditations on Adam and Eve, Cain and Abel, Abraham and Isaac, Jacob, Joseph, Moses, and Job. With these figures and stories in mind, Wiesel contends: "In Jewish history, all events are linked. Only today, after the whirlwind of fire and blood that was the Holocaust, do we grasp the full range of implications of the murder of one man by his brother, the deeper meanings of a father's questions and disconcerting silences. Only as we tell them now, in the light of certain experiences of life and death, do we understand them."[3] Biblical images, characters, stories, teachings—these have informed American history, too. Concentrating on Wiesel's renditions of them, focusing on the development of his own authorship and on his suggestions about a Holocaust God, we may discern some religious insights that can—and cannot—help us to address the multiple problems of evil stalking our path toward Century 21.

B. At the Risk of Being Defeated

Who's Who In America (1974-75) condenses Elie Wiesel to sixteen lines. Its sketch says that he was born in Sighet, Rumania on September 30, 1928, to Shlomo and Sarah Feig Wiesel. The paragraph tells that he studied in Paris at the Sorbonne from 1947 to 1950, and that he traveled to the United States in 1956, where he became a naturalized citizen in 1963. Many books authored by Wiesel are listed, along with the fact that he holds numerous honorary degrees. Mention is also made of his distinguished professorship, his marriage, and his winning of literary prizes such as the French Prix Medicis. Ironically, however, *Who's Who* is silent about the very fact that accounts for its entry about him. A seventeenth line should read: Jewish survivor of Auschwitz.

"I write in order to understand as much as to be understood."[4] Elie Wiesel does not see himself primarily as a philosopher, theologian, or political theorist. Instead, he is a storyteller. Storytellers can deal with ultimate questions without answering them straight out, and that possibility attracts Wiesel as a way of coping with the reality and meaning of the Holocaust. That reality and meaning defy words—at least any that are direct. Thus, the prospects offered by theory-building disciplines seem less fruitful to him than those offered by the indirect approach of telling tales. And yet, in the midst of recounting Holocaust stories that resist telling, philosophy, theology, and politics come to life in ways that theory alone never permits.

Speaking in God's name, Moses commanded his people to choose life. And after Moses, Wiesel believes, "nothing was the same again."[5] With the Holocaust as back- and foreground created by past responses to Moses's challenge, Wiesel's recurrent story from *Night* (1960) to *Messengers of God* (1976) is that of how men and women have chosen to live.[6] It is a tale that instructs not by explanations, but by setting before us life and death. The ultimate lesson-appeal stays constant: Choose life. However, as Wiesel has learned from Moses, that conclusion is always a beginning because it specifies too little. Indeed it quizzes us into troubling questions about ourselves and God. A Jew, writes Elie Wiesel, "defines himself more by what troubles him than by what reassures him.... To me, the Jew and his questioning are one."[7] To the degree that Americans are touched by Wiesel's writing, they are moved toward that strange identity.

Genèsis states that the earth was once "a formless void, there was darkness over the deep."[8] Darkness and the void— those realities were not erased by God's creating power. They were only refashioned so as to make the necessity of choice and creation new every day. And the accumulation of history from the time of Moses to the present has taken God and humanity together into a Nazi Kingdom of Night and into a Void of Crematoria that turn promises and hopes, bodies and spirits, to smoke and ashes. As event-symbol, the death camp taunts us with the question: What is ultimate reality and meaning?

Elie Wiesel's first works—*Night* (1960), *Dawn* (1961), and *The Accident* (1962)—travel through the destruction of a supportive universe, into the ambiguity, despair, and nothingness that accompany a realization that men and women must be their own providence. Life almost succeeds in fulfilling a choice to cancel itself, but failure on that score becomes a turning. The nature of that turning, however, remains blurred. The silence of God, the moral emptiness of the Void, the destructive form or formlessness of the Night—all of these shadow reasons for living.

Nonetheless, Wiesel asserts, the meaning of being Jewish is "never to give up—never to yield to despair."[9] That affirmation is one of his categorical imperatives, and it is to be applied in one's relations to human persons and God alike, irrespective of the temptations toward despair that they may provoke. Such a commandment is exceedingly difficult in a Holocaust Universe. To keep it Wiesel must wrestle long and hard, for-and-against the Jewish tradition that retains normative qualities for him and thereby for-and-against God and humankind together. Thus, effort to discover and to create trustworthy reasons and resources against despair is one thread that unites the four major novels that Wiesel has written thus far: *The Gates of the Forest* (1964), *The Town Beyond the Wall* (1964), *A Beggar in Jerusalem* (1970), and *The Oath* (1973).

These novels carry forward the testimony that ours is a Holocaust Universe. True, our times are penultimate; life continues to unfold. That unfolding, however, may never eliminate completely scars that are permanent. Indeed those scars must never be forgotten, even as we face the command to choose life in ways that build and heal beyond them. The edges of reality are ultimately jagged. *But how jagged does depend on the future.* God is real, humanity is real, evil and suffering and death are real—just as we experience them to be. But what they mean and thus what they become does rest in part with choices yet to be made. Jagged edges are in our hands and in God's. What and how they cut is forever unfinished business.

If a person will discover them by creating them, good reasons for choosing life can be found even in a world turned upside down by the Holocaust. Choose life because suffering and indifference are real, because love is possible and thus responsibility is put upon us. The truth of these reasons, however, is not self-evident. Their validity does not rest on natural law or on some indubitable foundation of a fully rational world. They are largely reasons of refusal, resistance, and rebellion, grounded in and against every power that yields needless, senseless waste. Learn the bonds between suffering and indifference, between love and responsibility. Oppose suffering with love; meet indifference with protest. Wiesel's novels re-echo the basic message that such acts constitute reasons enough to live hard and well.

At the same time, a counterpoint moves ahead. Especially in the essays, vignettes, and dramas of works such as *The Jews of Silence* (1966), *Legends of Our Time* (1968), *One Generation After* (1970), and *Zalmen, Or the Madness of God* (1974), memories, losses, lack of progress in our moral condition, continue to gnaw away. Hope must be renewed *because it is always being lost.* By way of illustration, consider *Zalmen.* Although "an abyss of blood separates Moscow from Berlin," Wiesel's play shows that the world of Soviet Jews is a Holocaust Universe nonetheless.[10] True, the hopelessness of Auschwitz is not so much the problem. Rather there is the hopelessness of seeing a way of life crushed out, not by some killing final solution, but the terror of being able to live— indeed of being required to do so—under terms set by enemies. And not even God seems to care. That knowledge weights the burden almost beyond belief.

"God requires of man not that he live, but that he choose to live. What matters is to choose—at the risk of being defeated."[11] Inside the U.S.S.R. an old rabbi, Zalmen his assistant, a doctor, a daughter, a grandson, and a son-in-law, the chairman of a synagogue and the rest of a fearful congregation are confronted by choices—choices imposed by an oppressive government intent on forcing silent submission. A troupe of visiting actors from the West wishes to witness Russian Jews at prayer. Concerned about appearances, government officials decide to permit the visit, but warnings are issued to the Jews. There must be no disturbances, no protests, nothing to suggest discontent. Almost everyone is willing to go along. The old rabbi, however, proves exceptional. Provoked by Zalmen, or the madness of God, he chooses to break silence and testify to the suffering of his people.

A dramatic scene . . . but nothing much changes—at least on the surface—except that futility gains a little ground. The government investigates; Jewish anxiety increases for a time. No plot is discovered, and fear subsides to a more typical level. The doctor dares the choice of visiting the visiting actors to drive home the protest made by the rabbi. Unfortunately, they have already gone on their way silently. Although the possibility remains that the rabbi can have a significant relationship with his grandson, his family may be more lost to him then ever, and the madness of his moving protest may have pushed him into permanent disorientation that will be useless. Zalmen begins to doubt that his provocation was worth the pain and fragmentation and emptiness it has caused. Madness compounds itself.

Such is the hopelessness that runs through this drama. Yet hope is intertwined. Slim though its chances may be, hope directs us to the power of an example, to the courage that can be contained in a choice, to the challenge that says: We must not leave the rabbi alone; we must not allow his sacrifice to be in vain. Maybe *Zalmen, Or the Madness of God* will provoke others to choose well—even at the risk of being defeated. With that hope as its premise, Wiesel's unwritten third act awaits direction by all of us.

C. Faces of a Holocaust God

Travel into nights of despair yields reasons for living, but the realism of Wiesel's reports, memories, and dialogues tells us that to live well is never to be far from hopelessness and that if we do not act with vigilant compassion and protest the future may not be worth having. All of those themes find repetition in a final group of Wiesel's writings: *Souls on Fire* (1972), *Ani Maamin* (1973), and *Messengers of God* (1976). In addition, these books bring the faces of his Holocaust God into sharpest focus.

"I never speak of God now," says Elie Wiesel, "I rather speak of men who believed in God or men who denied God."[12] The reasons are multiple. For one, his past experience—both in its Holocaust dimensions and in the religious training of his childhood—continues to underscore the point that one must not/cannot speak about God easily/directly: "To me, the essence of Jewish history is mystical and not rational."[13] For another, Wiesel holds the following convictions: "If you want difficulties, choose to live *with* God. Can you compare today the tragedy of the believer to that of the nonbeliever? The real tragedy, the real drama, is the drama of the believer."[14] Wiesel loves that "real drama." He seems to identify with it, at least enough to find its difficulties inescapable: "To be a Jew is to have all the reasons in the world not to have faith in language, in singing, in prayers, and in God, but *to go on telling the tale, to go on carrying on the dialogue,* and to have my own silent prayers and quarrels with God."[15] Thus, he has much to say about God, in spite and because of his disclaimer.

Wiesel's writings form a mediating mask that renders every theological interpretation uncertain. Nonetheless, as he explores the ranges of belief and unbelief within his characters and thereby in himself, faces of a Holocaust God are present throughout. Although glimpses of them are always momentary and broken, tentative and unsystematic, the blurring is reduced in these last three books. If it remains impossible to fix Wiesel's theology and religious stance once and for all, one can outline further some fundamental theological tendencies in his recorded thought..

1. *Paradox and Celebration.* "In the shadow of the executioner, they celebrated life."[16] In *Souls on Fire,* Elie Wiesel relates tales of the Hasidim. Born out of Jewish suffering, plus a passionate love for life and tradition that sought to find vigorous expression in eighteenth century Europe, Hasidism renewed the old and found ways to celebrate. Nourished by its examples and stories, succeeding generations kept Hasidic flames alive, even in Auschwitz. It is not clear that such faith has survived intact, but the Hasidic tradition does live on, perhaps even stronger than anyone might have guessed.

The Hasidism that Wiesel describes is fiercely humanistic. Its aim is always to affirm the world of life-here-and-now, to make life better-here-and-now. At the same time, the premise of that humanism is anchored in ties to God. Without God, humanity is and can be nothing. The catch—and the challenge—is that even with God humanity may also become nothing. Therefore, life must be lived so that it can be celebrated; it must be celebrated so that it can be lived. Otherwise we defeat ourselves and God too, causing hopeless tangles in the threads of the passionate story that he has chosen to weave with us. But what more can we see in Wiesel's portraits of the eternal face, and how do they relate to our Holocaust Universe?

Often the Hasidic tales recounted and embellished by

Wiesel speak of the need to force God's hand. The God in question is no weak idealist, helplessly watching the world run out of control and unable to respond except by hand-wringing. He is Creator and Master of the Universe. And yet, choosing stubbornly and persistently to be the creator and Master of *this* universe, the ultimate paradoxes in Wiesel's theological reflections emerge: God will not and, practically if not logically speaking, cannot move except through the characters he has brought to life to develop and tell his own uncompleted tale. This God is different from all of us, and yet he is present in each of us. He has a plan, but it is the plan of freedom working out its own course as it lives in individuals and communities. Thus, the plan is virtually no plan at all; it can unleash the worst as well as the best that is in us.

God listens and answers — usually in the mode of silence. He loves — but by needing our love because he is unloveable in his harshness, which is what we tend to experience most unforgettably. He is ally ... by being judge. He is judge ... not by intervention that metes out justice in total equity, but by letting events fall as they may to reveal the corrupt absurdity, as well as the grandeur, of what we do together. The presence of this God is like the absence of all Gods, and therefore obedience to his will is often to be found in rebellion against it. Depending on how that protest unfolds — and all of us, including God, take our chances on that score — we may discover in retrospect that the aim, divine and human, is indeed to celebrate life in spite and because of the executioner.

2. *Faith and Emotion.* "They leave heaven and do not, cannot, see that they are no longer alone: God accompanies them, weeping, smiling, whispering: *Nitzhuni banai,* my children have defeated me, they deserve my gratitude."[17] *Ani Maamin,* a song lost and found again, sings of faith in the Messiah. As Wiesel renders it, this cantata-poem tells of Abraham, Isaac, and Jacob, wandering Jews who return from earth to put God on trial with their Holocaust reports. The tale is told with all of the emotion and pain that the Patriarchs can muster, and yet apparently it cannot be told — at least not well enough to move God toward intervention, toward sending or permitting the Messiah to work. The three are beaten. They prepare to return to their forgotten people, remembering, experiencing, perhaps recounting once more in

amazement tales of Jewish belief—belief spawned and oriented not by what God has done apart from Abraham, Isaac, and Jacob, but by what they have done in the name of God and humanity together. Unseen, unnoticed by them, God begins to move.

The movement is in God's face. It is weeping, smiling, whispering. But to what effect? Although the collage of feeling expressed here is a tale too complex to tell, Wiesel suggests the following lines of reflection: God's tears are tears of grief, guilt, remorse, compassion, love, and joy all at once. His smile is one of knowing, of admiration and vindication, of stubborn and harsh determination that good is balanced enough against evil to let men and women continue on their heartbreaking way alone. The whisper says: "What am I doing? What are you going to do?" The effect overall is that the many emotions become one, and it is only God's face that moves. Once more the Messiah is delayed. The open account of his expected coming will have to move forward, leaving in suspense—in faith—the question of whether he has been on the way all along.

3. *Blessing and Burden.* "... It is given to man to transform divine injustice into human justice and compassion."[18] Abraham, Isaac, and Jacob—along with Adam and Eve, Cain and Abel, Joseph, Moses, and Job—are *Messengers of God.* The message that their tales repeat forms the portrait of God-man painted so clearly and starkly, so ambiguously and subtly, in a few words at the end of Elie Wiesel's fourteenth book.

Life is not fair. Although the Holocaust escalates that reality, unfairness was also a fact in the beginning. Not in detail perhaps, but in outline, things were intended to be that way. Seeds of error, deception, and guilt were planted originally in the Garden of Eden. Bias, favoritism, hurt feelings, vengeance, and murder formed the brotherhood of Cain and Abel. Promises, tests, obedience, trust, survival, hope—these did not add up to a world of rationality and justice for Abraham and Isaac, but they are the stuff that made a people.

In the beginning ... Auschwitz. Jacob fought to secure a blessing, and the world has shaken to the core in trying to fathom its nature and portent. Wily Joseph escaped jealous brothers, worked his way to the top, handled Potiphar's wife beautifully, made himself a *Tzaddik,* a Just Man. His success was too much. Unfairly, his people paid the price. Leadership and the law—these things we associate with Moses. But even this man, closest to God of all, had to glimpse the future from so far away that he had to wonder about the One in charge. And Job, our contemporary (Jewish or not, who knows?), maybe life had been unfairly good to him and so his testing should be (unfairly?) commensurate?

Wiesel implies that one face of God is that of unfairness and injustice. It is also a mask that reveals through the rebellion of *Messengers* that this same God intends for us to have hard, even impossible, moral work until and through death. So what about the face of this God who incites, permits, suffers, and perhaps endures and survives a Holocaust Universe? When everything is totaled, does the face belong to friend or foe? The messengers answer: Both . . . but the degree to which it is one or the other depends largely on how we choose to live.

Moses was instructed by God: "Say to Aaron and his sons, Thus you shall bless the people of Israel: you shall say to them, The Lord bless you and keep you: The Lord make his face to shine upon you, and be gracious to you: The Lord lift up his countenance upon you, and give you peace. So shall they put my name upon the people of Israel, and I will bless them."[19] Challenged to choose life well, all descendants and followers of Moses, Elie Wiesel, and thus of their God, have been left with one challenge more. It is to discover how to receive and to give that blessing so that it does indeed convey an affirmation of life. As the Hasidim suggest, discovery is in creation of the fact, and so Elie Wiesel's portraits and legends wind up where they began: with tales that cannot—and yet can and must—be told because they are in the making.

D. Answers: I Say There Are None

Holocaust experiences leave Elie Wiesel suspicious about finding answers to ultimate questions. Answers oversimplify, falsify, settle what is unsettled; they relax tension where it should be felt even more profoundly. "I have nothing against questions," writes Wiesel. "They are useful. What is more, they alone are. To turn away from them would be to fail in our duty, to lose our only chance to be able one day to lead an authentic life. It is against the answers that I protest, regardless of their basis. Answers: I say there are none."[20]

With our orientation toward problem-solving, that is a hard conclusion for us Americans to accept. This may be especially true where ingredients in our religious life are concerned. Whether our spiritual searchings take the form of a quest for God, a commitment to agnosticism or atheism, or a venture into forms of Oriental meditation, the drive is to settle questions, to transcend them, more than it is to confront them as ultimate. Elie Wiesel invites a spirituality of the latter kind, and if Americans really are discovering the Holocaust, we may come to agree with him that questions "alone are." As Wiesel himself shows, that outcome need not force hopelessness over a total lack of rationality in things, nor need it cause us to reject altogether philosophical and religious traditions that have nourished us. What it does require of us is to take seriously that the "whys?" are ultimately too thick and too many for us to handle.

Theories based on divine plans, abused freedom, punishment for human sin, the idea that some greater good will rise out of the testing ashes—all of them raise more questions than they satisfy. It is not that these "explanations" make no sense at all. The difficulty is that their sense is only partial. Whether freedom or necessity is at the ground of being, the result is the same. If things could have worked out differently, why didn't they? If they had to be this way and no other, why? God can answer by pointing to his will or by pointing beyond. After Auschwitz—before Auschwitz for that matter—neither act is sufficient to situate a principle of sufficient reason in the nature of things.

Such an outcome is not the end of religious thought and practice. It only clarifies too-easily-forgotten tasks that both have had all along: namely, that of informing life by raising questions instead of aiming to answer them; that of liberating and healing spirits, not by settling anything but by protesting and caring so that people—and even God—may move each other beyond despair or sheer numbness. Americans may continue to forget those possibilities, just as recent Holocaust concern may be one of our passing fads. But if Americans do come to see themselves more and more as situated in a Holocaust Universe, and if we can learn to follow Wiesel's leads in questioning, protesting, and caring, at least five aspects of our religious experience ought to feel and express an impact.

1. *Secular Humanism.* "One part of him yearned for God, the other for escape from God."[21] Such was Adam's condition after the fall. For many Americans that tension no longer exists. It relaxes in the conclusion that God is dead — or never was — and that we must place our bets on men and women or lose by default. The difficulty, though, is that our journey from the early sixties to the late seventies has been a slide away from optimism toward uncertainty. Instead of building The Great Society, political leaders counsel us to do more-with-less. Our recent political campaign has lacked passion, not because there are no issues, but because there is general indifference about the ability of anyone to solve them. Jimmy Carter offers to give the country "a leader, for a change"; Gerald Ford is supposedly "making us proud again." Belief on either score is lukewarm at best.

Elie Wiesel has suggested that "it was its own heart the world incinerated at Auschwitz.... Not only man died, but also the idea of man."[22] Any American who faces the Holocaust honestly is likely to find an already-shaking self-confidence eroded further. Perhaps that is a good reason for leaving the subject alone, but the event seems to find ways of its own to keep that from happening altogether. In any case, reaction to the erosion of humanism can take varied forms, including increased cynicism and despair, renewed determination to restore confidence, and even a revived yearning for God. Where the latter occurs, however, the need is likely to be rather different than religionists have tended to see in related spiritual expressions of past years.

This yearning will reinstate the tension that Adam felt. It will not be simply the response of a creature acknowledging faults penitentially to a perfect creator. A sense of having been beaten by God may be present, but having tasted the reality of our own freedom and power, our yearnings for God will also contain anger and rebellion against God for the uses made of his own creative urges. Times of trouble are often times of opportunity for religion. After Auschwitz, however, theologies that excuse God without trying him equally will fail to meet and inform raw emotion — feeling that could nourish a revival of religious humanism rooted in acceptance/protest of the fact that "it is given to man to transform divine injustice into human justice and compassion."[23]

2. *Civil Religion.* "This very ancient story is still our own and we shall continue to be bound to it in the most intimate way. We may not know it, but every one of us, at one time or another, is called upon to play a part in it. What part? Are we Abraham or Isaac? We are Jacob, that is to say, Israel. And Israel began with Abraham."[24] Americans pledge allegiance to a flag that symbolizes "one nation, under God." Our coins remind us that "in God we trust," and images of ourselves as a chosen people, a redeemer nation, still influence our behavior. Like Israel's, all of those stories began with Abraham, too.

Though we are famous for pioneering the separation of church and state, religion has long been perceived—rightly or wrongly—as a form of glue that holds our body politic together. It has been argued that religion functions most effectively in this fashion when it is non-sectarian, and there have been laments in some corners over the possibility that Americans may be losing a shared faith in a divine providence that watches over our national interest—judging it, to be sure, but protecting it even more so. Because it calls God's providence into question on all fronts, an encounter with the Holocaust will probably erode civil religion still further, thus creating new responsibilities for theology as well.

It is questionable whether anything valuable would be gained by a total elimination of civil religion in the United States. What seems more to the point is an effort to see if it can really be renewed and used to keep us vigilant and sensitive. Elie Wiesel's reading of Abraham could give us some handles for furthering that cause. Abraham was favored by God. He was, Wiesel suggests, "a man for all seasons, blessed with all talents and virtues, deserving of every grace."[25] He would be the father of a people. Yet the drama of this man's life centers on an original holocaust: God's commanding test that Abraham should offer his only son, Isaac, as a burnt offering. Such testing was contrary to reason; it was beyond reason, and yet Abraham acted obediently. But the point is that Abraham's obedience was not just obedience—at least as Wiesel tells the story. Abraham was also testing God to see how far God would go. And Abraham won—God relented.

It may be contested that such a reading of the story is a perverse reversal of the biblical account, not to mention the fact that it impugns God's goodness. After Auschwitz, however, Wiesel is suggesting that we may need to read the Bible with new eyes. Too many times God has not relented—his power has permitted needless waste or else that power is too minimal to worry about. Wiesel's reading favors the first option, and this leaves him close to Jung's observation that "God is not only to be loved, but also to be feared."[26] Abraham's discovery, then, was that God is guilty as well as humanity, and history lays that fact bare in a Holocaust Universe. But the greatness of Abraham is to be found in his non-rejection of God, indeed in his interceding with God for the sake of his people in spite and because of the hard responsibilities laid upon them. Civil religion that recognizes the unfairness of life—both in its blessings, which characterize the American experience, and in its burdens, which set an agenda of responsibility for us in our dealings with the poor and hungry and persecuted everywhere—that is a vision worth working for, and a goal for which American-theology-rooted-in-the-Holocaust should aim.

3. *Views of Covenant and the God of History.* "For, in fact, he filled two equally difficult roles: he was God's emissary to Israel and Israel's to God."[27] Meet Moses, who knew God as "a consuming fire" and as the One who sets people free.[28] Actually, for Americans to meet Moses is to keep an appointment with an old friend, for our nation's origins include visions of Exodus and the establishment of God's New Israel. How do things work out if we bring that tradition into contact with a Moses viewing us through Elie Wiesel's Holocaust eyes?

More than one writer has suggested that the God of History, not to mention convenants between that God and human creatures, is gone with the smoke from Nazi crematoria. That conclusion is hard to resist, if we restrict our concept of God to the traditional notions of full omnipotence and total goodness. At least in theory, we did learn to view God in that way, if not to believe that he really was with us as we claimed, but certainly Wiesel's Moses never lived with such illusions. He recognized the absolute power of God and knew that to confront God was to stand on sacred soil. He also learned that to enter self-consciously into relation with God is to initiate a battle for liberty that requires us to contend with God himself as well as with ourselves and other people.

Moses discovered that Gods of History come in many stripes and colors, and what he came to realize is that the One we are dealing with is a God who cares, but who does so largely through leaving us to sort out a gift of freedom that is at once incredibly vast and wonderful and yet destructively narrow and blind. True, directives are given and pacts are established as part of the bargain, but they increase the tension more than they dissolve it. Amazing that Moses did not reject God as a cosmic sadist, a hollow mask of indifference broken only by mocking laughter.

He did not, and there are two major reasons. First, Moses saw that people are forgetful, foolish, cowardly—and even worse that they are deceitful, calculating, ready to sell souls for almost any price. And yet the counterpoint was to remember that people could be different, Not perfectible, to be sure, but perhaps less imperfect. Second, an irreplaceable source of courage to struggle for good against evil could come through a sense of covenant with God, so long as it was understood that to serve God required one to be against God, too. Moses, so often pictured as the obedient leader who constantly had to deal with a rebellious people, that Moses was actually the most profoundly rebellious of all. Without God, Moses could be nothing. With God, Moses saw ways to bring people to places from which they could at least catch glimpses of a promised land. One religious task, Wiesel's Moses suggests, is to explore whether we can discern not a God of history who pulls the strings of events or even who uses people as instruments of his own judgment, but rather a God of history whose covenant with a world of freedom requires us to break it in moral rebellion if its goodness is to be preserved at all.

4. *Visions of Persuasion and Power.* "I could bring this farce to an end; that may even be what You want, what You are driving me to. But I shall not do it, do You hear me, Master of the Universe, I shall not do it, I shall not destroy, do You hear me, I shall not kill!"[29] Cain speaks to God ... and then he killed Abel. In Elie Wiesel's tale, Cain saw himself dared by God, pushed by God toward going against God. The only hitch is that this awareness did not forestall murder. And thus we may gain some new insight into the Christian prayer that petitions God to deliver us from evil.

Cain's feelings about divine persuasion rub us optimistic

Americans the wrong way. God has created structures in the world that drive us intentionally toward madness, violence, brutality of real-but-unimaginable-proportions. News—bad —to us. Of course those things do occur, but it isn't right to blame God; it's our fault. We tend to settle for a purely good God or no God at all. It is safer that way, more comforting perhaps. But those conclusions resist keeping when Cain is recognized as all-too-contemporary. We would like to buy a Whiteheadian portrait of God as "the ideal companion . . . the poet of the world, with tender patience leading it by his vision of truth, beauty, and goodness."[30] Indeed many of us have, as the hopes placed on "process theology" make clear. It is problematic, however, whether this God can really take the heat of Holocaust fires.

Committed to maintain the complete goodness of God, process theology is stuck with the implication that God is always doing the best he can. Given the way that the world's history unfolds, that notion is hard to swallow, at least if we also ascribe decisive power to God. In a Holocaust Universe, a God who is doing the best he can is either not as good as we thought or too weak to trust. And to the degree that he is the latter, which is the conclusion that the Whiteheadian process theology pushes to the fore in spite of itself, goodness is reduced in its influence. In that case, reasons for identification with God are also minimized, warm feelings to the contrary notwithstanding.

What we Americans have to ask religiously is whether we can settle for an innocent but ineffectual God, or whether we must run the risks of relating to a God who is really Master of the Universe but less than perfectly good by any standards we can comprehend. The fragmented, mystical quality of Wiesel's theology leaves any final statement clouded, but he seems inclined toward the second view. True, God's power is limited by virtue of his decision to underwrite human freedom, but this is a self-limitation that God elects in creation and there is ultimately nothing to suggest that the decision cannot be changed. Moreover, although Wiesel has said that "God does not want man to suffer; man suffers against God," he has also said of his people: "Who didn't persecute us in history? Even God made us suffer."[31] A God pure but weak, or One who is powerful but of questionable virtue—toward which end of that spectrum should we lean? Is one view more faithful to the facts than the other? Does one hold out more hope? We shall have to see. But I expect that Cain would favor the second option. Likewise for Abel.

5. *Jesus and the Suffering God.* "Job spoke his outrage, his grief; he told God what He should have known for a long time, perhaps since always, that something was amiss in His Universe. The just were punished for no reason, the criminal rewarded for no reason. The just and the wicked were subjected to the same fate—God having turned His back on them, on everyone. God had lost interest in His creation; He was absent."[32] If Wiesel's Job were with us today, how would he respond to the proposition that "Christ is the answer"? Would his car bear a "honk if you love Jesus" bumper sticker? Or in a more sophisticated vein, how would he react to a theology that finds Jesus testifying to the presence of a God whose love is revealed by suffering with us and whose power and victory are in weakness that the world finds impossible to overcome? With laughter, madness, tears? Would Job's response be: "Though he slay me, yet will I trust in him" and "I know that my Redeemer liveth"?[33]

It is not easy to say one way or the other. At least that is one conclusion to draw from Wiesel's interpretation, because he is struck by the fact that Job's final answer to God was that "now, having seen you with my own eyes, I retract all I have said, and in dust and ashes I repent."[34] For Wiesel's Job, however, that answer was no simple resignation. It was instead resistance and rebellion masked and expressed in hasty abdication. Ultimately, God cannot be defeated which is both our hope and our despair, but in confessing—when God, with greater reason to do so, did not—Job "continued to interrogate God."[35] Of this, therefore, we may be sure: Wiesel's Job would find Jesus a question, whatever the external relationship between them might appear to be.

Questioning does not leave relationships unchanged, but it need not cancel them and it can even push them deeper. Thus, to turn Jesus into a question instead of—or at least as well as—an answer might make the current enthusiasm and assurance of evangelical Christianity more profound. That move might also add worthwhile passion to the faith of Protestants and Catholics who see themselves as more liberal in outlook. Some of the issues could sort out as follows: (1) Even if we agree that all persons, "good and bad alike, are in the wrong before God and helpless without his forgiveness," can it suffice after Auschwitz to say that "in Jesus Christ God was reconciling the world to himself" when we see that action simply as the response of divine love to human sinfulness?[36] Or do we Christians have to play that theme of reconciliation in variations which include God's sinfulness and human love as well? (2) If we speak correctly in referring to "the gravity, cost, and sure achievement of God's reconciling work," must we not also compare the innocence and sacrifice of Holocaust victims against that of God himself, and in doing so see dimensions of gravity and cost—including Christian anti-Semitism—which render all sure achievements problematic?[37] (3) If "God reveals his love in Jesus Christ by showing power in the form of a servant, wisdom in the folly of the cross, and goodness in receiving sinful men," do not Holocaust flames give us pause to re-evaluate the love of love, the power of power, the wisdom of wisdom, and the goodness of goodness?[38] (4) And if we are right in saying that Jesus was "the perfect child of God. He was the fulfillment of God's promise to Israel, the beginning of the new creation, and the pioneer of the new humanity. He gave history its meaning and direction and called the church to be his servant for the reconciliation of the world"—if we are right in saying those words, then how shall things stand when we transfer to the crematoria cries of a Psalmist uttered from the cross: "My God, my God, why have you deserted me?"[39]

The list could go on and on, but always it leaves the same question: *Can we learn not to blame God as a way of covering over our responsibilities, but to be boldly honest with God and with ourselves as a means to deepen compassion?* The Holocaust offers that post-Bicentennial challenge to American religious life and waits for the response.

* * * *

Messengers of God did not appear on best-seller lists in 1976. Probably it will never attain the popularity of Elie Wiesel's novels, though rarely has he written with such depth and insight. The book is harder going than a novel; it forces the reader to meditate along with the writer, trying to hold together tensions and conflicts in biblical portraits and legends. One of Wiesel's great strengths is the ability to open up his readers to the predicament of having to live without final answers, of having to exist without the resolutions that we would choose, of having to acknowledge that life and death reflect a logic that defies our canons of rationality. However much we experience and know these messages, they are not easy to face. Elie Wiesel's tales help us to see how to do so well. *Messengers of God* is an important book for 1976, for 2001, and beyond. By urging us to see that the task—for Jews, Christians, Americans, and for every concerned man and woman—is "to transform divine injustice into human justice and compassion," it poses questions that leave nothing the same.[40] Yet those very questions can enable people to move closer than ever before in grasping that God may really be with us as we claim he is.

1.   The quips quoted here, plus others that follow in the paragraph, are from *The New York Times Book Review*, October 3, 1976, p. 45.

2.   A sampling of recent books on the Holocaust that have been widely read and discussed in 1976 would include: Harry James Cargas, *Harry James Cargas in Conversation with Elie Wiesel* (New York: Paulist Press, 1976); Lucy S. Dawidowicz, *The War Against the Jews 1933-1945* (New York: Bantam Books, 1976); Terrence Des Pres, *The Survivor* (New York: Oxford University Press, 1976); Lawrence L. Langer, *The Holocaust and the Literary Imagination* (New Haven: Yale University Press, 1975); Richard L. Rubenstein, *The Cunning of History* (New York: Harper & Row, 1975, Corrieten Boom, *The Hiding Place* (Old Tappan, N.J.: Fleming H. Revell, 1971); and Simon Wiesenthal, *The Sunflower* (New York: Schocken Books, 1976). In this context, Saul Bellow's winning of the 1976 Nobel Prize for Literature should also be noted. This Jewish writer, the first American novelist to receive a Nobel award since John Steinbeck in 1962, frequently develops his characters and themes in ways that reflect Holocaust realitites.

     The Holocaust also left an impression on American film audiences in 1976. For example, large numbers saw *The Hiding Place*, which is based on the experiences of a Dutch Christian, Corrie ten Boom, who helped to rescue Jews from the Nazis and barely escaped death in the Ravensbruck concentration camp as a result. Others witnessed the black comedy of Lina Wertmuller's *Seven Beauties,* and Bruno Bettelheim's long and highly critical review of the film in the August 2, 1976, issue of *The New Yorker* created sparks of its own. In addition, October, 1976, was the month in which Marcel Ophile's documentary on the Nuremburg trials, *The Memory of Justice,* opened its commercial run in Manhatten.

Three other events this October are also worth mentioning: (1) A professor at Yale University resigned under pressure when it was discovered that he had authored anti-Jewish newspaper stories in Europe during World War II. (2) In New York City, members of Concerned Jewish Youth took over the headquarters of the National Council of Churches in a nonviolent protest over the refusal of the Council to oust a board member, Archbishop Valerian Trifa of the Rumanian Orthodox episcopate, who has been accused of World War II crimes against Jewish people. (3) The United States Immigration and Naturalization Service filed deportation proceedings against three men accused of Nazi war crimes against Jews. These cases, part of a new campaign to handle charges against some eighty persons, are the first American deportation proceedings against Nazi war criminals in more than twenty years.

3.   Elie Wiesel, *Messengers of God,* trans. Marion Wiesel (New York: Random House, 1976), pp. xiii-xiv.

4.   Elie Wiesel, *One Generation After,* trans. Lily Edelman and the author (New York: Avon Books, 1972), p. 213.

5.   *Deuteronomy* 30:19-20 (Revised Standard Version.)

6.   *Messengers of God,* p. 181.

7.   *One Generation After,* p. 214.

8.   *Genesis* 1:2 (The Jerusalem Bible.)

9.   Elie Wiesel, "Against Despair." This essay, published as a pamphlet by the United Jewish Appeal, is a reprint of the first annual Louis A. Pincus Memorial Lecture, which was delivered by Wiesel on December 8, 1973. See p. 11 in the pamphlet.

10.   Elie Wiesel *The Jews of Silence,* trans. Neal Kozodoy (New York: Signet Books, 1967), p. 14.

11.   Elie Wiesel, *Zalmen, Or the Madness of God,* trans. Nathan Edelman (New York: Random House, 1974), p. 53.

12.   Elie Wiesel, "Talking and Writing and Keeping Silent," in Franklin H. Littell and Hubert G. Locke, eds., *The German Church Struggle and the Holocaust* (Detroit: Wayne State University Press, 1974), p. 271.

13.   "Against Despair," p. 5.

14.   "Talking and Writing and Keeping Silent," p. 274.

15.   *Ibid.,* p. 277. Wiesel's emphasis.

16.   Elie Wiesel, *Souls on Fire,* trans. Marion Wiesel (New York: Random House, 1973), p. 38.

17.   Elie Wiesel, *Ani Maamin,* trans. Marion Wiesel (New York: Random House, 1973), p. 105.

18.   *Messengers of God,* p. 235.

19.   *Numbers* 6:23-27 (Revised Standard Version).

20. Elie Wiesel, *Legends of Our Time* (New York: Avon Books, 1972), p. 222.

21. *Messengers of God*, p. 31.

22. *Legends of Our Time*, p. 230.

23. *Messengers of God*, p. 235.

24. *Ibid.*, p. 70.

25. *Ibid.*

26. C.G. Jung, *Answer to Job*, trans. R.F.C. Hull (Princeton: Princeton University Press, 1973), p. 99.

27. *Messengers of God*, p. 200.

28. *Deuteronomy* 4:24 (The Jerusalem Bible).

29. *Messengers of God*, p. 64.

30. See two books by Alfred North Whitehead: *Religion in the Making* (Cleveland: Meridian Books, 1965), p. 148; and *Process and Reality* (New York: Harper Torchbooks, 1960), p. 526.

31. *Harry James Cargas in Conversation with Elie Wiesel*, pp. 19-20.

32. *Messengers of God*, pp. 229-230.

33. *Job* 13:15 and 19:25 (King James Version).

34. See *Messengers of God*, pp. 231-232 and *Job* 42:5-6 (The Jerusalem Bible).

35. *Messengers of God*, p. 235.

36. The confessional language quoted here and in the sentences that follow is taken from *The Book of Confessions* (Second Edition, 1970) of The United Presbyterian Church in the United States of America. Specifically, I am quoting from "The Confession of 1967." I regard the quoted statements as expressing doctrines that most American Christians would accept. Following the reference system employed in *The Book of Confessions*, the passages quoted here can be found in paragraphs 9.13 and 9.07.

37. *Ibid.*, 9.09.

38. *Ibid.*, 9.15.

39. *Ibid.*, 9.19. See also *Psalms* 22:1 and *Matthew* 27:46 (The Jerusalem Bible).

40. *Messengers of God*, p. 235.

ELIE WIESEL:
CHRISTIAN RESPONSES

by Harry James Cargas

Elie Wiesel's impact on Christian thought cannot be estimated at this time. However I have attempted to find out something about his influence on individual Christians. I surveyed many by letter and and heve tried here to cull some patterns from the responses received from women and men throughout the country. (I have also incorporated the writings of half a dozen Christians who have commented, in print, on the significance of Wiesel the author, the Jewish survivor of the death camp.)

Certain themes do emerge, certain perspectives are shared in the letters I have received. The two topics most regularly mentioned are that of evil-suffering-death and second that of arguing with God.

Robert McAfee Brown summarized his thoughts in part, this way:

> ... Wiesel has perhaps done most for me in forcing me continually to confront the reality of evil in the world. I lead a "privileged" enough existence so that I can go for a time without confronting radical evil, except empathetically. But Elie's writings deny me that privilege, and it is important that they do so, else I am living in a pseudo-world. He forces me to take very seriously the charge that the spectator is the most culpable of all, since that is the role into which I most easily gravitate. I find with students also that this is where the resistances are greatest, and therefore where the impact has been most real.
>
> But I must say one other thing about the treatment of evil. For Elie does not *just* paint evil in its somberly vivid colors. He also points to ways in which we must deal with evil.[1]

Eden Theological Seminary Professor M. Douglas Meeks also refers to the hope he finds implicit in Wiesel's rendering of evil. Meeks specifically points to the tear which forms in God's eye in *Ani Maamin*, the tear brought about by the death of children in the Holocaust. He asks: did Abraham, Isaac, and Jacob see the tear? "Did they sense it? Does their faith, in spite of itself, still have to presuppose the tear? As a *Christian* who reads this in his own struggle to believe, I find it to be a symbol of the lost element in the Christian doctrine of God: the suffering of God. Wiesel's work may be an incentive for Jews and Christians, the children of Abraham, to collaborate in an experiment of grace, that is, a new openness to the power of suffering in history."

More briefly, Dr. John H. Tietjen, seminary president, (SEMINEX) noted that through Wiesel, "I have seen more deeply into the suffering, sacrificial love of God and His holy way of redeeming through the suffering and sacrifice of His servant people."

Professor John K. Roth (Claremont Men's College) wrote in an article that Wiesel "knows that no contemporary Jew—indeed no living person—can begin to fathom one's relation to God without passing through the world's death camps. He suggests to Christians that any simple or easy view of god's love is phony. If we are to understand God as love, this image must be tempered by the fact that fires of hell blaze on earth. It struck me as I read Wiesel that the faith of many Christians—myself included—is often shallow because we fail to bring the world's terror face to face with our claims about God's goodness."[2]

Process theologian Bernard Lee reminds us that "the Holocaust is that place in history where evil has been totally stripped of abstraction; and Elie Wiesel has insistently prevented it from losing its historical immediacy."

The Auxiliary Bishop of Detroit, Thomas Gumbleton, observes that Wiesel "shows clearly how evil is built into a societal system." Perhaps pessimistically, Gumbleton concludes his letter with a short paragraph: "Wiesel's biggest contribution is his forthright conviction that the Holocaust could be repeated, and his public witness that every effort must be made to see that it isn't."

I wish to quote the entire letter of Thomas E. Berry of the Riverdale Center of Religious Research:

Concerning Elie Wiesel. He has deepened my awareness of man's vocation to confront suffering, death, and the ultimate mystery beyond all human understanding. He has also profoundly affected my understanding of divine-human relations. I am not sure that he has affected the basic structure of my thinking to the degree that other thinkers of this century have affected the basic lines of my thinking, but he has considerably deepened my understanding and insight into everything that enters into my thinking. He is a kind of pervasive presence dealing with mysteries beyond mysteries in the historical realities of life. The terrifying dimensions of his concern constantly cast me into a deep reflexive mood in which amazing things happen somewhere in the depths of my being rather than on the surface of my thought. It is a high grace to live during his years of presence on earth.

Theologian Dennis Klass (Webster College) reveals that

I use Wiesel in my courses on death and dying because he is part of the literature from the camps and from the atomic bomb which has changed the symbols of death in our day. The grim reaper, the individual dance of death, and even the four horsemen are no longer adequate symbols for death. The new symbols are the instantaneous obliteration of the bomb and the mechanical, methodic dehumanization of the camps. The romance of individual death, against whom heroic myth could stand is no longer realistic. If my students can understand Wiesel, they can understand death in the modern world.

The second of the most frequently mentioned themes in my "survey" is that of arguing with God—an activity which would have seemed tinged with heresy to the Christian theologian of half a century ago. The author of *The Crucifixion of the Jews,* Temple University's Franklin Littell, told me how Wiesel radically changed his thinking.

... I was introduced by his writings to a profound theological reality: the right, indeed the duty, of a believing person *to debate with God.* Like most traditional Christians, perhaps more so because of my years of living with the Anabaptist/Mennonite tradition of *Gelassenheit/geleidsamkeid/*submission, I had come into a dead alley in the quest for and interpretation of G-d. Some of my close friends and colleagues had broken out of that dead end by radical denial of the God of whom the Bible speaks. This I could not do, for a complex of reasons I need not here go into. But Elie Wiesel helped me into a quite new dimension of religious life and thought, by opening to me what must be one of the permanent contributions of Hassidism: the debate with God. In Christian terms, I perceived that the traditional "submission" was more Muslim than Christian (i.e., a real heresy, however well established, and fundamentally un-Biblical), and that one of the blessings of Christian liberty is to be freed to argue and debate with God when he acts, or lets things happen, contrary to his own declared nature and promises. . . .

The superior of a religious order of women, Sister Anita Caspary, states that Wiesel's work is synonymous with reflections on the Holocaust and its meaning for all Jews. "Those of us who, although unwittingly, share the guilt of the terrible event must ask with Wiesel: 'Where was the God of Mercy to allow this to happen?'"

Prof. Terrence Des Pres (author of *The Survivor*) said in his letter that Wiesel

manages to personalize the Holocaust, to speak as if he were a voice within oneself, and his war with God— a traditional Jewish mode of relation to divinity— takes on at once the monumental aspect of the Holocaust and yet retains the particularity of a solitary voice. For me, the key to Wiesel's "war" is expressed in the contradictory but nevertheless true-to-experience statement that "there is no God and I hate Him." Acknowledgement and negation reside in the soul side by side, which is a very peculiar but widespread reaction, on the religious level, to the Holocaust.

June Yungblut of the American Friends Service Committee compares Wiesel and the late Catholic monk Thomas Merton. "Their work's personal meaning to me is, as their life's meaning, the challenge to wrestle with the Angel of God, knowing His Presence or loss of His Presence as the final, torturing, alluring frontier of this life and the one possible meaning beyond it."

Significantly, Lawrence S. Cunningham ended an article, "Elie Wiesel's Anti-Exodus" in *America* magazine, with this sentence: "God may still live, but if He does, He has much to answer for."[3] It is difficult to believe that any Catholic publication would have printed those words prior to the Holocaust.

Sr. Ann White who chairs Webster College's Department of Religion combines both of the two themes mentioned here in her reply to my inquiry: "I consistently assign *Night* to my religion students because Wiesel so powerfully encapsulates what religion in the modern world is all about—the struggle with God and the problem of evil."

Another pattern appearing in the letters and elsewhere is the acknowledgement by the writers of Wiesel's assisting them in becoming better Christians. Here is a paragraph by Protestant theologian A. Roy Eckardt:

> Elie Wiesel brought the Holocaust out of the shadowy sky and met me with it upon his face. Yet I did not become cynical. For he called me to act, to be responsible. Strangely, I felt joy and beauty. Here was this gentle man refusing to admit hell. He has fought back. Because I know him, I am kept much from despair.

John K. Roth concludes his article, previously alluded to, with thanks to Wiesel. "I am grateful to him for moving me, for setting my soul on fire."[4]

Here is Robert McAfee Brown again:

> Wiesel has helped me to see my own tradition more closely. The urgency of Jewish-Christian dialogue is now high on my agenda ... I am thinking not only of how I now see the issues that lie within the intramural life of Christianity must now be focused by me in a new way. Perhaps the simplest and starkest way to put this is to say that I am now, I hope, delivered by Elie Wiesel of any tendency to a cheap triumphalism in talking about "The Christian victory" or other terms that have historically been used to talk about "good news" or *evangelion*. Anything I am going to affirm about hope or promise or victory has to have gone through the crucible of *Night, Ani Maamin* and everything in between.

In a later paragraph, Brown concludes:

> So in a real sense Elie makes possible for me the life of faith—always an in-spite-of faith. He has earned the right to be heard, at the deepest levels, and I must continue to hear him, also at the deepest levels. Each re-

reading increases my debt to him. Each new book opens further doors, and my universe must once again be rearranged. So I remain very grateful.

Concluding another letter, Dean Walter Brueggemann of Eden Seminary writes that Wiesel "a) clarified to me a sense of vocation about my life and work and, b) raised questions I do not want to face about 'Good News' in our world of death." (Author Anthony Towne wrote me of rebelling against reading Wiesel at times. "This has to be because he insists upon rubbing my nose in unpleasant matters. Since I have a right not to have my nose rubbed in unpleasant matters why do I feel guilty that I avoid letting him do it? That has to do, I am sure, with the fact of his moral authority.")

A number of persons have commented on being affected by Wiesel's concept of story. The ethnicist and theologian Michael Novak put it succinctly: "Elie Wiesel helped to teach me the centrality of the concept of 'story' in the structure of each individual life."

Frank Littell elaborated in greater degree:

> Wiesel helped me to accept that in dealing with the Holocaust one can only—at least in this time—tell the story. For years I have been dealing with the mysteries of evil revealed in the assault of "post-Christian" ideologies on Christianity and Jewry. I had come to see that the generalizations and abstractions by which university-trained persons are want to handle such problems were both banal and immoral, not to say unaesthetic. But what is one to say when he is compelled to speak (or die spiritually), and yet the language is threadbare and inadequate? e.g.: "Man's inhumanity to man"; "theodicy"; "consequence of the history of Anti-semitism"; "totalitarian attack on traditional religions"; "racism"; "return to tribalism"—or the more patently absurd Social Democratic and Marxist socio-economic explanations. Elie Wiesel helped me to plunge ahead and simply tell the story again and again, and to demand that the events of the Church Struggle and the Holocaust be incorporated into Congregational liturgies (psalms, hymns, antiphonies, religious poems). And he helped me to be bold in stating flatly that the alpine event of this age was not the resistance of a comparatively small number of faithful Christians (Bonhoeffer, von Moltke, Delp,

Metzger, Lichtenberg, etc.) but the destruction of European Jewry. (As true for Christian history as for Jewish history!)

Others too have insisted that Wiesel somehow has brought the meaning of the Holocaust more deeply to them. Included among these are author Irving Sussman, Jesuit editor John Breslin and Brother Patrick Hart, who served as Thomas Merton's secretary at the Abbey of Gethsemani.

(Sussman says that "As for me, Wiesel's words [his works if you will] have made the Holocaust a never to be forgotten central event in my own life." Breslin writes of Wiesel: "He has certainly had an impact on my own thinking about the Holocaust by making it a real historical event whose effects are evident in even a casual meeting with him. Otherwise, it tends to be too large to grasp and so becomes an abstraction—a kind of negative proof text for original sin. Meeting Elie and reading his novels and essays have deepened my own understanding of that event and allowed me to see its ramification in contemporary life, and not just in the case of Israel." Brother Patrick's praise is this: "More than perhaps anyone else, Elie Wiesel's powerful and prophetic witness has opened my eyes to the atrocious Nazi pogrom of over six and a half million helpless Jews in this twentieth century.")

To return briefly to those who have written about "story," theologian Bernard Loomer has absorbed Wiesel's conclusion and mine: 'God made man because he loves stories.'" And A. Roy Eckardt once again: in his book *Your People, My People* he suggests ours as a post-Covenant time. "Prophecy has ceased; revelation has stopped; the Torah is, in a sense, gone. Perhaps all that is left is for the Jewish people to tell tales. It may well be that we Christians cannot do that. For us to tell the tale is only to speak of our shame. Perhaps all that we have left is the tale of meeting, between those who have survived and us who have survived nothing."[5]

Author/theologian Martin E. Marty of the University of Chicago's Divinity School sent this reply:

What has he meant to me? What Adorno and Solzhenitsyn have been saying: unless the story is told, suffering seems more meaningless and loses its dignity. He tells the story of the camps better than anyone else alive, knowing somehow exactly how far the reader can be carried and where nothing more can be said. He is a witness, in a time when few have credentials to be.

A final theme I wish to touch on is that of memory in the work of Wiesel. Philip Berrigan expressed his thoughts this way:

> Wiesel has taught me much of the essential nature of a transcendent history, a tradition-roots. He can write as he does of the Holocaust; he can quarrel with God as David did; he can isolate the right questions because he knows himself—he knows where he's come from. To be someplace, one has to be from somewhere.
>
> Our tragedy as Americans is our divorce from roots. We know neither our Biblical nor secular roots. And this prepares us to play god with our affluence and our weapons. Wiesel's message is the message of Israel—remember or perish. Remember God, remember The Fall, remember covenant—or perish.

Thomas A. Idinipulos of Miami University, touching on Wiesel, has written that "Wiesel, like the theologian Richard L. Rubenstein, recognizes that it is not in eschatology but rather in history that the Jew is to seek the basis of his unity with other Jews, living and dead."[6]

David L. Edwards sums it up in an article in the Lexington Theological Quarterly: "Elie Wiesel is a man who places memory at the center of humanity's being." The last sentence of Edwards' piece noted that "From Wiesel we learn that memory is a necessary step toward salvation."[7]

Not every letter I received or work I read could be included under the various topics so far listed: evil-suffering-death; arguing with God; becoming a better Christian; making the Holocaust more meaningful; memory. I would like to present some of these other thoughts, by Christians also influenced by Wiesel. I hope these do not appear to be dismissed or merely lumped under a miscellaneous category. They simply did not fit in the artificial scheme I made for convenience in organizing the material.

First, I must quote the complete letter I received from Father Malcolm Boyd:

> Wiesel's work has often been like a fingernail drawn across the full length of a blackboard in my conscious-

ness; an almost unbearable presence, sound, and effect being brought to bear upon my deepest feelings and conscience.

The Holocaust is the single most significant event in my life as a human being. Yet at the precise moment it occurred, I was virtually unaware of it. My repeated visits to Israel, coupled with deepening absorption in the elements that comprise Jewish experience, have stressed the centrality of the Holocaust in my own human experience.

Wiesel's is the dominant contemporary voice and presence that impinges ever anew upon my awareness of it, opening up new dimensions of the Holocaust for me; reminding me again and again when I might seek to relax the tautness of its hold on my spirit; and telling me quite simply that the agony of the Holocaust is imbedded beneath the facade of our resolutely smiling, outwardly secure, willfully complacent, self-absorbed caricature of life that is conveniently labeled 'Christian.'

This should be followed by a paragraph sent me by Father Theodore Hesburgh, Notre Dames's president:

I have not read everything that Elie Wiesel has written, but those things that I have read seem to me to speak to the heart. It is difficult not to be touched by his insight and concern for humanity, especially for the plight of those who suffer injustice.

Next, the text of a letter from a Regional Director of the National Conference of Christians and Jews, O'Ray C. Graber.

Someone has said, you don't know an individual or a people until you know what hurts them. There is a tension between knowing about someone or something and experiencing in some additudinal and life-changing way the forces and feelings that shape the history and the future of a people.

Bringing the two together is the supreme test in human communication. It means overcoming the barrier that allows us to see but not to feel, to hear but not to be touched, to exist in the presence of but not to be the Brother, to do justice, or to make peace.

More than anyone else, Elie Wiesel, the writer, speaker, and communicator has brought these polarities together for me in regards to the Holocaust and the aspirations of 20th century Judaism.

Philip Scharper, an Edith Stein Award recipient, writes that Rabbi Heschel taught him about certain theological problems and that "through the writings of Wiesel I came to feel these questions on my pulses, and to ask within my own Judaeo-Christian being the questions wrung from his Jewish soul."

Sister Stephanie Stueber, the superior of a religious community, has submitted these three paragraphs:

> I shall never forget that first meeting with Wiesel. At breakfast I asked him how one can possibly live through the holocaust experience. He looked at me with penetrating eyes and said very quietly, almost in a whisper: "One doesn't live through those things; one rises above them."
>
> That "rising above" is what Wiesel's life and thought and writing have meant to me. Here is a deeply religious man, a mystic, who has suffered intensely; whose bases for belief were shattered; whose doubts tortured him. At the same time, here is a man who has held on somehow, who has forgiven those at whose hands he suffered.
>
> Wiesel is a 20th century representative of the death-resurrection mystery; and the grace of that lived mystery fills his own life and the lives of those who meet and read him so that they too learn how to rise above.

Author Cornelia Sussman says that Wiesel reveals to her that "the authentic mystic does not only walk with God and talk with God and lose personality in the cosmic—but simultaneously he remains a person in the midst of death who dares stand up to death, invulnerable."

One of the true heroes of the Civil Rights movement in this country is John Howard Griffin. He tells that "My work and thought right now involve a synthesis (not completed yet) that seeks to pinpoint that moment in suppression that destroys: the harrowing moment when a person perceives and understands (regardless of the physical ramifications) that he is at the mercy of men or systems completely without mercy. That is the shattering perception. That is the moment. Wiesel is full of such moments and such perceptions—they confirm my own intuitions."

Richard Bauer, the actor who brilliantly performed the role of the beadle in Wiesel's drama *Zalmen, Or the Madness of God* wrote to me about what it has meant to him to live a Wiesel role for three years. Bauer's is the longest letter I received in answer to my query and he really opened his heart—more in response to Wiesel, of course, than to me.

> I'm not a great reader of religious (I use that in the loosest sense) works—in fact I'm not a great reader. But to me, as a Christian, Wiesel the man, the playwright and true writer has been life changing....
>
> Every great writer, knowingly or unknowingly reveals yet another facet of the face of God, perhaps an eye, part of the smile, the left nostril, or the chuckle. Thank you Elie for letting me see the tears, and, oh yes— thank You, God.

In a remarkable essay, soon to be published, on Wiesel's novel *The Oath,* Ted L. Estess, discusses the distinction he finds in Wiesel between fate (where there is no choice) and destiny (by which one can say "yes" or "no.")

To mention one final person who is trying to be a Christian, who has encountered Elie Wiesel, I believe that my meeting with him has been, for me, on the level of destiny. I hope that my "yes" will be in some measure an honest one. For me, Elie Wiesel has made the great act of faith of this century. Being who he is, having experienced what he has experienced, and reflecting as he has *on* that experience, he has written in *Ani Maamin:* "And the silence of God is God." There could be no more profound expression of belief.

1.   No notes in this paper will be used to refer to the letters I have received in response to my query. Where material is quoted, therefore, and note indicators are absent, the quotation is from a personal letter from the person being quoted and is in my possession.

2.   "Tears and Elie Wiesel," *The Princeton Seminary Bulletin,* (LXV, Dec., 1972), 43.

3.   April 27, 1974, p. 327.

4.   Roth, p. 48.

5.   (New York, 1974), p. 228.

6.   "The Holocaust in the Stories of Elie Wiesel," *Soundings* (LV, Summer, 1972), 210.

7.   "The Presence of Holocaust: The Vision of Elie Wiesel," (VII, April, 1973), 59.

NOTES ON CONTRIBUTORS

ROBERT ALTER is a frequent contributor to *The New York Review of Books, Commentary,* and *The New York Times.*

DR. MICHAEL BERENBAUM is Adjunct Assistant Professor and University Jewish Chaplain at Wesleyan University, Middletown, Connecticut. He is the author of *Elie Wiesel; The Vision of the Void* from which this article is taken.

DR. ROBERT McAFEE BROWN is Professor of Ecumenics and World Christianity at Union Theological Seminary, and author of *Theology In a New Key,* among his many books.

HARRY JAMES CARGAS has published fifteen books including *The Holocaust: An Annotated Bibliography, Harry James Cargas in Conversation with Elie Wiesel, Religious Experience and Process Theology.* He is chairperson of the Literature and Language Department at Webster College in Saint Louis.

LAWRENCE S. CUNNINGHAM is Associate Professor of Religion at the Florida State University, Tallahassee where he also serves as director of undergraduate studies in the Religion Department and professor in the graduate program in Humanities.

LILY EDELMAN directs the B'nai B'rith Lecture Bureau. Her published works include *Israel: New People in an Old Land* and *Japan in Story and Pictures.* She is also the translator from the French of Elie Wiesel's *Beggar in Jerusalem* and *One Generation After.*

TED ESTESS (Ph. D., Humanities, Syracuse University) is a member of the English faculty and is Director of the Honors Program at the University of Houston. Concentrating on the interrelationship of religion and literature, he has previously taught in the religious studies department of Le Moyne

College, Syracuse, New York. Other of his essays have appeared in *Journal of the American Academy of Religion, Parabola,* and *Arizona Quarterly.*

ELLEN FINE is an Assistant Professor of French at Kingsborough Community College, City University of New York and is completing her doctoral dissertation at New York University on "Elie Wiesel: The Theme of 'le Témoin.'" She has published articles on French literature and is doing research on Elie Wiesel's role in contemporary French thought. She is also preparing a complete bibliography of articles written on Wiesel in French.

MAURICE S. FRIEDMAN is Professor of Religious Studies, Philosophy and Comparative Literature at San Diego State University. His books include *Touchstones of Reality: Existential Trust and the Community of Peace* and *Martin Buber: Life of Dialogue.*

IRVING HALPERIN is Professor of English and Creative Writing at San Francisco State University. His volume *Messengers from the Dead* is a pioneering analysis of Holocaust literature. His work on this topic has appeared in *Congress Bi-Weekly, Jewish Life, Jewish Heritage* and *Judaism.*

THOMAS A. IDINOPULOS (Ph.D., University of Chicago) is Professor in the Department of Religion at Miami University, Oxford, Ohio, teaching in the areas of Philosophical Theology, Religion and Literature, and Modern Jewish Thought. He has written extensively on religion and politics in the Middle East today. He has published 50 articles and reviews in journals such as *Journal of Religion, Soundings, Scottish Journal of Theology, Cross Currents, Process Studies, Christian Century,* and *Journal of the American Academy of Religion.* He is also the author of *The Erosion of Faith: An Inquiry into the Origins of the Contemporary Crisis in Religious thought* (Quadrangle Books-New York Times, 1971).

LOTHAR KAHN is a professor of Modern Languages at Central Connecticut State College in New Britain. He is the author of *Mirrors of the Jewish Mind* and *Insight and Action: The Life of Lion Feuchtwanger* as well as numerous language text books. He has contributed to many publications here and abroad.

JOSEPHINE KNOPP, Professor in the Department of Religion at Temple University, is the author of the *Trial of Judaism in Contemporary Jewish Writing*. She has written for *Sh'ma* and other periodicals and is Research Director of the National Institute on the Holocaust.

LAWRENCE L. LANGER is Professor of English and holder of the Alumnae endowed Chair at Simmons College in Boston. He is the author of *The Holocaust and the Lite rary Imagination* and *The Age of Atrocity: Death and Modern Literature*.

JOHN K. ROTH is the Russel K. Pitzer Professor of Philosophy at Claremont Men's College. He was a fellow at the National Humanities Institute in 1976-77. His six books include *American Dreams, Problems of the Philosophy of Religion* and *The Moral Philosophy of William James*.

BYRON SHERWIN is a professor of Jewish Religious thought at Spertus College of Judaica in Chicago and the Project Director of the National Endowment for the Humanities he has a grant to develop an interdisciplinary curriculum in Holocaust Studies for American Colleges and Universities.